Principles of European Environmental Law

Edited by Prof. Richard Macrory

with Ian Havercroft and Ray Purdy

The Avosetta Series (4)
Proceedings of the Avosetta Group of European Environmental Lawyers

Europa Law Publishing is a young publishing company
specializing in European Union law, international trade
law, public international law, environmental law and
comparative national law.
For further information please contact Europa Law
Publishing via email: info@europalawpublishing.com
or visit our website at: www.europalawpublishing.com.

Typeset in Scala and Scala Sans, Graphic design by
G2K Designers, Groningen/Amsterdam

NUR 828; ISBN 90-76871-26-4

British Library Cataloguing-in-Publication Data
A catalogue record for this book is available from the
British Library

The Avosetta Serie publishes to
innovative discour

Acknowledgements

I am grateful to all my colleagues in the Avosetta group who so willingly developed the chapters in this book. Ray Purdy and Ian Havercroft of the Centre for Law and the Environment at University College provided invaluable editorial assistance in the preparation of the book. I would also like to thank Paul Bowden and his colleagues in Freshfields Bruckhaus Deringer who provided financial support, both for the 2003 London meeting of the Avosetta Group, which initiated this study and for the editorial work.

Richard Macrory
University College London
June 2004

Table of Contents

CHAPTER 4 **The Precautionary Principle before the European Courts**
Joanne Scott

CHAPTER 5 **European Environmental Law Principles in Belgian Jurisprudence**
Luc Lavrysen

CHAPTER 6 **Implementation and Application of Environmental Principles in Danish Law**
Peter Pagh

CHAPTER I

Principles into Practice

Richard Macrory

The chapters in this book are concerned with the legal significance of core environmental principles in contemporary European legal systems. It arose from a meeting of the Avosetta group of European environmental lawyers in 2003, where participants wished to learn from each other how national courts were handling environmental principles in practice. In developing the written chapters for a wider audience, we deliberately resisted trying to impose too inhibiting a structure asking the same questions of each country. Certainly, there were some common issues – such as the identification of key national case law and national constitutional or legal provisions that referred to environmental principles; but we also allowed each writer to develop their analysis from their own perspectives and experience. This has led to variations in style and emphasis (as well as length), which may not meet the strictures of some comparative methodologies, but probably more accurately, reflects the richness of distinctive national legal traditions in contemporary Europe.

The starting point for the study was the core environmental principles stated in Article 174 of the EC Treaty and notably polluters pay, prevention, and precaution. In Chapter 3, Kramer traces the historical development of these provisions in the European Treaty, and the political background to their inclusion. He also considers the forms of policy response by the European Commission, which they have stimulated. The main focus of the book, however, is not so much with the substance of Community environmental policy. Instead its concern is how these and equivalent core environmental principles are currently being used and applied by the judiciary in European countries in assisting the resolution of legal disputes. It is already clear that the Treaty environmental principles have influenced the approach of the European Court of Justice in a number of significant cases. In Chapter 4, Scott considers the precautionary principle and its interpretation and application by the ECJ. Under the Treaty, the principle is stated within the context of the environmental policy of the European Union, but by dint of application of another significant environmental principle, the so called 'integration' principle, currently stated in Article 6 of the EC Treaty, the European court has now endorsed the application of the precautionary principle to other areas of Community policy such as agriculture and the protection of public health. This does not answer the question of precisely what application of the principle requires of decision-makers and Scott considers the implications of the recent case law in this context. She is particularly concerned as to whether the current emphasis of the European judiciary on the need for 'rational' risk assessment and the avoidance of governments taking steps against hypothetical risk, may be unduly influenced by the approach of the WTO appellate bodies faced with similar issues.

Much of the book, though, is concerned with how environmental principles are being handled by courts at national level. This of necessity raises general issues concerning the legal nature of principles – a question, of course, that strays well beyond the boundaries of environmental law and touches on core questions of the nature and structure of legal systems. The American legal philosopher, Ronald Dworkin, in a famous passage in *Taking Rights Seriously*[1], explicitly draws a distinction between legal rules and legal principles:

> *'Both sets of standards point to particular decisions about legal obligation in particular circumstances, but they differ in the character of direction they give'.*

Legal rules, even those that include exceptions, are applicable in 'an all or nothing fashion', while a legal principle 'states a reason that argues in one direction, but does not necessitate a particular decision.' Different principles may argue in a different direction, and a further distinction between principles and rules, according to Dworkin, is that given the need to weigh up the significance of different principles in determining the outcome of any particular decision it becomes necessary to consider their weight or importance. Some rules may be functionally more significant than other rules, but this dimension of weight or importance s not an inherent characteristic.

The core environmental principles stated in the EC Treaty such as precaution and polluters pay certainly appear in many ways to fit Dworkin's characterization of a principle as opposed to a rule. Nevertheless, as Winter points out in Chapter 2, there may be some important distinctions. Many of Dworkin's examples of legal principles, taken from the US common law tradition, have been developed by the judiciary themselves. In contrast, the core environmental principles have been largely expressed in formal legislation, as in the EC Treaty, international treaties, or, as examples in the national chapters demonstrate, sometimes in national legislation. Dworkin, however, does not confine his concept of principles to those that are developed by the judiciary, but includes examples from both the US Constitution and legislation. Dworkin also makes a distinction between principles and policies. In his terminology, a principle has a moral dimension and represents a moral standard to be observed because it is a requirement of justice or fairness, one that tends to be associated with the rights of individuals. In contrast, a policy is a type of standard that represents a collective goal to be reached, normally some improvement in social, economic or political features in a society.

As both Winter and Wegener (Chapter 7) observe, the environmental principles have more in common with Dworkin's notion of a policy in this sense, though the exception might be the polluters pay principle. From a policy-makers perspective, this originally had the characteristic of a collective environmental goal to ensure full internalization of environmental costs. In litigation before the courts, however, as a number of the national chapters illustrates, it has tended to be invoked by potential polluters to challenge unjust burdens being imposed upon them. In this sense, it appears to be treated in the courts more in accordance with Dworkin's conception of a principle. As to the distinction between legal principles and legal policies, Dworkin admits that for some purposes this

---

[1] R. Dworkin, *Taking Rights Seriously*, Harvard University Press, Cambridge, (1977), Chapter 2.

may not be significant, at least compared to their shared distinction from the 'all or nothing' nature of legal rules. The difference, though, may be highly significant in providing insights as to the legal and political system in which they operate. Wegener notes the distinction made by the German legal writer, Alexy,[2] between a directly applicable rule and an obligation to reach a goal as far as possible ('*Optimierungsgebote*') and suggests that this may be more useful than Dworkin's terminology in this context.

Another way of analyzing the legal significance of these expression of principles is to take a distinction, more familiar to lawyers dealing with written constitutions, between directory duties and mandatory requirements.[3] Directory duties are essentially exhortatory statements not intended in themselves to be legally enforceable, though they may colour the interpretation of other duties. In contrast, mandatory requirements are self-executory, in the sense that they impose duties that are enforceable and with the requirement of further legislation. Most of the EU environmental principles appear to be more in the nature of directory duties in this sense, though some of the examples in the chapters indicate that national courts have been prepared to treat them as directly legally binding.

De Sadeleer (Chapter 14) offers a quite distinctive analysis of the legal significance of environmental principles. As with Winter, he notes that in contrast to more general principles of law which have often been developed by the courts through an inductive process, the core contemporary environmental principles are boldly stated in both hard and soft law. He characterizes much of contemporary environmental law as representing classic features of 'post modern' law where the rigidity, rationality and certainty of modern law is giving way to fragmentation, flexibility and dispersion. Core environmental principles, can, he suggests, provide a means of providing a degree of underlying coherence and stability in a new legal world that requires being adaptable and fast-moving and in this way act as a bridge between modern and post-modern law.

Dworkin's distinctions between principles, policies and rules were developed in a precise manner, as part of an intellectual challenge to a purely positivist construction of legal systems. In practice, policy makers and legislators do not necessarily use the terminology so precisely. Bándi (Chapter 13) gives a salutary reminder by quoting Dhondt: 'terms such as rules, principles, legal principles, objectives and guidelines are used incoherently to mean similar and different things.'[4] Hence the significance of considering environmental case law where these concepts have been raised as it is only here that one will begin to discern

---

[2] R. Alexy, *Theorie der Gundrechte*, Suhrkamp, Frankfurt, (1994).

[3] See Hession and Macrory (1998) The Legal Duty of Environmental Integration, in T. O'Riordan and H. Voisey (eds), *The Transition to Sustainability: The Politics of Agenda 21 in Europe*, Earthscan, London, (1998), Ch 5.

[4] N. Dhondt, *Integration of Environmental Protection into other EC Policies: Legal Theory and Practice*, Avosetta Series, Europa Law Publishing, Groningen, (2003).

their true legal nature in practice by seeing how they are handled and treated by the judiciary in influencing the outcome of disputes.

The national chapters do not cover every European country, but the picture they reveal remains rather mixed. Here, again, it is necessary to draw a number of distinctions. The first concerns the status of the EC Treaty environmental principles themselves within national legal systems. Most of the examples suggest that national courts are reluctant to give the Treaty principles any independent legal status or direct effect. This appears to be the current position, for example, in Germany, the United Kingdom, the Netherlands, and Spain. Both Grassi and Montini, however, quote a recent Italian court decision where a national decree was suspended because it conflicted with the prevention and precautionary principles in Article 174 of the EC Treaty, but acknowledge there is also conflicting case-law in Italy on this point.

The position is likely to be different where a national court is dealing with national provisions that are explicitly transposing European Community legislation, which have been based on the core principles. Here principles may be legally significant in the interpretation of the national laws. Van Middelkoop (Chapter 10), for example, quotes a Dutch case where the relevance of the precautionary principle in the context of public bodies taking appropriate steps under the Habitats Directive was raised; similarly, in the United Kingdom (Chapter 12) the relevance of the polluters pay principles to national decisions implementing the Nitrates Directive was raised in the *Standley* case. Both these cases were referred to the European Court of Justice, the Dutch case still pending.

But as many of the national chapters illustrate, the significance of environmental principles is not confined to cases involving European Community issues. Moreno (Chapter 8) notes that in civil law systems, the emergence of general principles purely through judicial made law is a more complex process than in common law countries. However, even in a common law system such as the United Kingdom, as Macrory and Havercroft suggest (Chapter 12), the more that contemporary environmental law is dominated by national legislation, the less likely are the judiciary to invoke environmental principles independently, unless the legislation or its accompanying policy is expressly related to those principles. Few of the countries studied have expressed environmental principles in their written constitution, though as Moreno observes, the polluter pays principles is enshrined in the Spanish constitution and has been significant in constitutional cases concerning the division of powers concerning the raising of taxes. Aragão (Chapter 11) points to the principle of 'solidarity between generations' as the sole true environmental principle contained in the Portuguese Constitution. A number of constitutions contain general provisions concerning the right to life and physical integrity and here the core environmental principles have had some influence on the interpretation of these provisions, as noted, for example, by Wegener in Germany (Chapter 7) and Grassi in Italy (Chapter 9).

It is also clear that the environmental principles may assist courts in the interpretation of more general principles of administrative law. In the Netherlands (Chapter 10), for example, general legal principles such as sound administration, the duty of care and justification are codified in law. The precautionary principle has been invoked to colour the interpretation of the duty of care and justification principle, though van Middelkoop notes that the Dutch courts are more confident in handling the principle where it has been explicitly express in an element of environmental law or policy. In Germany (Chapter 7) the polluter pays principle has been associated with the general concept of causation, and often integrated with the general principle of proportionality.

A number of countries have developed what are described as basic framework environmental laws and these are likely to contain an expression of core environmental principles, not necessarily limited to those contained in the EC Treaty. Principles contained in the Portuguese Basic Environmental Law, for example (Chapter 11) include, inter alia, prevention, equilibrium, participation and liability. In the Netherlands (Chapter 10), there are currently proposals to amend the key Environmental Management Act to include explicit reference to core environmental principles. Bándi (Chapter 13), in his study on accession countries, noted the extent to which the 1990s saw the development of core environmental laws in many Central and Eastern European countries which contained references to environmental principles such as precaution, participation, polluters pay, cooperation and participation. He ascribed this in part, to the influence of the Model Environmental Act, developed under the auspices of the Council of Europe Directorate for Environment and Local Authorities and originally specifically designed as a model for CEE countries as they developed modern environmental laws. He accepts that in the absence of detailed regulations and laws, such statements of general environmental principles may have little real legal value, but are nevertheless important as representing a political commitment for the framework of future development and design of environmental legislation.

As many of the chapters illustrate, environmental principles are only likely to have real legal bite where they are referred to in more detailed national environmental legislation or in policy documentation. In a number of countries, they can be described as only implicitly affecting the structure and content of environmental laws as in Denmark (Chapter 6). On the other hand, as in Germany (Chapter 7) for example, both the prevention and precautionary principles are found in the Federal law on air quality and emissions and their distinctive use – the former in the context of air quality standards and the latter in emission standards – has been important in the context of the interpretation of standing issues by the German courts on the basis of violation of rights. Wegener also notes that the principle of cooperation, implying a restraint on conventional regulatory tools in favour of voluntary schemes, a system of open choices and a principle not found in the EC Treaty, has proved significant in Germany. In a controversial decision in 1998, the constitutional court interpreted national waste legislation as being based on the cooperation principle with the result that the use of certain subsidiary mechanisms within the context of the law such as local taxes were restrained.

The examples in the national chapters of how courts are currently handling environmental principles, present an intriguing picture at present. Clearly actual practice is subtler than more simplistic views, which presents the principles as, on the one hand, no more than political statements, or on the other as a binding set of legal norms, which must be respected at all times. There are some some common themes that cut across different jurisdictions. It is notable, for example, the extent to which the precautionary principle has been raised in litigation in different European countries concerning electro-magnetic emissions from telecommunications installations; equally the polluters pay principle has been used in the context of challenging fiscal and similar financial measures across different jurisdictions. Equally there are important national distinctions in the constitutional relationship of the courts to the executive and legislature and the extent to which, environmental principles are expressly referred to in national legislation or policy. These differences can vitally affect the legal significance of the principles.

We are still at a fairly early stage of the development of environmental jurisprudence dealing with the types of principles discussed here. Yet comparative legal study in the environmental field is no longer simply a matter of academic interest. In August 2002 over 100 senior judges adopted the Johannesburg Principles on the role of law and sustainable development, which called, *inter alia*, for improvements in legal and judicial capacity in the field of environmental law. Detailed programmes of work in UNEP are now following up this initiative. As one of the regional responses, a new European Union Forum of Judges for the Environment held its inaugural meeting in April 2004 in Luxembourg and was open to all judges in the European Union and EFTA. The exchange of information between national judges, on how environmental cases are in practice being handled in different jurisdictions, will be a significant element of these initiatives in judicial cooperation. This study will, it is hoped, be an initial contribution to that process which is set to continue for many years.

The Legal Nature of Environmental Principles in International, EC and German Law

Gerd Winter

Much has been said about the semantic content of environmental principles, but there is less clarity regarding their legal nature. This chapter shall contribute to the related discussion. I will propose a general concept of principles, which can be applied to all levels of the law, national, regional as well as international. I will begin with a short overview of basic propositions called principles (I) and proceed with an analysis of their legal nature (II).

I Overview of environmental propositions called principles

In general international law two environmental propositions are widely recognized as customary law, namely the procedural duty between states to co-operate in mitigating environmental risks and emergencies and the substantive duty to prevent, reduce and control imminent and serious environmental harm.[1]

Precaution, meaning the duty to take measures even in situations of uncertain, but possibly serious risks, has much been discussed as a candidate for a third norm of international law. However, neither the International Court of Justice[2] nor other international dispute settlement bodies, like the WTO Appellate Body,[3] have yet been bold enough to take this step. Although many scholars call precaution a principle[4], few are prepared to call it a rule because the requirements of the three sources of international law recognized in Article 38 ICJ Statute – treaty law, customary law and general principles of law – set the hurdle of recognizing a binding rule very high. It is true, there is ample treaty law citing the precautionary principle[5], but treaties only apply *inter partes*. Precaution is neither customary law because although *opinio necessitatis sive iuris* may be widespread it is not at all *consuetudo*. Nor is it a general principle of law (as long as by "law" it is understood national law) because not many domestic environmental law systems have as yet ventured into precautionary legislation.

More environmental propositions have been established by issue-related treaties and named principles, notably, the polluter pays principle, the principle of transparency and participation, the principle of joint but separate responsibility and the principle of sustainability.[6] Equitable access to natural resources and the state's duty of effective management are significant complementary prin-

---

[1]   P. Birnie, A, Boyle, *International Law and the Environment*, 2nd ed. Oxford (Oxford UP) 2002

[2]   ICJ, Judgment of Sept. 25, 1997, Case concerning the *Gabcikovo-Nagymaros Dam*, at paras 111-114.

[3]   WTO Appellate Body, Report of Jan. 1998, WT/DS26/AB/R and WT/DS48/AB/R (Measures concerning meat and meat products) at paras. 120-125 and fn. 93.

[4]   Cf. Birnie/Boyle, *op. cit.* p. 120.

[5]   For an overview see N. de Sadeleer, *Environmental Principles*, Oxford, (Oxford UP) 2002, p. 94 *et seq.*

[6]   Cf. Birnie/Boyle, *op. cit.* p. 79 *et seq.*; N. de Sadeleer, *op. cit.* p. 23 *et seq.*; A. Epiney, M. Scheyli, *Umweltvölkerrecht*, Bern (Stämpfli) 2000.

ciples emphasized by those authors who write on the background of societies where inequality is tremendous and the administration widely ineffective.[7]

At EU level, environmental propositions have been codified in the EC Treaty, Article 174. Some of them, precaution, prevention, rectification at source, and polluter pays, are called principles; others, preserving, protecting and improving the quality of the environment at a "high level" are called objectives. These objectives and principles may seem to be uncompromising, however Article 174(3) puts them on a more realistic footing. According to Article 174(3), in preparing its policy the Community law shall take account of, inter alia, the available scientific and technical data, advantages and drawbacks, regional factors, and the economic and social development of the Community.

Environmental protection requirements do not only shape genuine environmental policies but shall also be integrated into the other policies of the Union. This so-called integration principle is established in Article 6 EC, but also found, with slight variations, in Article 37 of the Charter of Fundamental Rights. As will be explained later in this paper integration is not a principle in the definition of the term here proposed but rather a rule, because in building a bridge between opposing principles it is strictly to be followed. It is noteworthy that sustainability is not directly named as a principle of environmental policy, but is seen as both a task of the Community (Article 2 EC) and a qualification of the "principle" of integration (Article 6 EC).

The draft treaty, submitted by the Convention, retains the principles and objectives as listed above. Only slight changes have been made. The integration principle stages even twice, namely as a basic right (Article II-37) and as a principle (Article III-4). Sustainability has been included in the objectives of the relations of the EU with the wider world. The new somewhat pretentious formula is that the Union shall 'contribute to the sustainable development of the earth'.[8]

On the national level Germany and Brazil may be cited as two opposing cases, Germany being parsimonious and Brazil rich in constitutional principles of environmental protection. In the German constitution (*Grundgesetz*), disregarding the rules on competences, there is only one article referring to the environment. In Article 20a it is provided that the state must protect the natural conditions of life. In addition, jurisprudence of the Federal Constitutional Court has developed an objective duty of the state to protect human health and a subjective right of the individual demand such protection. There is, however, no subjective right to a habitable environment. German law rarely provides principles by ordinary legislation, the principles are mostly doctrinal constructions abstracted out of more precise norms of specific laws. For instance, precaution is part of a complex norm of the German Federal Emission Prevention Act, which

---

[7] See P. A. Leme Machado, *Direito ambiental brasileiro*, Sao Paulo (Malheiros Editores), 11th ed. 2003, p. 47 *et seq.*, 87 *et seq.*

[8] Part I Title I Article 3 paragraph 4.

carefully circumscribes how far precaution can go and what other interests must
be considered. The same is true with regard to laws concretizing the principles
of rectification at source, polluter pays, and sustainable use of natural resources.

By contrast, Article 225 of the Brazilian constitution, establishes a much
greater number of propositions which are called principles by legal doctrine
including; everyone's right to an ecologically balanced environment; prevention
and precaution; the duty of public authorities to defend the environment and
to preserve it for future generations; the duty to prepare environmental impact
assessments; the duty of the polluter to repair environmental damage and the
precautionary management of risks.[9]

At the levels of international, regional and national law the term "principle"
is used in very different ways; an attempt to clarify the legal nature of principles,
by consulting legal philosophy, is made below.

II The legal nature of environmental principles

Definitions of principle abound in legal and philosophical discourses. In such a situation it is advisable to build a definition, which best suits
the hermeneutic context in which the term shall be used. That context can be
characterised by the following questions:

1) What distinguishes principles from policies and what is the source of
   their binding force?
2) What is the difference between principles and rules?
3) How do principles range in the hierarchy of norms and what follows from
   any positioning in the hierarchy?
4) How does the operational context influence the normative weight of principles?

I shall discuss these questions in turn.

1. Principles and policies

A principle is undoubtedly a candidate for legal effect, if it is
contained in a law or sublegal norm. The legislator must however have intended
to give the principle such effect. This distinguishes principles from policies.
Policies may also be mentioned in a law, but if so, they are not intended to be
binding. The policy character of a proposition contained in a legal text, can be
deduced either from its express wording (*e.g.* if a postulate is called a task, a
value, an objective, or something else) or from the vagueness of the language

---

[9] Although precaution is not explicitly mentioned, jurisprudence has read it into Article 225. See P. A.
Leme Machado, *op. cit.* p. 67.

expressing it. For instance, sustainable development is called a task of the Community in Article 2 EC and if understood in the broadest sense of bridging ecological, social and economic concerns, it lacks determinable content. For these two reasons it is not a principle. It may rather be called a policy or an ideal.[10]

Besides legislation, principles of legal value can also emerge from legal practice, *i.e.* the common sense of the legal profession and broader societal discourse based on the experience derived from cases. This is the very source of principles in the common law systems, but it is also well known in the civil law systems as a corollary to statutory law.[11] Many land-mark judgments which have created new principles have based their arguments on experience and common sense rather than on the text of laws. It is true that judges, like policy-makers, may have a vision of good policies. To establish a principle of legal value they must, however reason that the principle shall be binding as law.[12]

Sometimes, principles will emerge, like a phoenix from the ashes, in full development and clarity. This is the case when they appear in constitutions and codifications, or in landmark decisions of courts.[13] More often principles emerge incrementally, being carved out of a number of small steps taken in more specific legislation or case law. For instance, precaution was introduced into German law by one specific statute in 1974. Later on, other laws were gradually also orientated towards precaution. Only if one takes all of the laws together one can say that German legislation is characterised by the precautionary principle, and that it should be interpreted in that way.

The philosopher Ronald Dworkin suggests that the content of principles can only be individual rights, not public interests. According to Dworkin principles are to be distinguished from 'policies' that serve not individual but collective goals; 'Arguments of principle are arguments intended to establish an individual right; arguments of policy are arguments intended to establish a collective goal. Principles are propositions that describe rights; policies are propositions that describe goals.'[14] However, there is ample evidence that legal practice has also established principles of respect for the public interest. For instance, the public interest in occupational and consumer health protection has for long been accepted as a counter-principle to economic freedoms. Public interests in environmental protection are more recent examples.

---

[10] See for a distinction of ideals and policies J. Verschuuren, *Principles of Environmental Law*, Baden-Baden (Nomos) 2003, 19 *et seq.*

[11] For an in-depth analysis of the relationship between principles and codified law see Josef Esser, *Grundsatz und Norm*, Tuebingen (Mohr) 1964, p. 141 *et seq.* See also his observation (p. 223) that there has emerged a convergence of continental axiomatic and anglo-american topical thought.

[12] Esser, *op. cit.* p. 137.

[13] Like for example the principle of strict liability in the famous judgment *Rylands* v. *Fletcher* (1868) LR 3 HL 330. Cf. Stuart Bell, Ball & Bell on *Environmental Law*, London (Blackstone) 4th ed. 1997, p. 193 *et seq.*

[14] R. Dworkin, *Taking Rights Seriously*, Cambridge (Harvard UP) 1977, p. 90.

The question of sources of environmental principles is particularly difficult
in relation to international law. The traditional categories of treaties, customary
law and general principles of domestic law, are too conservative to adequately
respond to the demands of worldwide environmental change. The sources of
rules and principles of international law, *consuetudo* and *opinio iuris sive necessitatis*, common features of domestic law, and consensus for international treaties,
lack the proactive dynamism needed today.[15]

Some international lawyers react by using the term principles in a looser
form. Discussing 'principles' of sustainability, precaution, etc., they do not imply
that these have already a legal effect.[16] Rather, such ambitious 'principles' are
regarded as a kind of proto-law. I submit that thereby the terminology is somewhat confused. The term principle should be reserved for principles of law. Non-
legal principles should rather be called ideals, objectives, policies, etc.

2.   Principles and rules

Principles and rules have often been opposed as different
compositions of the law. There is wide agreement among legal philosophers
that *principles are open for balancing against other principles whilst rules have to be
applied in any case.* Whilst principles are committed to one objective or value and
must be compromised if conflicting with opposing principles, rules are conclusive.[17]

Rules may however provide that exceptions are possible. Often such exceptions will be door openers for concerns, which represent a counter principle to
the principle which primarily stands behind the rule.[18] For instance, according
to the German Federal Emission Prevention Act (*Bundesimmissionsschutzgesetz*) the competent authority is entitled to order a firm to take improvement
measures, if after the issuance of the primary authorisation scientific progress
has revealed new environmental risks. The order is however, not allowed if the
economic burden involved is unproportional. Here, the rule reflecting the principle of environmental protection is relativised by an exception representing the
principle of economic freedom.

Rules can even be formulated in a way, which allows the balancing of opposing concerns *within* the scope of the rule. For instance, fundamental rights such
as the right to economic freedom are constructed to include first the *prima facie*
protection of certain activities (such as economic undertakings) and second the

---

[15] G. Winter, Anachronien von Gesellschaft, Natur und Recht, in: H. Faber, G. Frank (ed.) *Demokratie in
      Staat und Wirtschaft, Festschrift für Ekkehart Stein zum 70. Geburtstag,* Tübingen (Mohr) 2002, p. 327.

[16] Epiney/Scheyli, *op. cit.* p. 75 *et seq.*

[17] R. Alexy, *Theorie der Grundrechte,* Frankfurt, Suhrkamp, 2nd. ed. 1994, p. 71 *et seq.*; Martin Borowski,
      Grundrechte als Prinzipien, Baden-Baden (Nomos) 1998, p. 67 *et seq.*

[18] Alexy, *op. cit.* p. 88.

possibility of interference with the protected realm if resaons of public interest (such as environmental concerns) so require.[19]

Sometimes principles can be uncompromising. This is the case if they are of extremely high value, and if the core of the principle is at stake. For instance, according to the German constitution the essential requirements of human dignity are absolute. They may not be relativised by other principles. In international law principles with peremptory effect (such as the prohibition of apartheid, of torture, of aggression, etc.) are of this kind. The uncompromising principles should at the same time be conceived as rules, because they have to be strictly applied.

Principles stand in the background of rules and influence their interpretation and application. They enhance the normative power of rules, advise how to interpret them, help to fill regulatory gaps, guide discretionary powers and inform about necessary exceptions to a rule.[20] For instance, according to the German Federal Law on Soil Protection, the authorities have discretion to deal with past land contamination. They have the choice of making one or more out of the following persons responsible: the original polluter, his or her legal successor, the owner of the land and the holder of physical control of the land. The polluter pays principle, which is regarded as a principle although not explicitly stated by the law, has been used to fetter this discretion to the effect that the original polluter, if still available, should primarily be addressed.

If two or more principles contradict each other, rules solving such conflict are often available or could be established. This is I believe, the core characteristic of rules; that they are made in order to solve conflicts of principles in relation to more specific issue areas.

There is however, no rule establishing absolute cardinal or even ordinal ranks between principles. The law may nevertheless characterise a principle to be of particular importance. If so, the principle has, in the concrete case, a *prima facie* priority over conflicting principles.[21] In consequence, the burden of proof

---

[19] This is very controversial in the German debate on the doctrinal construction of basic rights. Many authors understand a basic right as a conglomerate of principles. They regard basic freedoms as principles, which can be balanced against public concerns and conflicting basic rights. They speak of rules only with regard to those specific propositions which case law develops for certain categories of cases. Cf. U. Ruehl, *Tatsachen – Interpretationen – Wertungen*, Baden-Baden (Nomos) 1998, p. 384 *et seq.* I believe that this conception neglects the specific terms of balancing constitutions often provide. There is no reason why rules should not be conceived to be open for balancing if they circumscribe the kind of conflicting interests to be considered and give direction on how to do the balancing. There is also room to distinguish between more general and open rules on the one side and more concrete and closed rules on the other.

[20] For more functions of principles, *e.g.* in relation to extra-legal negotiation and self-regulation, see Verschuuren, *op. cit.* 38 *et seq.*

[21] Alexy, *op. cit.* p. 88 *et seq.*

is shifted to the defender of the counter-principle.[22] For instance, German land use planning law prescribes that the authorities must consider and adequately balance, all interests affected by a zoning plan. Those interests include interests of housing, trade and industry, transportation, environmental and nature protection, etc. The law says that some of the interests are to be respected as far as possible. For instance land used for agriculture, forestry, or housing shall only, if unavoidable, be converted for other uses.[23] This means that to destin such land for *e.g.* industrial or transportation purposes, would be a prima facie violation of the principle. The burden of proving that in the case industrial use is preponderant will be shifted to the development interests.

Without legal prioritisation, all principles are equal in an abstract sense. The relative weight of principles will then change with the given individual circumstances and can therefore, only be determined in the concrete case. One rule recognized in such circumstances is that, the greater one principle will be impaired by a solution, the weightier the prevailing principle must be.[24]

An example of a quite sophisticated rule of balancing opposing principles is contained in Article 6(4) of the Habitat Directive 92/43/EEC: As a starting point the protected demands of the rare species and habitats are given priority over interests in their use. However, compelling public interests in the project can overcome this protection. Such interests must again give way, if the affected species or habitats are listed as priority. The priority is again reversed if the public interest in the project is particularly indispensable (such as the interests of public health and safety).

3. Principles and the hierarchy of norms

a) General remark

Principles and their corresponding rules can be situated on the same level of a hierarchy of norms. This is the normal situation where principles play their proper role by serving as a source for interpreting rules, filling gaps in the rules, guiding the use of discretion, etc. For instance, as mentioned before, the precautionary principle stands behind its more precise and complex emanation laid down in the German Federal Emission Prevention Act.

Principles and rules can also be situated on different hierarchical levels of the law. There are internal hierarchies of the levels of national, regional and even international law between ordinary law and higher ranked law controlling the ordinary law; *i.e.* constitutional law prevailing over national ordinary law, EC primary law commanding EC secondary law, and international peremptory law commanding international ordinary law. This internal constitutional

---

[22] Alexy, *op. cit.* p. 146.

[23] Article 1 para 5 sentence 3 Construction Code.

[24] Alexy, *op. cit.* p. 146.

hierarchy *within* each level is to be distinguished from the external hierarchy *between* levels which we might call the federal hierarchy: EC law has supremacy over national law and depending on certain conditions international law can also have supremacy over national or regional law. The higher level can be one of constitutional law or one of EC or international law. I have mentioned examples of such higher ranked principles earlier, for instance, the protection of the natural conditions of life contained in Article 20a of the German constitution, the achievement of a high level of environmental protection in Article 174 EC and the prevention of serious harm as a principle of international customary law.

If a principle has been laid down on a higher 'constitutional' or 'federal' level the crucial question is whether these principles have the power to render rules ranked on a lower level in the hierarchy inapplicable if they contradict the principle. I suggest that the answer is: not directly. *The constitutional, supranational or international principle must first have been transformed into a rule. Only rules can be attributed the effect of invalidating lower rank rules.*[25]

International peremptory law	Principles Rules
International ordinary law	Principles Rules
Regional constitutional law	Principles Rules
Regional ordinary law	Principles Rules
National constitutional law	Principles Rules
National ordinary law	Principles Rules

This implies, first of all, that we must be more careful with calling propositions, rules or principles. The higher the level in the norm pyramid the more

---

[25] For a different view see R. Alexy who proposes to directly apply principles if only in a more open way which allows for the balancing of principles with colliding other principles. I do not follow Alexy because his theory would hinder the emergence of principles out of common sense and common practice. The discourse about new principles would be loaden with the "threat" that all what is accepted would already be applicable law. The dynamic potential of principles is, I believe, based on their somewhat elusive status behind the scene.

willing we are to call a proposition a principle, although upon closer look it may
be framed as a rule which already contains the balancing of different opposing
principles.

b) German law

For instance, Article 20a of the German constitution contains
a qualification stating that the principle of environmental protection is binding only 'in the framework of the constitutional order', 'constitutional order'
meaning the entirety of the constitution. This is generally understood to mean
that environmental protection must be balanced against other principles such
as property and economic freedoms.[26] Article 20a *Grundgesetz* is therefore a
rule, an open one, but not a principle. Basic rights can also be understood to
establish rules on balancing opposing principles. For instance, the basic right to
health may be relativised by other principles of public interest. The fact that one
principle (the protection of human health) was made a basic right has the effect
that the protected freedom has a *prima facie* priority over the principles protecting public interests. The latter bear the burden of proving their *secunda facie*
preponderance.

c) EC law

In relation to the principles contained in Article 174 EC, I
submit that they too can only become operative if transformed into rules. This
means that they must be formulated in a more complex way, than by merely
restating the principle. Opposing principles must be integrated into the rule,
such as the principles of proportionality and the principles representing
economic freedoms. Only via a complex and more precise rule, can a principle render a national law inapplicable. This can be shown if we consider ECJ
jurisprudence on fundamental rights under Article 6 EU and basic economic
freedoms under Article 28 EC.

As for basic rights it is true, that European courts have only rarely had the
opportunity of expressing themselves on rules combining the basic right principle with environmental protection principles. In comparison to the frequent
opposition of basic rights and environmental protection in German domestic
law (in particular guaranties of economic freedom and property), it is astonish-
ing how seldom fundamental rights in the Community have been invoked as a
bulwark against Community environmental measures (though this can sometimes be explained by the restrictive standing requirements of Article 230(4)
EC).

---

[26] Hans D. Jarass, *Grundgesetz für die Bundesrepublik Deutschland*, 5. ed., München 2000, Article 20a note
9.

Standley however can be seen as a case, which does oppose fundamental rights and Community environmental principles. Standley, a farmer, brought an action against British laws, which were founded upon a Community Directive. That Directive prescribed that the Member States must designate bodies of water, with high levels of nitrate and limit intensive animal husbandry in the corresponding zones. Standley argued (unsuccessfully) that this was an interference with his property right. In response, the ECJ stated that the exercise of basic property rights could be subject to limitations in so far as

'*those restrictions in fact correspond to objectives of general interest pursued by the Community and do not constitute a disproportionate and intolerable interference, impairing the very substance of the rights guaranteed*'.[27]

The protection of public health can be such a goal. The Directive serves these ends, as the Court briefly indicated, in a way that follows the principle of proportionality.[28] Thus, the principle of protection of public health was integrated into the basic right to private property. This right was constructed as a complex rule on balancing property and human health interests. In the *Standley* case this rule was not considered violated, by the incriminated Directive.

As for basic freedoms, since *Danish Bottles* the principle of environmental protection has been recognised as a justification for encroachments by Member States on the basic freedom of movement of goods.[29] The same is true of the principle of the protection of human health. The *Toolex* case shows this in particular; human health is affected in this case not directly through products, but indirectly through environmental causational chains such as air and water pollution.[30] In the *Bluhme* case the protection of biodiversity, as a legally protected interest was recognised.[31] In *PreussenElektra* the climate was similarly recognised.[32] With respect to the principles of Article 174(2) EC, there is case law as to the rectification-at-source principle, this was evident in *Walloon Waste* as an admissible justification for Belgian import restrictions on waste.[33]

However, in other cases the opportunity to corresponding recourse was missed. For example in *Dusseldorp*, which addressed Dutch export restrictions

---

[27] Case C-293/93 *Standley* [1999] ECR I-2603 (para. 54).

[28] Case C-293/93 *Standley* [1999] ECR I-2603 (para. 54, 56).

[29] Case 302/86 *Commission* v. *Denmark* [1988] ECR 4607 (No. 9). For an overview *see:* H. Temmink, From Danish bottles to Danish bees: the dynamics of free movement of goods and environmental protection – a case law analysis (2000) *Yearbook of European Environmental Law* Vol. 1, p. 61-102.

[30] Case C-473/98 *Chemical Inspections* v. *Toolex* [2000] ECR (No. 38). The case concerns the prohibition of Trichlorethylen which also spreads via environmental processes.

[31] Case C-67/97 *Ditlev Bluhme* [1998] ECR I-8033 (para. 33).

[32] Case C-379 *PreussenElektra* [2001] ECR I-2099 (para. 73).

[33] Case C-2/90 *Commission* v. *Belgium* [1992] ECR I-4431 (para. 34).

[34] Case C-203/96 *Dusseldorp* [1998] ECR I-4075.

for waste intended for recycling[34], the ECJ could have relied on the effectiveness
of recycling in domestic or foreign installations as a criterion for allowing or
disallowing export restrictions; this criterion could have been derived from the
principle of rational use of resources provided by Article 174(3) 3rd indent EC.[35]

In relation to the doctrinal construction of principles and rules we can
conclude that the Court has used principles in order to form a complex rule on
the admissibility of transborder trade restrictions. The rule is about the following: Trade restrictions are *prima facie* prohibited but can, *secunda facie*, be justified if based on environmental protection principles.

d) International law

At international law level, the distinction between principles
and rules can also play a clarifying role. International lawyers have not yet
adopted a clear distinction between principles and rules. Often the term principle is used, but in fact what is discussed is a rule. This is true for the general
principles of international law, some of which have the character of rules and in
particular, those which even have the status of peremptory norms.[36] For the sake
of clarity they should better be called 'general rules (or norms) of international
law'. Even the 'general principles of law', in the sense of Article 38(1) lit. c) ICJ
Statute, if consulted as a source of international law will not lead to a principle,
but to a rule based on those principles.[37] The environmental propositions cited
earlier as recognised international law, *i.e.* the duties to prevent serious harm
and to cooperate, are also not principles but rules. By contrast, precaution is
certainly not yet a rule. It can, however, be regarded as a principle, if by principle
we mean a proposition which is open for balancing against conflicting principles. Bed on such principle, we may even consider precaution to be part of a
rule of international law which also takes opposing principles such as economic
freedoms into account. If so it could be stated as follows[38]:

*'States cannot rely on scientific uncertainty to justify inaction when there is
enough evidence to establish the possibility of a risk of serious harm, even if there is
as yet no proof of harm. In determining whether and how far to apply precautionary
measures, states may take account of their capabilities, their economic and social
priorities, the cost-effectiveness of preventive measures, and the nature and degree of
the environmental risk'.*

---

[35] The Dutch government did not raise the issue of recycling effectiveness. As a consequence the court
    was not compelled to invoke that criterion. *See*: G. Winter, Die Steuerung grenzüberschreitender Abfall-
    ströme, *Deutsches Verwaltungsblatt* 2000, 657 ff.

[36] See *e.g.* Ian Brownlie, *Public International Law*, Oxford (Clarendon Press), 5th ed. 1998, p. 19.

[37] Esser, *op. cit.* p. 140.

[38] The phrasing is based on Birnie/Boyle, *op. cit.* p. 120.

If specified in this way, precaution may be more easily acceptable as a rule of international law. Of course, it does not have a peremptory character in relation to treaty law. It can, however, influence domestic legislation, depending on how the national constitutions decide on the relationship between international and national law.

As a consequence, environmental principles, distinct from rules, would also be able to play their proper role in international law, *i.e.* to inform the interpretation of rules and to fill possible gaps in the body of treaty and customary law. They can emerge out of world-wide public discourses and experiences. They are transmission belts between common experience and common sense on the one side and rules of international law on the other. If widely accepted by international doctrine and court practice, they can instigate *opinio iuris sive necessitatis* and *consuetudo* in order to bring about new customary law. They can even be regarded as general principles of the law, if by 'law' we do not only understand national but also international law.[39] In conclusion, principles can be a genuine source of rules also on the international level and may as such accelerate the process of international law-making. In that respect they show the same potential of the self-creation of law, which is well known from common law systems.[40]

4. Judicial review of principles

We have seen that there is a difference between policies, principles and rules. Principles are legally binding. They inform the interpretation and development of rules. They may be built into rules, by which they may also be assigned a specific legal weight in relation to possible countervailing principles. For instance, as we have seen, the rules of the EC Treaty on basic freedoms provide that environmental concerns may prevail over the free transboundary movement of goods.

There is one more dimension to the legal value of principles, *i.e.* how thoroughly the courts will review governmental action based on environmental principles. If the governmental body has actually made use of a principle, the courts will tend to have a close look at the case. In other words, if the principle is used to empower an authority, the review will be thorough. By contrast, if the governmental body has refused to act, although the principle may oblige it to, the courts will tend to tolerate such passivity. Thus, if the principle would compel an authority to act, the court will not impose its own understanding of the principle. The reason for this reaction is as follows; if the governmental body has already applied the principle it will normally have already weighed it against opposing principles in its decision. The courts are then prepared, to check if

---

[39] See on the history and potential of this source of international law A. Cassese, *International Law*, Oxford (Oxford UP) 2001, p. 155 *et seq.*

[40] Esser, *op. cit.* p. 139.

the balance was correctly struck. If on the other hand, the governmental body
has desisted from acting, it is undecided what opposing principles would have
to be taken into consideration. As this is widely a political matter reserved for
the democratically legitimated bodies, the courts will normally defer to their
opinion.

I shall prove this hypothesis by recalling some ECJ judgments.

a) The context of providing powers

Principles can inform rules empowering governmental activities;
· when a competence basis is required
· when a member state wishes to go further than a Community measure
provides.

aa) Empowering the exercise of community competences

In the *BSE* ("mad cow disease") case, the Community had taken legal
measures directed against the export of British beef to other member states.
The ECJ was asked by Britain to check if the competence basis, namely that for
agricultural policy, had been duly applied. Referring to the environmental policy
principles and the principle of integration of these principles into other policies,
the court pronounced itself quite precisely on the legal concept of "acting under
uncertainty":

*'Where there is uncertainty as to the existence or extent of risks to human health,
the institutions may take protective measures without having to wait until the reality
and seriousness of those risks become fully apparent.'*[41]

Secondary legislation can however, also exceed the margin of competence rules
and the principles of the treaties, including the environmental principles, can
then serve as guidance on when the Community organs exceed their competence. One example of this given by the ECJ, is the already cited *Standley* case.[42]

---

[41] Case C-180/96 *United Kingdom* v. *Commission* [1998] ECR I-2265 (No. 99); the phrase was again
invoked in the case *Artegodan* v. *Commission*, Court of First Instance, Joined Cases T-74/00, T-76/00,
[2000] ECR II-327, at no. 184.

[42] Case C-293/93 *Standley* [1999] ECR I-2603. The relevant passage is in paragraphs 55 and 56 which read:
'It is true that the action programmes which are provided for in Article 5 of the Directive and are to
contain the mandatory measures referred to in Annex III impose certain conditions on the spreading of
fertiliser and livestock manure, so that those programmes are liable to restrict the exercise by the farmers concerned of the right to property. However, the system laid down in Article 5 reflects requirements
relating to the protection of public health, and thus pursues an objective of general interest without the
substance of the right to property being impaired.'

Standley invoked the polluter pays principle against an EC Directive, which limited his animal husbandry. On this point the ECJ stated:

> *'As regards the polluter pays principle, suffice it to state that the Directive does not mean that farmers must take on burdens for the elimination of pollution to which they have not contributed.'*[43]

From this, one can interpolate that the court would have appreciated the act as a violation of the polluter pays principle, if the Directive had burdened the person who was not the source of the pollution.

bb) Empowering member states to go further than secondary law

In the area of secondary law, member states can according to Article 95 paras. 4 and 5 EC and/or Article 176 EC, under certain circumstances enact law, which goes further than Community law. The particular preconditions are of no interest here. The only relevant point for our consideration is the question of the applicability of environmental principles. They come into play as specifying the direction in which complementary member state action can move. Thus Article 95 paras. 4 and 5 EC, allow for complementary action 'relating to the protection of the environment'. The same is implicit in Article 176 EC. Any complementary action must result in greater environmental protection. The principles contained in Article 174(2) EC are drawn into Article 95 paras. 4 and 5 EC by the integration clause and into Article 176 EC through direct reference to Article 174 EC. They open up the potential space for, but also mark the limits of complementary acts. For example, a member state making use of Article 176 EC can draw upon the precautionary principle when the Community legal act is limited to defence against imminent and serious danger.

Environmental principles can also guide the use of safeguard-clauses established on the ground of Article 95(10) EC. The Court of Justice in the *Monsanto* case expressed this.[44] The court once more going into some detail said that the safeguard clause introduced by legislation on novel food could be used for precautionary measures, but that such measures had to be based on a risk assessment:

> *'Nevertheless, those measures can be adopted only if the Member State has first carried out a risk assessment which is as complete as possible given the particular circumstances of the individual case, from which it is apparent that, in the light of the precautionary principle, the implementation of such measures is necessary in order to ensure that novel foods do not present danger for the consumer, in accordance with the first indent of Article 3(1) of Regulation No. 258/97.'*[45]

---

[43] Case C-293/93 *Standley* [1999] ECR I-2603 (para. 51).

[44] Judgment of September 9, 2003, Case C-263/01 *Monsanto*.

[45] No. 107 of the judgment.

b) The context of commanding action

aa) *Triggering action by Community organs*

A commanding function can be attributed to the principles, when they make specifications for the exercise, by Community organs, of a rule on competences, thereby encouraging rather than limiting action. The obligation that the commanding function imposes is even more marked when, in a situation of otherwise complete passivity or even political resistance, it constitutes a rule compelling the Community's organs to act.

The ECJ gives the Community organs wide discretion in such cases. In *Safety High Tech*, following its usual jurisprudence, it stated that;

'in view of the need to strike a balance between certain of the objectives and principles mentioned in Article 130r and of the complexity of the implementation of those criteria, review by the Court must necessarily be limited to the question whether the Council, by adopting the Regulation, committed a manifest error of appraisal regarding the conditions for the application of Article 130r of the Treaty.'[46]

The judicial self-restraint exposed in this rule, is explained by the necessity to strike a balance between opposing principles and the complexity of the implementation of those principles. In more general terms, we can conclude that if the rule is very open; *i.e.* if it is only providing for a fair balancing of principles without giving specific guidance, the courts allow for wide legislatory discretion, thereby avoiding the need to replace the legislator's appreciation with their own.

Nevertheless further guidance, other than the mere arbitrariness test, may be derived from a closer look at the meaning, aim and conditions of the principles. A core and a penumbra of the principles may be distinguished, the core fettering the discretionary margin of the legislator. The core could be defined somewhat in the way of *a maiore ad minus*: when measures combating uncertain risks may be regarded as an extension of the principle of environmental protection measures to defend against imminent and serious dangers should be taken as a legal obligation. If in this way the core of principles is identified, it can also be taken to already constitute the relevant rule. For if the core is affected there will hardly remain space for bringing opposing principles into the shaping of the rule.

Genuine cases in which a Community measure remains below an attainable level of protection, have not yet received explicit treatment by the European

---

[46] Case C-284/95 *Safety High Tech* [1998] ECR I-4301 (No. 37). The German Federal Constitutional Court has expressed itself in a similar way. See, for instance, the case where the neighbour of an airport complained that the authorities had not taken appropriate protection measures. The court ruled that there was no "evident" violation of the constitutional duty of the state to protect the individual (BVerfGE 56, 54 *et seq.*, at 80).

Courts. However the ECJ in the case of *Safety High Tech* does imply the possibility that an environmental protection measure can fail to attain the high level of environmental protection required by Article 174 EC. In the case the court found this standard was in fact met as a comparison with the laxer measures of a pertinent international agreement (the Montreal protocol) showed. Since the court treated this issue only implicitly, the question cannot be considered as decided.

The ECJ has expressed itself on commanding functions mostly in the somewhat ironical cases, where it was the addressee of a Community measure, which complained that the Community measure did not go far enough. The plaintiffs in such cases, whose environmentally injurious acts were enjoined by Community law, argued that the Community failed to also (or instead) punish the other "sinners". The argument can be designated as a version of the NIMBY ("not in my backyard") principle. The more normal case – where a Community organ, a member state or a third party who would benefit from the Community measure, but deems it insufficient, files the complaint – has not yet been decided by the courts.

Safety High Tech is particularly relevant as an example of the NIMBY situation. A regulation for the protection of the stratospheric ozone layer prohibited the use of partially halogenated CFCs. The producer, *Safety High Tech*, argued that CFCs could not be singled out and forbidden without also forbidding halons, for halons have a higher potential than CFCs for destruction of the ozone layer and in addition, unlike CFCs, also have a green house effect. The failure to consider the green house potential of halons, meant that the general command of the protection of the environment was violated; further, because of the failure to consider halon's higher potential to destroy the ozone layer the specific command of a 'high level of protection' was also violated. The ECJ replied, on the basis of ex Article 130r (now Article 174), that

> '*it does not follow from those provisions that Article 130r(1) of the Treaty requires the Community legislature, whenever it adopts measures to preserve, protect and improve the environment in order to deal with a specific environmental problem, to adopt at the same time measures relating to the environment as a whole.*'[47]

Although this answer is basically reasonable, the court could have gone somewhat further by making use of a German legal construct, namely the *Konzeptgebot* (planned approach). The *Konzeptgebot*, which was introduced by the Federal Administrative Court (*Bundesverwaltungsgericht* – BVerwG), may be invoked in situations in which a complex set of problems must be solved urgently, but are difficult to handle because of limited instrumental and administration capacity. Due to this complexity, the issues do not have to be solved in one stroke; rather, the public authorities may go step-by-step singling out individual actors if this is based on a broader plan providing for systematic further action in the future.

---

[47] Case C-284/95 *Safety High-Tech* [1998] ECR I-2603 (para. 44).

In *Safety High Tech* the application of the *Konzeptgebot* would have meant, a requirement for an overall plan for the phasing out of both CFCs and halons. It seems that in fact, there was such a plan in fulfillment of the obligations of the Montreal Protocol. It was defensible to first tackle CFCs, where ready substitutes exist and then to address the thornier question of halons (which have since indeed been banned).

In *Standley*, the *Konzeptgebot* would have required asking whether the Directive stood in the framework of a general concept of combating all nitrate sources in order to judge the burdens which arose there, from agriculture. Instead the Court of Justice satisfied itself with an isolated consideration of the contribution of farming to nitrates.

bb) Directing member states

Directive functions of the environmental principles vis-à-vis the member states, are less apparent than commanding functions. Certainly the member states are not bound in so far as their own area of competence is concerned. However, in so far as they apply Community secondary legislation and thereby have a certain margin of appreciation, they are also under a duty to pay heed to the environmental law principles of the Community.[48] This would be a consequential application of the case law in *Wachauf* (which is also codified in Article 51 of the Charter of Fundamental Rights), namely that the member states when applying Community law are bound by the fundamental rights and principles of the Community.[49] The fact that the integration principle of Article 6 is not anchored anywhere, in the national constitution of any member state is of particular interest in this regard. This could lead to consequences for member states when applying Community law outside the realm of environmental law (say for example energy law), for they would have to respect the environmental principles of Article 174 EC, including *e.g.* the principle of rational use of natural resources.[50]

III Conclusion

The analysis of the legal nature of environmental principles above, can be summed up as follows:

1) Principles should be understood to have a legal value. Non-legal principles should be called policies, ideals, objectives, etc.

---

[48] See: Jans/ von der Heide, *op. cit.* p. 23.

[49] Case 5/88 *Hubert Wachauf* v. *Bundesrepublik Deutschland* [1989] ECR 2609 (para. 19).

[50] Similar suggestions have been made by: R. Macrory, *Environmental integration and the European Charter of Fundamental Rights*, Paper presented to the Avosetta Group, Jan. 12/13, 2001, p. 8 (www.avosetta.org); N. de Sadeleer, Les fondements de l'action communautaire en matière d'environnement, in: *L' Europe et ses citoyens*, Peter Lang 2000, p. 112, with further examples.

2) The legal value is derived from legislation or court jurisprudence. In the first case it is based on political decision, in the second on common experience and common sense.

3) Principles are to be distinguished from rules. Principles can be balanced against conflicting principles, rules are conclusive even though they may provide for exceptions or for the balancing of conflicting concerns.

4) Rules that provide for the weighing of principles may give one principle a prima facie or even conclusive priority over countervailing principles.

5) Principles help to interpret rules, fill gaps in rules, and develop new rules.

6) The distinction between principles and rules can be applied to all levels of the hierarchy of norms, be the hierarchy internal to one level or related to different levels.

7) If applied to international law, the distinction between principles and rules may help to accelerate the development of the law. Principles can serve as a transmission belt between common experience and common sense on the one side and rules on the other. They may be more readily accepted if understood as being open for balancing against other principles. Rules may be more readily accepted if formulated more precisely as bridges between conflicting principles.

8) The exactness of judicial reviews of governmental action, for applying or not applying, environmental principles differs; depending on whether a principle was used by an authority to empower it to act or whether the authority desists from action although the principle may oblige it to act. The courts tend to apply a more rigourous check in the first instance and defer to the authority's attitude in the latter. The reason for this is to be found in the separation of powers between the judiciary and democratically legitimated govenmental bodies.

CHAPTER 3

The Genesis of EC Environmental Principles

Ludwig Krämer

1 **The birth**

1.1 The origins

The EC Treaty in its present version contains a number of environmental principles. The following contribution will try to retrace the origins of these principles in the EC Treaty and how they were developed by the EC institutions and in particular by the Commission. This discussion concerns the principles of integration[1], prevention[2] and precaution[3], the principle that environmental damage should as a priority be rectified at source[4] and the polluter pays principle.[5]

As is well known, the original EC Treaty of 1957 did not contain any provision on environmental policy or law. In 1971, the Commission submitted the first communication to the Council on a Community policy for the environment,[6] which was soon followed by a proposal for an environmental action programme.[7] Neither of these documents contained any reference to environmental principles. It was the German delegation which, in a Council note of 25 September 1972[8], requested that the Council's resolution should be based 'on a general environmental conception', and that the Council's document on environmental policy should contain 'a general part which determines the basic principles of a European environmental policy' and an action programme with specific concrete actions.[9] 'The general part should contain general principles and objectives which are recognised in the same way for specific EC measures and as guidelines for specific actions in Member States [...] the basic principles should have long-term effects.' The document formulated ten basic principles, among them the prevention principle, the polluter pays principle and the integration principle.

---

[1]   Article 6 EC Treaty: 'Environmental protection requirements must be integrated into the definition and implementation of the Community policies and activities referred to in Article 3, in particular with a view to promoting sustainable development'.

[2]   Article 174(2.2) EC Treaty: 'It (Community policy) shall be based [...] on the principles that preventive action should be taken'.

[3]   Article 174(2.2) EC Treaty: 'It (Community policy) shall be based [...]on the precautionary principle'.

[4]   Article 174(2.2) EC Treaty: 'It (Community policy) shall be based on the principles that environmental damage should as a priority be rectified at source'.

[5]   Article 174(2.2) EC Treaty: 'It (Community policy) shall be based on the principles that the polluter should pay'.

[6]   Commission SEC (71) 2616 of 22 July 1971.

[7]   Commission proposal, (1972) OJ C 52/1.

[8]   Council, R/1879/72 (ENV 37) of 25 September 1972.

[9]   'umweltpolitische Gesamtkonzeption' (all translations, also in the following, by the author). In 1972, English was not an official EC language.

In mid-October 1972 the Heads of State or Governments of the Member States met in Paris and invited the EC institutions to elaborate an environmental action programme. On 31st October 1972 the EC ministers for the environment, at a meeting in Bonn, agreed eleven 'principles of a Community environment policy', which took over the environmental principles mentioned in the German note and, in supplement, some wording on the necessity to rectify damage at source.

1.2   Principles in action programmes

The first EC environmental action programme followed the German proposal; it was split into a general part, which dealt with objectives, principles and generalities of EC environmental policy and a specific part which gave a detailed description of the specific actions which were to be undertaken within the next two years.[10] The eleven "principles of a Community environment policy"[11], agreed in Bonn, were incorporated into the general part, without any clarifying wording.

The second, third and fourth EC environmental action programme also referred to these principles, though the separation of the programme into a general and a specific part was abandoned.[12] There was also no detailed discussion of the principles in these programmes. The Commission also showed in other documents, which it issued in this period that it did not attach much importance to the principles, and hardly ever mentioned them.[13]

EC environmental legislation between 1975, when the first environmental directive was adopted, and 1985, only mentioned the environmental principles when this appeared convenient in order to justify the approach chosen.[14] There

---

[10]   Programme of action of the EC on the Environment (1973) OJ C 112 p. 1.

[11]   These principles were: 1. Preventing the creation of pollution or nuisances at source; 2. Taking into account of effects on the environment at the earliest possible stage in planning and decision-making processes; 3. Avoiding exploitation of natural resources or of a nature which causes significant damage to the ecological damage; 4. Improving standards of scientific and technological knowledge; 5. Polluter pays principle; 6. Activities in one State should not cause degradation of the environment in another state; 7. Taking into account of the developing countries; 8. Improving regional and global cooperation and research; 9. Improving information and education on environmental issues; 10. Intervening at the most appropriate level (local, regional, national, EC); 11. Coordination environmental policies within the EC.

[12]   Second environmental action programme (1977) OJ C 139 p. 1; Third programme (1983) OJ C 46 p. 1; Fourth programme (1987) OJ C 328/1.

[13]   Commission, State of the Environment: first report, Luxembourg 1977; Second report, Luxembourg 1979; Progress made in connection with the Environment Action Programme and assessment of the work done to implement it, COM (80) 222 of 13 May 1980.

[14]   See for examples below the discussion of the specific principles.

is not a single directive or regulation where the chosen approach was directly based on one of the principles. This attitude finds its explanation mainly in the fact that there was no explicit legal basis for environment measures in the EC Treaty and that legislation therefore proceeded very pragmatically, and also that the insertion of the principles in the programme had been done at the specific request of one Member State. Similarly, the legal literature prior to 1985 hardly discussed the environmental principles.[15]

There was thus little scientific, administrative and political preparation of the ground for environmental principles, when in 1985, the EC Treaty was amended and a chapter on environmental policy (Articles 130r to 130t) was introduced. On the request of the Intergovernmental Conference the Commission drafted provisions inter alia on principles, which were incorporated in the final text without much discussion.[16] These principles correspond to those, which are now enshrined in Article 174 EC, with two exceptions: the Maastricht Treaty of 1993 added the precautionary principle to Article 174(2) EC. And Article 130r in its version of 1987 also contained a provision on the integration principle, which was, by the Amsterdam Treaty of 1999, placed into Article 6 as will be explained below.

2   The integration principle

2.1   Origins

The Commission's first proposal for an EC environmental policy programme stated that environmental concerns affected more or less all EC policies; it expressly mentioned commercial,agricultural, competition, social, transport, development, energy and regional policy.[17] The first environmental action programme then stated that 'the activities of the Communities in the different sectors in which they operate (agricultural policy, social policy, regional policy, industrial policy, energy policy, etc.) must take account of concern for the protection and improvement of the environment. Furthermore, such concerns must be taken into consideration in the elaboration and implementation of these policies'.[18]

---

[15] See for instance House of Lords, Select Committee on the EC: *EEC Environment Policy.* (London 1980); K. v. Moltke, a.o. *Grenzüberschreitender Umweltschutz in Europa,* Heidelberg 1984; E. Rehbinder-R. Stewart, *Environmental Protection Policy.* Berlin-New York 1985; R. Romi, *L'Europe et la protection juridique de l'environnement.* Paris 1990.

[16] See also J. de Ruyt, *L'Acte Unique European.* Bruxelles 1987, p. 216.

[17] Commission (n. 7) p. 6 *et seq.*

[18] First action programme (n. 10) p. 11 *et seq.* These phrases are placed in Title III, chapter 2, outside the section on principles of environmental policy, which constitute Title II.

The second environmental action programme stated that without environment protection measures, it would not be possible to achieve the EC's objectives of Article 2 EC;[19] it discussed some activities in the agricultural, energy and social sector, but did not specify in detail any integration requirements. In 1983, the Council and Member States' Resolution on the third environmental action programme declared 'that it is important for Community actions to be carried out particularly in the following areas: (a) integration of the environmental dimension into other policies [...]'.[20]

2.2 Treaty amendments

In March 1985, the Commission presented to the meeting of Heads of State and Governments in Brussels a memorandum on an EC-wide environment policy[21] in which it asked the European Council to endorse three main guidelines of such a policy, the first of which declared: 'Protection of the environment is to be treated as an integral part of economic and social policies both overall (at macroeconomic level) and by individual sectors (agricultural policy, industrial policy, energy policy, etc.)'. At the end of that Brussels meeting the European Council affirmed 'its determination to give this policy [environmental policy, L.K.] the dimension of an essential component of the economic, industrial, agricultural and social policies implemented by the Community and by its Member States'.[22] The discussions on the amended EC Treaty, which started in the same year, 1985, led to the provision of the new Article 130r (2.2) EC which entered into effect in 1987, and which stated that 'environmental protection requirements shall be a component of the Community's other policies'.

The Maastricht Treaty of 1993 reformulated this provision as follows: 'Environmental protection requirements must be integrated into the definition and implementation of other Community policies'. The Amsterdam Treaty of 1999 transferred this provision into the new Article 6 EC which now reads: 'Environmental protection requirements must be integrated into the definition and implementation of the Community policies and activities referred to in Article 3, in particular with a view to promoting sustainable development'. This transfer was a reaction to the Commission's request at the Intergovernmental Conference to insert a reference to environmental requirements into the chapters on agriculture, transport, competition etc.

---

[19] Second programme (n. 12) p. 5.

[20] Third action programme (n. 12), p. 2; see also European Parliament Resolution of 20 November 1981 (1981) OJ C 327 p. 83, which strongly pleads for integrating environmental requirements in all other relevant EC policies.

[21] Bulletin of the EC (1985) 3, p. 101.

[22] European Council, Bulletin (n. 21) p. 13.

The fourth environmental action programme, drawn up in 1985/86 at a time, when it was already apparent that there would be a chapter on environmental policy inserted in the EC Treaty, contained a full chapter on integration requirements[23] though it did not go beyond general statements that such integration was necessary. For the internal market aspects, the Commission set up a specific Task Force, which came up with a detailed thorough analysis on the integration of environmental requirements in the internal market, but was poor as regards operational conclusions.[24]

2.3   Procedures inside the Commission

In 1991, the Commission published guidelines for legislation in internal market matters[25] which generally suggested that future internal market legislation should fix strict binding standards for a first period and at the same time guide standards which were to be reached in a longer period. The Council should fix the standards for the first period, the standards for the second period by the Commission. Tax incentives for an accelerated application of the first standards, and within certain limits, the second set of standards should be allowed. These guidelines had the disadvantage that the Commission itself did not make one single proposal for legislation where it suggested their application. They quickly fell into oblivion.

In 1993, the Commission adopted a number of internal operational measures with the aim of reaching better integration of environmental concerns into its decisions.[26] The main measures suggested were the following:
- all Commission proposals were to be assessed on their environmental effects. Where such an impact was likely, an environmental impact assessment was to be made;
- proposals for new legal measures should, in the explanatory memorandum, describe and explain environmental effects and environmental costs and benefits;
- the Commission work programme had to identify with a green asterisk, measures with a significant impact on the environment;
- in all Commission departments, contact persons for the integration of environmental requirements into that sector had to be designated;
- an environmental network of director generals was set up inside the Commission which was to ensure coordination of measures and the integration of environmental requirements;

---

[23] Fourth action programme (n. 12), 9 et seq., chapter 2(3).

[24] Task Force Report: 1992 – The Environmental Dimension. Bonn 1990.

[25] Bulletin of the EC (1991) 3, p. 49 no. 1.2.156.

[26] Commission, SEC (93) 785 of 2 June 1993; see also Written Question E-0649/97 (Carmen Diez de Rivera Icaza) (1997) OJ C 367 p. 33.

· the Commission's annual report had to include, for key political areas, an indication of how environmental considerations were taken into account;
· a number of measures concerning the Commission's handling of its own waste management, waste recycling and purchase policy ('green accounting') were taken.

Overall, the effect of these measures on the orientation of the Commission's policy was insignificant. No environment impact assessment was made for any new proposal. Also other measures were not applied by the Commission administration and the guidelines were, with the political renewals of the Commission in 1995 and 1999, progressively forgotten.

2.4 Sectoral initiatives

Another attempt of integration was made under the fifth environmental action programme, which ran from 1993 to 2000.[27] In this programme, which had the heading 'Towards Sustainability', the Commission selected five target sectors – manufacturing industry, energy, transport, agriculture and tourism – with a particularly significant impact on the environment. The programme fixed, for the very first time, a number of targets for each of these sectors, which were to be reached by 2000.

The programme did not change the EC's administrative and political practice and, in particular, did not lead to any specific initiative in any of the five sectors. In view of the modest results, the Commission's report which was to assess the results of the fifth action programme, did not examine these five sectors in any detail but, limited itself to mentioning that integration had had a 'limited success' and, for the rest, preferred to look at these in the future.[28]

Since the appearance of environmental provisions in the EC Treaty, one of the actions taken by the Commission was the publication of communications, greenbooks or white papers on the relationship between specific sectors of EC policy and the environment. The first of such papers dated from 1988 and concerned 'Environment and agriculture'.[29] The thoroughness and quality of these communications differed greatly. Normally, the analysis of the interrelationship between the environment and the specific sector of policy was acceptable. However, since almost no operational or political proposals for amending the sectoral policies were made, the communications had more an alibi effect than a significant impact.

---

[27] Fifth environmental action programme (1993) OJ C 138 p. 1.

[28] Commission, Europe's environment: what directions for the future? The global assessment of the EC programme of policy and action in relation to the environment and sustainability development, 'towards sustainability', COM (99) 543, section 9.

2.5   Cardiff process; impact assessments

The above-mentioned insertion of Article 6 into the EC Treaty once more underlined the importance of the integration principle, and the European Council, meeting in Cardiff in June 1998, took a fresh view of that question. It invited the transport, energy and agriculture Councils to elaborate strategies for integrating environmental requirements into their sectors and to report on it. Later European Councils extended this request to the internal market, industry, development, fisheries, economic and general affairs Councils.

However, the work was not done by these Councils, but rather by the Commission, which submitted a number of papers[30] that were subsequently 'approved' by the different sectoral Councils and discussed by the Heads of State and Governments. Neither the different Councils nor the Commission felt bound by these papers and the subsequent political conclusions. And while this 'Cardiff process' of developing and discussing 'strategies' was never formally brought to a halt, it progressively turned more into a political declaration than leading to a work programme with objectives, priorities and timetables[31]. This led the sixth environmental action programme to state that further integration efforts were needed and request that the different strategies produced under the Cardiff process 'are translated into effective action'.[32]

In 2003, the Commission started a new attempt. It submitted to an impact assessment all legislative proposals, which had an economic, social or environmental impact and all non-regulatory proposals, which had significant impacts. Where such impacts appeared, after a first scrutiny, to be likely, an extended impact assessment was to be made which included consultations with interested parties. This procedure, which is more oriented on the 'sustainable development' approach than on integration of environmental requirements, is still in its infancy and it is too early to assess its effects. It appears, though, that the extended impact assessments might turn into a cost-benefit assessment

---

[29] Commission, COM (88) 338 of 8 June 1988.

[30] Commission, COM (98) 716 of 1 December 1998 and COM (99) 640 of 1 December 1999 (transport); COM (98) 571 of 14 October 1998 (energy); COM (99) 22 of 27 January 1999 and COM (2000) 20 of 26 January 2000 (agriculture); COM (99) 263 of 8 June 1999 (internal market); COM (99) 36 of 28 January 1999 and COM (2000) 264 of 20 May 2000 (development); COM (2001) 143 of 16 March 2001 (fisheries); COM (2000) 576 of 20 September 2000 (economic questions); SEC (2002) 271 of 7 March 2002 (external affairs).

[31] See the statement of the then environmental Commissioner, R. Bjerregaard, of 26 November 1998 (quoted after ENDS Environment Daily of 27 November 1998 p. 1): 'a few nice words about the environment, but it's not what we are looking for' (referring to the strategies for energy, agriculture and transport).

[32] Decision 1600/2002 laying down the Sixth Community Environment Action Programme (2002) OJ L 242 p. 1, Article 3(3).

of measures; and as there are still no means to precisely assess the economic impact of environmental impairment, there is a risk that the process will be limited to an assessment of economic costs for economic operators.

3 The principle of preventive action

The description of the evolution of this principle can remain short. Indeed, from the very beginning of the EC environmental policy, prevention of environmental deterioration, impairment and damage played an important role in all official documents. Thus, the first principle of the first environmental action programme stated[33]; 'The best environmental policy concerns preventing the creation of pollution or nuisances at source, rather than subsequently trying to counteract their effects'.

The second action programme repeated this principle. The third action programme declared it necessary that 'the preventive side of environmental policy be strengthened in the framework of an overall strategy'.[34] After the insertion of the preventive principle into the EC Treaty, the quoting of the necessity to take preventive action became even more frequent. A number of directives – such as on environment impact assessment, on industrial permitting or standards for products or installations – expressly saw their raison d'etre in the application of the prevention principle – and quite rightly so.

4 The precautionary principle

4.1 Birth of the principle

Matters became more complicated when the Maastricht Treaty added to Article 174 (ex Article 130r) EC the precautionary principle. This principle had not been mentioned in any of the EC environmental action programmes prior to 1991 nor, as far as I can see, in any other official EC document. The clause was proposed by Belgium[35] and apparently adopted without much discussion. As EC law is autonomous and cannot be interpreted by referring to national notions or concepts, its interpretation is difficult, in particular as regards how the precautionary principle related to the prevention principle.[36]

---

[33] First action programme (n. 10) p. 6.

[34] Council Resolution on the third action programme (n. 12) p. 2.

[35] J. Cloos-G. Reinesch-D. Vignes-J. Weyland, *Le Traité de Maastricht*. Bruxelles 1993, p. 321.

[36] H.G. Sevenster, *Milieubeleid en Gemeenschapsrecht*. Deventer 1992, mentions that environmental organisations had suggested, in a publication, to substitute the prevention principle by the precautionary principle. Other sources refer to the German principle of *'Vorsorge'* as the model for this principle.

The question of the origins of the principle will not be discussed in this contribution, which is limited to the tracing of the development of the principles.

4.2   Precaution and prevention

At present, the precautionary principle is interpreted as concerning cases of scientific uncertainty.[37] Its disputed interrelationship with the prevention principle on the one hand and the German notion and concept of '*Vorsorge*' will not be discussed further. It appears, though, that prior to the insertion of the precautionary principle in the EC Treaty all cases of scientific uncertainty, which are now subsumed under this principle were subsumed under the notion of prevention. The best illustration for this is the landmark judgment of the Court of Justice in the *BSE* case. In that judgment, the Court upheld an export ban for British beef, because of the risk that British beef was infected with BSE and stated: 'Where there is uncertainty as to the existence or extent of risks to human health, the institutions may take protective measures without having to wait until the reality and seriousness of those risks becomes fully apparent. That approach is borne out by Article 130r(1) of the EC Treaty, according to which Community policy on the environment is to pursue the objective *inter alia* of human health. Article 130r(2) provides that that policy is to be based in particular *on the principles that preventive action should be taken* and that environmental protection requirements must be integrated into the definition and implementation of other Community policies' (emphasis added).[38] The same approach is adopted in Directive 2001/18 on the deliberate release of genetically modified organisms where considerant four mentions prevention and considerant eight the precautionary principle.[39]

4.3   Content

Even if a clear distinction in law between precaution and prevention might not be able to be drawn as to where the precautionary principle is understood as applying in cases of scientific uncertainty, the principle is open to broad interpretation. For this, it may be sufficient to compare the wording of the precautionary principle in the USA influenced Rio Declaration[40] on the

---

[37] See, for instance, T. Christoforou, The origins, content and role of the precautionary principle in European Community Law, in: E. Freytag-T. Jakl-G. Loibl-M. Wittmann (eds.) *The Role of Precautions in Chemical Policy*. Vienna 2002, p. 23: 'The precautionary principle is about scientific uncertainty'.

[38] Case C-157/96 *Regina* v. *Ministry of Agriculture* [1998] ECR I-2211, paras 63-64. It is interesting, but also significant that the English version of this judgment only refers to the prevention principle, whereas the German and other language versions mention both the precautionary and the prevention principle.

[39] Directive 2001/18 (2001) OJ L 106 p. 1.

[40] Rio de Janeiro Declaration on Environment and Development, 16 June 1992. Principle 15.

one hand, and the definition in the Convention on the Protection of the Marine Environment in the North-East Atlantic (OSPAR), to which the EC adhered[41], on the other:

Rio Declaration: 'In order to protect the environment, the precautionary approachshall be widely applied by States according to their capabilities. Where there are threats of serious or irreversible damages, lack of full scientific certainty shall not be used as a reason for postponing cost-effective measures to prevent environmental degradation'.

OSPAR-Convention: '(The precautionary principle is a principle) by virtue of which measures are taken when there are reasonable grounds for concern that substances or energy introduced directly or indirectly into the environment may bring about damage to human health, or harm living resources, even where there is no conclusive evidence of a causal relationship between the inputs and effects'.

The EC interpretation more closely follows the OSPAR-definition.[42] In 2000, the Commission adopted a communication on the precautionary principle where again it followed the broader definition of the OSPAR-Convention.[43] The prolonged discussions with the USA on a moratorium for the marketing of genetically modified products and of meat that contains chemical growth promoters (hormones) that took place in the context of the World Trade Organisation, probably prompted the Commission to elaborate that Communication. The Communication explained how and to what extent the Commission intended to use the principle and established guidelines for its application. The Commission also undertook to build a common understanding on the principle and warned against using it as a disguised form of protectionism.

It should be noted that under Article 95(5), the Commission rightly does not allow Member States to apply the precautionary principle in order to introduce national legislation which deviates from common EC provisions that had been fixed under Article 95 EC; the Commission rather requests the conditions of Article 95(5) EC and in particular those of 'new scientific evidence' to be complied with in full.[44]

---

[41] Convention on the protection of the marine environment in the North-East Atlantic (1998) OJ L 104 p. 3.

[42] See for example Directive 1999/39 on baby food (1999) OJ L 124 p. 8, fourth considerant: 'Whereas, taking into account the Community's international obligations, in cases where the relevant scientific evidence is insufficient, the precautionary principle allows the Community to provisionally adopt measures on the basis of available pertinent information, pending and additional assessment of risk and a review of the measure within a reasonable period of time'.

[43] Commission, Communication on the precautionary principle, COM (2000) 1 of 2 February 2000.

[44] See Commission Decision of 3 September 2003, by which a request from Austria was rejected which intended to introduce regional legislation in Oberösterreich according to which the fragile Alpine environment was to be temporarily protected against the import of genetically modified plants or animals.

5   The rectification of environmental damage at source

5.1   Origins

This principle appeared for the first time in the list of general environmental principles of the first environmental action programme.[45] This stated that: 'The best environmental policy consists in preventing the creation of pollution or nuisances at source, rather than subsequently trying to counteract their effects'. The same idea is expressed in the second principle: 'Effects on the environment should be taken into account at the earliest possible stage in all the technical planning and decision-making processes'. The wording of both principles indicates their proximity to the prevention principle.

However, nowhere in the first or, indeed, the second action programme was there any conclusion drawn from the existence of this principle. Also, the two reports on the state of the environment of 1977 and 1979[46] did not mention this principle, though there would have been good reason to do so. Indeed, the first report mentioned in detail the controversy between the United Kingdom and the other Member States on whether discharges into water should be tackled on the basis of emission standards – this approach was, at that time, favoured by the Commission and eight Member States – or quality standards, which were favoured by the United Kingdom.[47] One argument in favour of emission standards in this controversy would have been that environmental impairment should, if any possible, be rectified at source. However, this argument was neither raised in the directive on discharges itself[48] nor in the 1977 report on the state of the environment. In its chapter on air pollution, the 1977 report even used the title 'reduction environmental pollution at source' and described measures on gasoil and used oil, without ever mentioning the principle.[49]

The Council's resolution on the third action programme declared that EC action should be carried out particularly in the area of 'reduction of pollution and nuisance if possible at source'.[50] With small drafting amendments, this formula became, in 1985/87, the principle in Article 174(2) (ex Article 130r) EC. The fourth action programme discussed 'source-oriented controls' without mentioning the principle[51] and without making any concrete proposals. The Council's resolution on this programme declared that the EC should concen-

---

[45] First environmental action programme (note 10), p. 6.

[46] See above n. 13.

[47] First report (n. 13) p. 42.

[48] Directive 76/464 on pollution caused by certain dangerous substances discharged into the aquatic environment of the Community, (1976) OJ L 129 p. 23.

[49] First report (n. 13). p. 75.

[50] Resolution on the third action programme (n. 12) p. 1.

[51] Fourth action programme (n. 12) p. 19, no. 3.4.

trate, under the heading 'pollution prevention' on the 'reduction at source of pollution and nuisance' regarding air, water and soil pollution and hazardous waste.[52]

5.2 Application

The fifth and sixth environmental action programmes did not touch on this principle any more, despite a judgment of 1992, where the Court of Justice declared that the principle of rectifying damage at source 'means that it is for each region, commune or other local entity to take appropriate measures to receive, process and dispose of its own waste. Consequently, waste should be disposed of as close as possible to the place where it is produced in order to keep the transport of waste to the minimum practicable'.[53] The Commission rightly considered that specific judgment to be politically influenced[54] and therefore did not generalise its conclusions.

An illustrative example of practical application may be found in Directive 96/61 on integrated pollution prevention and control. The Commission had made a proposal for this directive where it mentioned in the considerants all the principles of Article 130(2), and proposed that that permits for industrial installations exceptionally need not be based on the best available techniques where environmental quality standards could nevertheless be respected.[55] The European Parliament opposed this approach, invoking the principle that environmental damage should be rectified at source, and asked for a deletion of that clause.[56] The Commission did not amend its proposal,[57] but the Council, while maintaining the need for the inclusion of the 'rectification' principle, deleted the clause in the final version of Directive 96/61.[58]

---

[52] Resolution on the fourth action programme (n. 12).

[53] Case C-2/90 *Commission* v. *Belgium* [1992] ECR I-4431, para. 34.

[54] The case considered a temporary import ban of hazardous waste into Wallonia. The Court did not discuss the fact that the temporary ban already lasted for nine years; it did not discuss, why a principle of Article 174 (ex Article 130r) EC applied to national measures and not only to EC measures; it did not discuss whether the measure was discriminating, as waste from other Belgian regions was not covered by the ban; it quoted the Basel Convention on the shipment of hazardous waste in support of his reasoning, though the EC was not party to that Convention at the time of the judgment; and it did not distinguish between waste that was shipped for being recycled and waste that was to be eliminated; etc.

[55] Commission (1993) OJ C 311 p. 6, first considerant and Article 9.

[56] European Parliament (1995) OJ C 18 p. 82; in the same sense Economic and Social Committee (1994) OJ C 195 p. 54 which considered the proposal 'not in tune with the objectives of Article 130r of the EC Treaty, as amended by the Maastricht Treaty (prevention principle, high level of protection, combating of environmental pollution at source)'.

[57] Commission (1995) OJ C 165 p. 9.

[58] Directive 96/61 on integrated pollution prevention and control (1996) OJ L 257 p. 26.

For other environmental Directives, the Commission never took any initiative to explain in detail the meaning and relevance of this 'rectification at source' principle or to examine to what extent it required the elaboration of EC-wide emission standards rather than quality standards, though this problem was discussed in legal literature. Generally, the EC has orientated itself, since the end of the eighties, towards quality rather than emission standards for water, air, and soil[59], without having established an explicit strategy in this regard.

Overall, the rectification principle has not played any significant role in the legislation and practice of EC institutions in the area of environmental policy.

6   The polluter pays principle

6.1   Origins

The polluter pays principle appears at a very early stage of EC environmental policy. This can by explained by the fact that the Commission wanted to assure Member States that the introduction of an EC environmental policy did not mean that their contribution to the EC budget would have to be increased. In its proposal for an environmental programme in 1972, the Commission therefore declared that the market economy required that persons who damaged or polluted the environment should pay the costs of this pollution and for remedial measures.[60]

The environmental principles of the first action programme included this aspect in principle 5: 'The cost of preventing and eliminating nuisances must in principle be borne by the polluter. However, there might be certain exceptions and special arrangements, in particular for transitional periods.'[61] Subsequently, the polluter pays principle was discussed in two Council Recommendations addressed to Member States[62] and in a Commission Report.[63] Recommendation 75/436 explained it as 'a principle under which natural or legal persons who are responsible for pollution must pay the costs of such measures as are necessary to eliminate that pollution or to reduce it. Environmental policy should not in principle depend on policies which rely on grants of aid and place the burden of

---

[59] See in particular Directives 96/61 (n. 45); Directive 96/62 on air pollution (1996) OJ L 296 p. 55; and 2000/60 on water (2000) OJ L 327 p. 1.

[60] Commission proposal (n. 7), p. 5.

[61] First action programme (no. 10) p. 6; see also p. 9 where the EC requests to work out EC-wide details of that principle and exceptions, in order to avoid distortion of trade and investment, and p. 31 et seq., where measures for allocating the costs of anti-pollution measures are announced.

[62] Recommendation of 7 November 1974, (1974) OJ C 68 p. 1; Recommendation 75/436 of 3 March 1975 (1975) OJ L 194 p. 1.

[63] Commission, Fourth Report on Competition Policy, Brussels-Luxembourg 1975, no. 175 et seq.

combating pollution on the tax-payer'.[64] The Recommendation also discussed possible charges for emissions and envisaged a harmonisation of such charges. Furthermore, it discussed exceptions to the application of the polluter pays principle.

6.2   State aids

As these Recommendations were not binding nor addressed to Member States, the Commission sent, in November 1974, a memorandum to Member States setting out its approach to state aids in environmental matters.[65] These provisions were to apply for a transitional period that ended in 1980; afterwards, it must be understood, the Commission intended to apply the polluter pays principle in full. In the meantime, however, state aids in environmental matters had increased rather than diminished, and this transition period was prolonged by a further six years.[66] This process was repeated in 1986.[67] For the first time the Commission then published in 1994 'guidelines for State aid for environmental purposes'[68] which were renewed in 2001[69]; they are intended to apply until 2007. The guidelines state that environmental policy could no longer be understood as a corrective policy – which it had never been, but as a long-term policy with the aim of promoting sustainable development. 'In general, the 'polluter pays' principle and the need for firms to internalise the costs associated with protecting the environment would appear to militate against the granting of State aid. Nevertheless, aid can be justified in two instances: (a) in certain specific circumstances in which it is not yet possible for all costs to be internalised by firms and the aid can therefore represent a *temporary second-best solution* by encouraging firms to adapt to standards; (b) the aid may also act as an *incentive* to firms to improve on standards or to undertake further investment designed to reduce pollution from their plants'.

The guidelines constitute at present the basis on which the Commission assesses the compatibility of national aids for the environment with the requirements of the provisions of Article 87 *et seq.* and bind in this sense, in a way of self-commitment, the Commission.

---

[64] The English version uses the word *'Community'* which is, however, just an incorrect translation of *'collectivit'* or *'Allgemeinheit.'*

[65] A resume of this memorandum is found in the Fourth Competition Report (n. 63 above) no. 181.

[66] Commission, 10th Report on Competition Policy, Bruxelles-Luxembourg 1981, no. 222 *et seq.*

[67] Commission, 16th Report on Competition Policy, Bruxelles-Luxembourg 1987, no. 259 *et seq.*

[68] (1994) OJ C 72 p. 3.

[69] Guidelines for state aid for environmental purposes (2001) OJ C 37 p. 3.

6.3   EC law

In primary law, the polluter pays principle was introduced into Article 174 (ex Article 130r) by the Single European Act 1985/1987, however with rather different wordings in the different languages.[70] In 1991/1993, the Maastricht Treaty added paragraph 5 to Article 175 (ex Article 130s) EC, according to which the Council could, without prejudice to the principle that 'the polluter should pay', decide on financial support for a Member State, where an environmental measure decided under Article 175 EC 'involved costs deemed disproportionate *for the public authorities'*. The financial support was to be granted by the Cohesion Fund under Article 161 EC. The imperfect drafting of this provision which only took into consideration the costs for public authorities, but not the costs of the measure itself, meant that until recently this provision was not applied at all.

The Regulation which set up the Cohesion Fund[71] does not refer specifically to the polluter pays principle, though it also co-finances projects where the environmental impairment was caused by a specific polluter and where thus the polluter pays principle might be applied. No case is known, where EC authorities recovered clean-up costs in full or in part from a polluter.

The Regional Funds regulations[72] also do not refer to the polluter pays principle, though under regional policy the EC co-finances projects where specific, identifiable polluters or group of polluters may be responsible for environmental damage.

In my opinion, it would be appropriate, if both under the Cohesion Fund and the Structural Funds the polluter pays principle were applied in full: in cases where public funds are used for restoring an impaired environment and the polluter can be identified, the cost for restoration should be borne by that polluter.

---

[70] The wording is as follows: English: principle that the polluter should pay; German: *Beruht auf dem Verursacherprinzip* (is based on the causer principle); French: *est fondée sur le principe du pollueur-payeur* (is based on the polluter-payer principle); Italian: *fondata sul principio 'chi inquina paga'* (is based on the principle 'who pollutes pays'); Dutch: *berust op het beginsel dat de vervuiler betaalt* (is based on the principle that the polluter pays); Danish: *bygger paa principperne at forureneren betaler* (builds on the principle that the polluter pays); Greek: *stirisetai stin archi 'o ripainon plironei'* (builds on the principle 'the polluter pays'); Spanish: *se basará en el principio de que quien contamina page* (will be based on the principle that the polluter pays) Portuguese: *fundamenta-se no principio do poluidor-pagador* (is built on the principle of the polluter-payer).

[71] Regulation 1164/94 (1994) OJ L 130 p. 1; amended by Regulations 1264/99 (1999) OJ L 161 p. 57 and 1265/99 (1999) OJ L 161 p. 62.

[72] Regulations 1260/1999 on general provisions (1999) OJ L 161 p. 1; 1261/1999 on the Regional Fund (1999) OJ L 161 p. 43; 1263/1999 on a financial instrument for fishery (1999) OJ L 161 p. 54.

The polluter pays principle was mentioned, explicitly or implicitly, in all six EC environmental action programmes. In secondary law, it was mentioned in a number of directives, in particular in the waste sector.[73] Some more recent directives contain more detailed provisions which try to elaborate which costs should be borne by polluters;[74] Directive 2000/59 on waste from ships[75] expressly deviates from the polluter pays principle, by requesting ships to pay a fee for port installations of ship waste independently whether they use the installations or not.

6.4   Environmental liability

In early 2002, the Commission made a proposal for a directive on environmental liability[76], where it proposed, in particular that, as a principle, Member States 'shall either require the operator to take the necessary restorative measures or shall itself take such measures' (Article 5). In certain cases Member States had even to 'ensure that the necessary preventive or restorative measures are taken' (Article 6). Member States had to recover the costs incurred from the operator that had caused the environmental damage. The proposal expressly invoked the polluter pays principle.[77] In Council this was considered to be too far-reaching. The Common Position therefore stated that the operator should be liable: '[...] the remedial measures are taken by the operator'(Article 6); the 'operator shall bear the costs for the preventive and remedial actions taken' (Article 8).[78] Any reference to an obligation of Member States to restore the damaged environment was deleted.

One can clearly see the reasons behind the Council's decision, though in my opinion an obligation for public authorities to restore the damaged environment

---

[73] See among others, Directive 75/439 on waste oils, (1975) OJ L 194 p. 31, Article 15(2); Directive 75/442 on waste (1975) OJ L 194 p. 47, Article 11; Directive 91/156 on waste (1991) OJ L 78 p. 32 ; Directive 94/62 on packaging and packaging waste (1994) OJ L 365 p. 10, Article 15; see also Directive 96/61 (n. 58) first considerant.

[74] Directive 2000/60 (n. 59) Article 9; implicitly also Directive 1999/31 on waste disposal installations (1999) OJ L 182 p. 1 (Article 10).

[75] Directive 2000/59 (2000) OJ L 332 p. 81, Article 8.

[76] Commission (2002) OJ C 151E p. 132.

[77] *Supra*, Articles 5 and 6 and considerants 2, 14 and 15.

[78] Council, Common Position of 19 September 2003 (not yet published). See also considerant two: 'The prevention and remedying of environmental damage should be implemented through the furtherance of the 'polluter pays' principle, as indicated in the Treaty and in line with the principle of sustainable development. The fundamental principle of this Directive should therefore be that the operator whose activity has caused the environmental damage or the imminent threat of such damage is to be held financially liable, in order to induce operators to adopt measures and develop practices to minimise the risks of environmental damage so that their exposure to financial liabilities is reduced.'

and then to recover the costs from the responsible operator, is not in contradiction with the polluter pays principle.

7   Concluding remarks

1. The environmental principles, which are now laid down in Articles 174(2) and 6 EC were, in substance, all laid down in the first EC environmental action programme of 1973 and in subsequent programmes, with the exception of the precautionary principle.

2. Between 1972 and 1986, EC environmental policy hardly attached any importance to the existence and meaning of environmental principles. A recommendation on the polluter pays principle of 1975 remained without significant effect at EC level.

3. It does not appear that the express introduction of environmental principles in Article 174 EC in 1987 led to a significant change in EC environmental policy or with regard to specific files.

4. The integration principle – now Article 6 EC – which has been a principle of environmental policy since 1973, and was established in 1987 in Article 174 (ex Article 130r) EC, remained a subject of political declamation rather than changing policy orientations.

5. Its transfer to Article 6 EC in 1999 increased its visibility and led to some efforts by the Commission to make it operational. A final assessment of its effect cannot yet be made.

6. The precautionary principle, which was inserted in Article 174 in 1993, had no explicit antecedents in EC law. Probably due to international developments, the Commission issued a communication on its meaning. Nevertheless, the precise legal contours of the principle remain open for interpretation.

7. Where the EC has legislated and taken into account the problems of scientific uncertainty, Member States may not introduce different legislation by invoking the precautionary principle. Rather, they are confined to the application of Article 95 EC.

CHAPTER 4

The Precautionary Principle before the European Courts

Joanne Scott[*]

Over recent years the European Courts have been active in laying down the parameters for the application of the precautionary principle. This case law offers important insights into the 'European' understanding of this all-important principle. The implications of the case law will be felt beyond the European Union, most notably in the WTO. This chapter will focus upon this case law. Though it is limited to analysis of this one principle, much of what follows will have implications beyond this. We see the European courts – notably the Court of First Instance (CFI) – embracing the precautionary principle as an 'autonomous' principle and characterising it as a 'general principle'. We see it emerging as an instrument of interpretation, as a tool in the assessment of legality. There is no reason, having regard to the structure of the EC Treaty, to imagine that the precautionary principle will enjoy a status and function in Community law, which is distinct from the other principles laid down in Article 174 EC. Thus, the case law under discussion may be thought to bear also upon our understanding of the place of other environmental principles in the European Union legal order.

This chapter will address three themes, *viz.*, the status of the precautionary principle according to the case law of the European courts, its content according to this case law and finally the impact of the WTO on this case law and the constitutional issue which this begs.

I   The status of the precautionary principle according to the case law of the European courts

Article 174(2) EC identifies a number of principles upon which European Union environmental law is to be based. The precautionary principle is included among them. It has been accepted that these principles, along with the objectives and criteria laid down in this same article, are binding upon the Community institutions, albeit that the intensity of judicial review of compliance with them is low:

'That provision [Article 174 EC] thus sets a series of objectives principles and criteria, which the Community legislature must respect in implementing environmental policy.

However, in view of the need to strike a balance between certain of the objectives and principles mentioned [...] and of the complexity of the implementation of those criteria, review by the Court must necessarily be limited to the question whether the Council, by adopting the Regulation, committed a manifest error of appraisal regarding the conditions for the application of [Article 174] of the Treaty.'[1]

---

*   Thanks to Richard Macrory for his help in the writing of this paper.

[1]   Case C-341/95 *Gianni Bettati* v. *Safety Hi-Tech Srl* [1998] ECR I-4055, paras. 34 and 35.

Though the precautionary principle only applies explicitly in respect of European Union environmental policy, the European courts have endorsed its application also in relation to other policies, notably in relation to the protection of public health.[2] To take a recent example, in *Pfizer*, the Court of First Instance acknowledged that this principle must be taken into account when the common agricultural policy is implemented by the Community institutions, in pursuit of a public health objective.[3] In a yet more recent case, the CFI might be thought to go further. In *Artegodan* the CFI concludes that the precautionary principle 'is intended to be applied in order to ensure a high level of protection of health, consumer safety and the environment in all the Community's spheres of activity'.[4] The scope of the concept of consumer safety remains uncertain. It is not a notion found in the EC Treaty, which refers instead to the attainment of a high level of consumer *protection*.[5] While consumer protection self-evidently extends beyond the protection of the health of the consumer, to encompass broader welfare concerns,[6] the more attenuated notion of consumer safety may not. The CFI's judgment is slippery in this respect. It talks of consumer safety while seeking justification in a Treaty article concerning consumer protection. Within the space of a paragraph it drops the language of consumer safety in favour of 'public health, safety and the environment', thus arguably aligning 'safety' to the precursor 'public' and rendering this part of a broader, and already accepted, public health dimension.[7]

In reviewing the scope of application of the precautionary principle it would seem that it bites not only in respect of the environmental dimension of all areas of Community policy (transport, agriculture and the like as laid down in Article 3 EC), but that it has teeth also whenever public health or safety objectives are

---

[2] See especially, Case C-180/96 *United Kingdom and Northern Ireland* v. *Commission* [1996] ECR I-3903, concerning BSE ('Mad Cow Disease'). Here the judgment of the Court is thoroughly infused with the language of precaution, though the principle is nowhere explicitly mentioned. See also, as regards the Court of First Instance, Case T-199/96 *Bergaderm SA and Goupil* v. *Commission* [1998] ECR II-2805, para. 66 citing the ECJ judgment in the *BSE* case. See also COM(1) Communication on the Use of the Precautionary Principle, p. 10 for a more detailed discussion of the justification for this extension in the reach of the precautionary principle.

[3] Case T-13/99 *Pfizer Animal Health* v. *Council* [2002] ECR II-3305, para. 114. See para. 115 for a list of the ECJ cases relied on by the CFI in reaching this conclusion.

[4] Case T-74/00 *Artegodan GMbH and Others* v. *Commission* [2002] II-ECR 4945, para. 183. See also, for the ECJ judgment on appeal, Case C-39/03 *Commission* v. *Artegodan GMbH and Others* [2003] I-7885.

[5] See Article 153 EC.

[6] This is apparent from the scope of the legislation adopted on the basis of Article 153 EC and from the scope of application of the 'mandatory requirement' relating to consumer protection, as invoked as a defence in of restrictions on free movement. See generally, S. Weatherill, *EC Consumer Law* (Longmans, 1997).

[7] *Supra* n. 4, para. 184.

being pursued. The extension in the scope of application of this principle is justified by the CFI by reference to the environmental integration obligation in Article 6 EC. The relevance of this principle is clear in so far as the institutions concerned are pursuing environmental objectives, albeit within the framework of other Community policies. Its relevance is less obvious when it comes to the pursuit of public health or safety objectives, except in so far as these might be understood as environmental in nature. In this sphere, a second rationalisation put forward by the Commission in its Communication on the precautionary principle seems more compelling;[8] namely that the Community institutions are charged with ensuring a high level of protection in respect not only of environment, but also in relation to health, safety and consumer protection.[9] In so far as the precautionary principle may be viewed as a necessary part of a high level of protection, this serves to explain its extension to these additional policy spheres.

In a series of recent cases, the CFI have entered some far-reaching observations in respect of the status of the precautionary principle. Two such observations merit consideration.

First, the nature of the precautionary principle remains uncertain. In particular, doubts persist as to whether it is purely permissive in its connotations or whether it might generate positive obligations for the relevant authorities. In the recent case law of the CFI, the language goes beyond the merely permissive ('Community institutions may, by reason of the precautionary principle...'[10]) and is from time to time expressed in mandatory terms. Thus, for example, in *Pfizer*, the CFI observes that a public authority can, by reason of the precautionary principle, be *required* to act even before any adverse effects have become apparent.[11] This is a point to which we will return in section II below.

The *second* notable feature of the CFI's jurisprudence is its insistence upon the autonomous nature of the precautionary principle, and upon its status as a general principle of European Union law.

It follows that the precautionary principle can be defined as a general principle of Community law requiring the competent authorities to take appropriate measures to prevent specific potential risks to public health, safety and the environment, by giving precedence to the requirements related to the protection of those interests over economic interests. Since the Community institutions are responsible, in all their spheres of activity, for the protection of public health, safety and the environment, the precautionary principle can be regarded as an autonomous principle stemming from the above mentioned Treaty provisions.[12]

---

[8]   COM (2001) 1.

[9]   See Article 95(3) as well as Articles 152, 153 and 174(2) EC.

[10]   *Supra* n. 3, para. 139. See also paras. 144.

[11]   *Supra* n. 3, para. 444.

[12]   *Supra* n. 4, para. 184.

It is not entirely clear what it means to say that the precautionary principle is an autonomous principle. One possibility would be that this emphasis upon autonomy highlights the independent nature of the principle. Though it originates in the Treaty, it has subsequently broken loose of this and, as noted above, it has come to apply even in areas where no explicit reference is to be found. Likewise, in the case of specific legislation, the role and relevance of the principle is not contingent upon their being an explicit reference to it. Thus, for example, the principle would be binding upon the Commission in the adoption of implementing acts in the relevant spheres, regardless of whether the empowering legislation contains any explicit endorsement of it.

Another possibility is that autonomy speaks to the freestanding nature of this principle, relative to other principles of Community law. Thus, whereas the European Court has, in the past, conflated environmental principles with the general principle of proportionality – the former being presented as mere reflections of the latter – emphasis upon autonomy serves to highlight the independent content of these environmental principles and the distinctive obligations which they impose.[13]

The claim that the principle is a general principle would seem to be more exact in its connotations, the notion of a general principle having a somewhat settled meaning in European Union law.[14] Traditionally, such principles have played a two-fold role in the EU legal order. They serve as instruments for the interpretation of law and wherever possible legal norms are to be construed to be consistent with them. Second, and more dramatically, general principles constitute a benchmark against which the legality or validity of secondary norms will be assessed. General principles represent a hierarchically superior source of European Union law and may serve as the basis for the invalidation of Community legislation. All of this is relatively uncontroversial.

There is one additional connotation associated with the concept of a general principle. Such principles are said to be binding not only upon the institutions of the European Union but also – in certain circumstances – upon the Member States. More specifically, they are said to bind the Member States in so far as they are acting within the scope of Community law. At the very least, Member States will be deemed to be so acting when they are implementing Community law, or when they are seeking to derogate from one of the fundamental freedoms, such as the free movement of goods. Thus, were it to be accepted by the European Court of Justice that the precautionary principle constitutes a general principle, imbued with a status equal to that of the other general principles, this would serve to clarify the long-running debate regarding the status of the precautionary principle in the Member States, and perhaps even shed some

---

[13] See in particular, Case C-293/97 *Standley and Metson* [1999] ECR I-2603.

[14] See generally, for an excellent discussion, P. Craig & G. de Búrca, *EU Law: Text, Cases and Materials* (OUP, 3rd ed., 2002), chapters 8 & 9.

light upon the status of the other Treaty based environmental principles in the Member States. In *Artegodan*, the CFI skips around this issue through careful use of terminology.[15] The precautionary principle is said to impose obligations on the 'competent authorities'. This phrase is found frequently in Community legislation, and is deployed therein to connote Member State authorities. Nonetheless, in the context of the challenge in *Artegodan*, it would seem to refer to the relevant Community institutions. The European Court has likewise dodged the question of the status of the environmental principles vis-à-vis the Member States.

We know however that environmental law principles, notably the precautionary principle, may be used to delimit and to clarify the obligations imposed on Member States by virtue of their role in the interpretation of Community law. This may serve the Member States well in so far as they are able to invoke the principle in mounting a defence of a national restriction on, say, the movement of goods. Denmark appears to be the latest beneficiary in this respect.[16] However, the interpretative impact of the precautionary principle will not be all one way as far as the Member States are concerned. It may result in the imposition of more far-reaching obligations on them.[17] This may be true even where the relevant principle is not explicitly referred by the legislative instrument in question. Thus, in *Palin Granit Oy*[18] the European Court eschewed a restrictive interpretation of the concept of waste on the basis of the objective of the waste framework directive (protection of human health and environment), and in the light of Article 174(2) which provides that Community environmental policy is to aim at a high level of protection and is to be based, in particular, on the precautionary principle and the principle that preventive action should be taken. Clearly, here the precautionary principle is just one element among several in producing this result.

In this example, the precautionary principle serves indirectly to impose obligations on the Member States, in that it shapes a specific Community law obligation. It is not an autonomous source of obligation, but a dependent one in so far as it finds expression by attaching to an existing concrete obligation. General principles, by contrast, constitute an autonomous source of obligations, not just for the European Union institutions but also for the Member States in so far as they are acting within the scope of Community law. As such we see that there may be a link between the two core attributes identified by the CFI, autonomy and status as a general principle. For the Member States (and Community insti-

---

[15] *Supra* n. 4.

[16] See Case C-192/01 *Commission* v. *Denmark* judgment of 23 September 2003.

[17] Recourse to the environmental principles will not invariably imply the most far-reaching interpretation. See Case C-203/96 *Dusseldorp* [1998] ECR I-4075, for a case in which the European Court found that the principle did not apply, in relation to waste for recovery as opposed to waste for disposal.

[18] See, for example, Case C-9/00 *Palin Granit Oy* [2002] ECR I-3533, para. 23.

tutions), such principles may be cited, in and of themselves, as grounds for the unlawfulness of national measures falling within the scope of Community law. It would suffice that a national implementing measure fails to comply with a general principle, for that national implementing measure to constitute a breach of European Union law. It would not be necessary to point to a more specific provision of European Union law (such as a specific obligations laid down in a directive) in order to demonstrate that breach.

The European Court has had only limited opportunities to comment upon this ambitious case law developing before the CFI. *Artegodan* is subject to pending appeal. It has neither endorsed nor distanced itself from the perspective of the CFI that the precautionary principle represents an autonomous, general principle. It might have taken the opportunity to do so in the recent *Monsanto* case.[19] Though the European Court is careful in *Monsanto* not to speculate about the nature of the precautionary principle, it does however attach strong importance to it. We will examine this case in Section II below.

II The implications of the precautionary principle

The precautionary principle has recently suffered a strong attack. Mounted by a leading US scholar, Cass Sunstein, the attack is rendered all the more powerful by dint of Sunstein's explicit endorsement of the goals which motivate adherence to this principle.[20] These include, Sunstein suggests, 'the importance of protecting health and the environment even from remote risks; the need to attend to unintended adverse effects of technological change; and the need to ensure that wealthy countries pay their fair share for environmental improvement and risk reduction'.[21] Sunstein's attack rests upon the

---

[19] Case C-236/01 *Monsanto*, judgment of 9 September 2003.

[20] 'Beyond the Precautionary Principle' Public Law and Legal Theory Working Paper No. 38: The Law School, The University of Chicago, at: http://www.law.uchicago.edu/academics/publiclaw/index.html. p. 2. For a more positive reaction to the precautionary principal see: See the statement of the Royal Commission on Environmental Pollution on setting environmental standards (CM 4053, 1998 4.41) where a conception of the precautionary principle as 'anti-science' or 'political' is rejected. RCEP conceives the principle as a perfectly rational response to the scientific uncertainty inherent in many environmental issues. RCEP points out that a key factor for a decision-maker is the question of what sort of uncertainty is in place – and in particular whether the uncertainty is open to resolution through further scientific inquiry or whether it is inherently irresolvable until it is 'too late' having regard to the objective being pursued. I am grateful to Richard Macrory for this point

[21] *Ibid.* Thus unlike certain opponents of the precautionary principle, Sunstein does not suggest an alternative approach to be applied in all situations. He rejects Aaron Wildavsky's 'resilience principle' as 'a heuristic, one that favours inaction in the face of possibly damaging technological change. Like most heuristics, the resilience principle will work well in many circumstances, but it can also lead to systematic and even deadly errors'. (p. 44).

claim that the precautionary principle does not resolve hard choices in risk regulation. On the contrary, he argues, the principle 'leads in no direction at all... [threatening] to be paralysing, forbidding regulation, inaction, and every step in between'.[22] Risks, he points out, are 'on all sides of social situations' and consequently any attempt to be 'universally precautionary' will threaten to paralyse in this way.[23] Sunstein points out that in many situations – and he offers countless examples – regulatory intervention will not only serve to guard against risk but it will also generate different risks. These different risks will often take the form of 'opportunity costs' or benefits foregone. These lost benefits may even result in loss of life. He points to the infamous 'drug lag' example, associated with a so-called precautionary approach to the approval of new medicines:

If a government takes such an approach, it might protect people against harms from inadequately tested drugs; but it will also prevent people from receiving potential benefits from those very drugs. Is it "precautionary" to require extensive pre-marketing testing, or to do the opposite?[24]

Critical though he is of the precautionary principle, Sunstein accepts that a 'weak version' is 'entirely unobjectionable' (though the question remains as to how useful it would be). It is the 'strong version', which forms the subject matter of his attack. This he defines as a principle, which requires regulation 'whenever there is a possible risk to health, safety, or the environment, even if the supporting evidence is speculative and even if the economic costs of regulation are high'.[25] Inherent even in this strong version is a 'threshold of scientific plausibility', but in this version 'the threshold burden is minimal', and once met it creates a presumption of stringent regulatory control.[26]

Extrapolating from Sunstein, it seems reasonable to conclude that the following elements would be found in his strong version of the precautionary principle:

· regulation is *required* or mandated in the face of the relevant risk;
· the economic costs of regulation are not a paramount consideration in deciding how to act;
· the threshold level of anticipated harm is set low according to the strong version; anticipated harm need not be serious or irreversible, for example;
· the risk threshold is also set low, albeit that there must be a scientifically plausible risk;
· according to the strongest versions, steps to guard against the risk will

---

[22] *Ibid.*

[23] *Ibid.,* p. 5.

[24] *Ibid*, p. 18 (footnotes omitted). See pp. 15-21 of Sunstein's paper for additional examples.

[25] *Ibid*, p. 13.

[26] *Ibid*, p. 13.

be taken other than where the party wishing to engage in the relevant activity, or to deploy the new technology, can demonstrate that there is no scientifically plausible risk; in other words there is a shift in the burden of proof.[27]

According to Sunstein, this strong version can only be made workable by virtue of a series of 'blinders that people wear when they use the precautionary principle to support concrete outcomes'.[28] Given that it is not feasible to guard against all risks, and given that guarding against some risks may or will imply different risks, including those associated with the human costs of economic benefits foregone, precautionary regulation may only proceed with the assistance of 'blinders' or biases. It is only thanks to these more often than not unacknowledged biases, that priorities may be identified and so-called precautionary action may find its route through the maze of multiple and often competing risks. Drawing upon the work of Paul Slovic and others,[29] Sunstein identifies five such sets of 'blinders'. Without engaging in a full discussion of these it may be useful to note that these include, for example, the 'availability heuristic' whereby 'people focus on some risks simply because they are cognitively "available", whereas other risks are not'.[30] This is, in part, a question of familiarity: 'The hazards associated with heat waves, for example, receive little public attention, while the hazards associated with air travel are a significant source of public concern; one reason is that the latter hazards come readily to mind'.[31] This example reminds us that the question of cognitive availability is not fixed. As we leave behind the memorable (for its hot weather) European summer of 2003, the risks associated with heat-waves are, tragically, all too 'available'. Significant too, in terms of Sunstein's 'blinders', is the fact of 'probability neglect'. '[S]ometimes people will attempt little assessment of probability at all, especially when strong emotions are involved'.[32] He points too to 'system neglect', resulting from a focus 'on the "target" risk, and not on the systemic, risk-related effects of being precautionary'.[33] This leads to 'tradeoff neglect' whereby risks are seen in

---

[27] Drawing on WTO literature, I use this to mean that both the burden of production (of evidence) and the burden of persuasion would rest with this party. See, for example, V. R. Walker, Keeping the WTO from Becoming the "World Trans-Science Organization", and Factfinding in the Growth Hormones Dispute. (1998) 31 *Cornell Int. LJ* 251.

[28] Sunstein, *supra* n., p. 27.

[29] This is a book I was introduced to thanks to Sunstein's piece. It is invaluable in thinking about risk regulation, for example (topically) in thinking about the place of public opinion in the regulation of GMOs. See P. Slovic, *The Perception of Risk* (Earthscan, 2000).

[30] Sunstein, *supra* n., p. 6.

[31] *Ibid*, p. 6. (footnotes excluded)

[32] *Ibid*, p. 33. See Slovic, *supra* n. 27.

[33] *Ibid*, p. 42.

isolation, and not balanced against benefits or against the different risks, which might be anticipated to spillover from intervention.[34]

Leaving Sunstein on one side for a moment, it is useful in the light of this account to turn again to the case law of the European courts and to their conception of the precautionary principle.

The *Pfizer* case highlighted above offers a typical, if unusually full, illustration of the approach of the CFI to the application of the precautionary principle. Though a judgment of the CFI, many of its observations regarding the precautionary principle draw upon the jurisprudence of the European Court, or have been subsequently endorsed by it.[35] In essence, *Pfizer* concerned the withdrawal of authorisation by the Council of the use of certain additives in animal feed. The substances concerned took the form of antibiotics. The decision to withdraw authorisation was based on the 'possibility' that their 'use would give rise to adverse effects on human health, namely a transfer of antimicrobial resistance from animals to humans, and consequently, a reduction in the effectiveness of certain medicinal products in human medicine'.[36]

Drawing upon the earlier case law of the European Court, the CFI confirmed that, by virtue of the precautionary principle, the Community institutions, faced with scientific uncertainty, were entitled to take protective measures without having to wait until the reality or seriousness of risks to human health became fully apparent.[37] In such a situation a risk assessment could not be required to provide the Community institutions with conclusive scientific evidence of the reality of the risk and the seriousness of the potential adverse effects were that risk to become a reality'[38] 'The fact that it is impossible to carry out a full scientific risk assessment does not prevent the competent authority from taking preventive measures, at very short notice if necessary, when such measures appear essential given the level of risk to human health which the authority has deemed unacceptable for society'.[39] It is for the institution concerned to determine the level of protection, which it considers appropriate for society, depending upon the circumstances of the particular case.[40]

---

[34] Sunstein also highlights 'loss aversion' whereby, '[p]eople tend to be loss averse, which means that a loss from the status quo is seen as more undesirable than a gain is seen as desirable' (27), and 'the myth of a benevolent nature' whereby 'people think that safety and health are generally at risk only or mostly as a result of human intervention [as opposed to nature]'. See *ibid*, pp. 5-7 and pp. 27- 41 for a full discussion of these five sets of 'blinders'.

[35] In terms of the latter, see especially *Monsanto supra* n. 19.

[36] *Supra* n. 3, para. 138.

[37] *Supra* n. 3, para. 139 and 140.

[38] *Supra* n. 3, para. 142.

[39] *Supra* n. 3, para. 160.

[40] *Supra* n. 3, paras. 151 and 153.

It is apparent from this that the precautionary principle casts a blanket of protection around political institutions wishing to act in the face of scientific uncertainty, in pursuance of one of the relevant objectives. That said, any decision to act is subject to a host of constraints inherent in European Union law, and identified by the courts. The protection offered is contingent not absolute.

First, the precautionary principle may only be used to justify action where there is a risk, which, though not fully demonstrated, is not founded on mere hypotheses that have not been scientifically confirmed. '[P]reventive measure[s] cannot properly be based on a purely hypothetical approach to risk, founded on mere conjecture which has not been scientifically verified'.[41] On the contrary, the risk must be 'backed up by the scientific data available at the time when the measure was taken', though the reality and seriousness of the risk have not been fully demonstrated. The CFI laid emphasis upon the impossibility of proving scientifically that there is no current or future risk and as a result upon the inappropriateness of basing regulating upon a 'purely hypothetical approach to risk'.[42] It is in this sense that the European courts preclude a 'zero-risk' approach, this being understood as an approach, which would permit steps to guard against purely hypothetical risk. To preclude a zero-risk approach would not – it seems – be such to preclude the adoption of measures designed to eliminate *entirely* a risk which is more than purely hypothetical and which has been scientifically confirmed.[43]

Second, when Community measures are based upon complex scientific and technical assessments, a scientific risk assessment must be carried out before such measures are adopted:[44]

'[...]the Community institutions must show, first, that the contested regulation was adopted following as thorough a scientific risk assessment as possible, which took account of the particular circumstances of the present case, and, second, that they had available, on the basis of that assessment, sufficient scientific indications to conclude, on an objective scientific basis, that the use of virginiamycin as a growth promoter constituted a risk to human health.'[45]

Risk assessment is understood as a scientific process consisting in the identification and characterisation of a hazard, the assessment of exposure to the hazard

---

[41] *Supra* n. 3, para. 143.

[42] *Supra* n. 3, para. 145.

[43] This point merits emphasis as the Appellate Body of the WTO uses the language 'zero-risk' to refer to this latter scenario, namely the total elimination of an existing risk. On the basis of language alone one might think that the European courts and the Appellate Body adopt a different stance as regards zero-risk. This would be misleading as they simply use the same language to mean different things.

[44] *Supra* n. 3, para. 155.

[45] *Supra* n. 3, para. 165.

and the characterisation of the risk. Risk is in turn defined as 'a function of the probability that use of a product or procedure will adversely affect the interests safeguarded by the legal order'.[46] Risk assessment must be entrusted to experts who will provide the institutions with scientific advice. This scientific advice must be based on the principles of excellence, independence and transparency.[47] Decisions must be taken in the light of best scientific information available and be based on the most recent results of international research.[48] The scientific advice must provide the institutions concerned with sufficiently reliable and cogent information to allow it to understand the ramifications of the scientific question raised and to decide upon a policy in full knowledge of the facts. That institution may not adopt arbitrary measures 'which cannot in any circumstances be rendered legitimate by the precautionary principle' and the measures adopted must be based on as thorough a scientific risk assessment as possible.[49] Nonetheless, as noted previously, in order that the precautionary principle not be rendered nugatory, 'the fact that it is impossible to carry out a full scientific risk assessment does not prevent the competent authority from taking preventive measures, at very short notice if necessary, when such measures appear essential given the level of risk to human health which the authority has deemed unacceptable for society'.[50]

As a matter of procedure, while the Community institutions are not bound by the opinion of the Community's scientific committees (or presumably by the opinions of the relevant agencies such as the European Food Safety Agency), to the extent that they opt to disregard these opinions, they are obliged to provide specific reasons. This statement of reasons must be at a scientific level at least commensurate with that of the opinion in question.[51]

It is then clear that institutions seeking recourse to the precautionary principle incur obligations in respect of risk assessment. Additional obligations arise also in respect of what the CFI characterises as risk management.[52] In relation to both (risk assessment and risk management) the CFI nonetheless acknowledges

---

[46] *Supra* n. 3, paras. 147 and 156.

[47] *Supra* n. 3, paras. 157 and 159.

[48] *Supra* n. 3, para. 158.

[49] *Supra* n. 3, para. 162.

[50] *Supra* n. 3, para. 160.

[51] *Supra* n, 3, para. 199. The duty to give reasons will always bind the Community institutions. These reasons must be appropriate to the issue at hand and disclose in a clear and unequivocal fashion the reasoning followed in order to enable persons to defend their rights and the courts to exercise their powers of review. *Supra* n. 3, para. 510.

[52] This follows the familiar distinction. This distinction was rejected by the Appellate Body of the WTO, as not being inherent in the SPS Agreement. See *EC Measures Concerning Meat and Meat Products (Hormones)* Jan. 16 1998 (WT/DS26/AB/R). For a critique of the premises underpinning the distinction, see J. Adams, *Risk* (UCL Press, 1995).

that the institutions concerned enjoy broad discretion, review by the courts being confined to examining whether the exercise of discretion is vitiated by a manifest error or misuse of powers, or whether the Community institutions clearly exceeded the bounds of their discretion.[53]

Significant in this regard is the principle of proportionality, which serves to temper precaution in a European Union setting. This requires that the measures adopted by the Community institutions should not exceed what is appropriate and necessary in order to attain the legitimate objectives pursued by the measures in question and that where there is a choice between several appropriate measures, recourse must be had to the least onerous. In requires also that the disadvantages caused must not be disproportionate to the aims pursued. That said, the importance of the human health objectives pursued in the case at hand may justify adverse consequences, even substantial adverse consequences for certain traders.[54] Crucially, the CFI laid emphasis upon cost-benefit analysis as a 'particular expression' of the proportionality principle in risk management decisions and hence made it requirement of decision-making in this setting, that such an analysis was conducted prior to the adoption of the contested act.[55]

It is notable that while the CFI talked the language of deference, in fact it subjected the Council's decision to intense and detailed scrutiny. Thus, to illustrate, in assessing whether the withdrawal of the antibiotic in question was manifestly inappropriate to achieve the stated human health objective, it examined a variety of arguments relating to the alleged negative effects of this ban on, for example, animal health and, ultimately, human health. Evidence of what Sunstein calls 'system neglect' was put before the court, but rejected by it in the face of 'differing points of view'.[56]

Looking to *Pfizer* the European courts conception of precaution falls on the weak side of Sunstein's line. It is true that the risk threshold to be transcended for the adoption of precautionary measures would seem to be low – more than merely hypothetical risk; though this is an issue to which we will return in Section III below. However, there is no suggestion of any reversal in terms of burden of proof and, critically, in such a case the precautionary principle merely leaves space for political actors to exercise their judgment with respect to risk. It does not paralyse because it does not mandate. It liberates rather than mandates. Even then, liberation comes at a price and, we saw, is contingent upon conformity with a whole host of obligations designed to ensure that the rhetoric of precaution is not used to sustain arbitrary decisions. So, in *Pfizer*, the existence of a link between the use of antibiotics as growth promoters and the development of resistance in humans had not yet been scientifically proven. Nonethe-

---

[53] *Supra* n. 3, para. 406. This refrain is repeated frequently throughout the judgment as a whole.

[54] *Supra* n. 3, para. 456.

[55] *Supra* n. 3, para. 410.

[56] *Supra* n. 3, para. 425.

less, in view of the fact that it was 'corroborated by a certain amount of reliable scientific data, it was for the Council, on a proposal from the Commission, to exercise its discretion and assume its political responsibilities in the face of a particularly complex and delicate situation'.[57]

Perhaps though these remarks smack of complacency. The question remains as to whether, in different circumstances, the precautionary principle may be susceptible to application by the European courts in a manner, which is mandatory rather than permissive; that is to say whether the principle may impose positive duties upon political actors. *Monsanto* is interesting in this regard.[58]

In the recent *Monsanto* case the European Court seemed to be willing to examine the legality of the Novel Foods Regulation (and specifically the 'simplified procedure' laid down therein) on the basis of an inquiry as to whether this 'is coupled with detailed rules sufficient to ensure a high level of protection of human health and the environment [...] and to guarantee compliance with the precautionary principle and the principle of proportionality'.[59] As regards the precautionary principle, the Court pointed out that the safeguards clause contained in the Regulation – maintaining emergency powers for the Member States – gives specific expression to it and that the conditions governing recourse to this clause must therefore be interpreted in the light of it. In addition, Member States seeking recourse to this clause must ensure that the precautionary principle, where relevant, forms an integral part of their decision making process. Even as regards the 'normal procedure' for authorisation, which was not regarded as constituting a specific expression of the precautionary principle, this principle must nonetheless be taken into account where relevant. Thus, the European Court, in attesting to the legality of the Regulation, reads it in such a way as to impose obligations on the relevant institutions (Member State and EU) to act in accordance with the precautionary principle; this though the Novel Foods Regulation does not contain any reference to this principle. In so far as the Regulation is deemed to give specific expression to the precautionary principle, it must – where relevant – form an integral part of the decision making process. Otherwise, it must – where relevant – be taken into account. It seems likely that relevance will be assessed on the basis of the objective being pursued (human health, consumer safety and environmental protection) and in the light of there being evidence of potential (though uncertain) risks.

It is not at all clear what is meant by the assertion that the precautionary principle must be an integral part of decision-making or that it must be taken into account. It tells us that this principle is mandatory in the sense that it must form a constituent element of decision-making. Where relevant the decision maker must be open to the space, which the precautionary principle provides, to

---

[57] *Supra* n. 3, para. 443.

[58] *Supra* n. 19.

[59] *Supra* n. 19, para. 128.

permit the adoption of preventive measures in the face of scientific uncertainty. But the decision maker must be open to the possibility that it *may* act in such circumstances. It is mandatory to be suitably aware of the additional degree of discretion, which the precautionary principle provides!

This then leaves the question of whether the precautionary principle also implies a substantive bottom-line, according to which the legality of action may be assessed, even where the principle has, as a procedural matter, been appropriately integrated into the decision making process, or adequately taken into account. On occasion the language of the CFI would seem to indicate that this might be so. Thus, in *Pfizer* it states that a public authority can, by reason of the precautionary principle, be *required* to act even before any adverse effects have become apparent.[60] *Artegodan*, similarly, defines the precautionary principle as *requiring* the competent authorities to take appropriate measures to prevent specific potential risks to public health, safety and the environment, by giving precedence to those requirements over economic interests.[61]

To the extent that the precautionary principle is conceived here as requiring a given course of action, it will be apparent that we are entering the territory of what Sunstein calls 'strong' precaution and that, consequently, it is rendered vulnerable to his powerful critique. That said, the concept of 'appropriate measures' is an open-ended one, leaving substantial discretion to the political actor concerned; discretion which we now know must be exercised in a manner which is consistent with the panoply of constraints imposed by European Union law. These constraints were outlined above, and include the requirement of a scientific risk assessment, and recourse to cost-benefit analysis as an element of proportionality. In view of the fact that no institution is *entitled* to act without securing compliance with these requirements, it will be apparent that no institution can be *required* to act without so doing. Thus, if the most that we can say is that the institution concerned is obliged, pursuant to the precautionary principle, to take appropriate measures in the face of scientific uncertainty and that it is for European Union law to structure decision making in such a way as to facilitate responsible determination of what is appropriate in these supremely 'complex and delicate' situations, it would seem unlikely that the precautionary principle will threaten paralysis in the manner feared by Cass Sunstein.

This, however, is not the end of the story. In one respect at least, the European courts prescriptions would seem to take us further. Recall the above quotation:

'*It follows that the precautionary principle can be defined as a general principle of Community law requiring the competent authorities to take appropriate measures to prevent specific potential risks to public health, safety and the environment, by*

---

[60] *Supra* n. 3, para. 444.

[61] *Supra* n. 4, para. 184.

giving precedence to the requirements related to the protection of those interests over economic interests.'[62]

This statement of precedence has been endorsed on many occasions, in a wide variety of different settings, by both the CFI and by the European Court.[63] Read literally it would seem to provide for the absolute and unqualified primacy of public health and environmental concerns. Yet, as Sunstein puts it so nicely, though not with specific reference to the EU: 'Precautions cannot be taken against all risks, not for the important but less interesting reason that resources are limited, but simply because efforts to redress any set of risks might produce risks of their own.'[64]

This speaks not merely to the palpable absurdity of this slogan, in so far as it would seem to imply a total disregard for the economic consequences of measures contributing to the achievement of public health or environmental objectives. In so far as proportionality is about balancing, on this perspective, economic considerations would not feature in the equation. On this analysis, drinking alcohol and smoking would be banned, as indeed would most if not all forms of transportation. Life as we know it would come to an end!

At any rate, the apparent and appealing simplicity of the slogan belies a complex reality. Sunstein teaches us this. Steps to guard against one risk to public health, often generate different, sometimes little understood, risks. *Pfizer* is illustrative. It was argued that the ban on the antibiotic concerned would lead not merely to higher production costs, and to an increase in the price of meat, but that it would also necessitate an increase in the use of antibiotics in farming for therapeutic (as opposed to growth promotion) purposes. It was argued that, ultimately, this would pose a more significant risk to human health. The legislature was thus confronted with the challenge of balancing different and differently understood, risks to public health. This task is rendered more complex and less certain, the more holistic the perspective adopted. In a *Pfizer* scenario the risks flowing from regulation are manifested directly in the form of a closely related threat to human health. Often, though, the countervailing risks will be remote in time or place, or – significantly in our world of ultra specialisation – the new risks will be cognitively remote. Not unrelated to this is the fact that it is not at clear what it means to say that health concerns must be given priority over economic considerations. Here 'health' is somehow represented as the 'soft' and the socially concerned, while hard-nosed selfish economics can look after itself. But as all those who despair at the AIDS crisis in many parts of Africa are acutely aware, health care requires resources and resources foregone *may* (or may not according to patterns of distribution and spending) accentuate this loss of life.

---

[62] *Supra* n . 4.

[63] Case C-473/98 *Toolex* [2000] ECR I-5681.

[64] Sunstein, *supra* n. 20, p. 39.

The point here is not to delve into the complex and highly normative world of risk regulation and risk management. It is merely to emphasise that hard choices cannot be avoided through recourse to slogans. Such slogans obfuscate rather than assist. The point equally is not to argue against the pursuit of a high level of protection for public health and for the environment, or to suggest that the European courts are wrong to concede that these objectives may serve to justify gravely adverse consequences for certain traders. The point rather is to emphasise that decision makers are faced with hard choices necessitating a balancing of many, not easily commensurable, objectives and concerns and that these choices cannot be reduced to a slogan which sounds good but which, in concrete terms, means nothing.

Before moving on it is comforting to be aware that the slogan in question is not reflected in the actual approach adopted by the CFI in the cases under discussion. Not only, as noted above, is emphasis placed upon a balancing of competing risks to human health, but also economic considerations are it seems to be reflected in the cost-benefit analysis required as an element of proportionality.

The Court notes in limine that the contested regulation is founded on a political choice, in respect of which the Community institutions were required to weigh up, on the one hand, maintaining while awaiting further scientific studies, the authorisation of a product which enables the agricultural sector to be more profitable and, on the other, banning the product for public health reasons.[65]

In this respect the regulation in question has some redeeming features, which seem to weigh heavily in the court's acceptance of it. First, the contested decision withdrawing authorisation, is subject to the Community institutions' duty of 're-examination'. The legislative framework granting the relevant powers establishes this. Second, the introduction of the ban was subject to a transitional period of six months.[66] Furthermore, the court was persuaded that the use of such antibiotics is not 'strictly necessary in animal husbandry and that there are alternative methods of animal husbandary even if they can lead to higher costs for farmers, and ultimately, consumers'.[67] It is from 'that perspective' that the measure is not found to be disproportionate, although it does entail serious economic consequences for *Pfizer*.[68] Similarly, in assessing whether a cost-benefit analysis had been conducted, the CFI points, for example, to the detailed analysis contained in the Swedish report submitted to the Council during the procedure leading to the adoption of the contested regulation. This report examined the experience in Sweden of the economic effects of ceasing to use

---

[65] *Supra* n. 3, para. 468.

[66] *Supra* n. 3, para. 460.

[67] *Supra* n. 3, para. 459.

[68] *Supra* n. 3, para. 461.

antibiotics for growth promotion.[69] Thus, although the CFI allowed the Council a wide degree of discretion in this regard, citing the mantra of the precedence of human health objectives, in examining its 'reasonableness',[70] it does appear to have regard to the fact that economic analysis was conducted in the course of the adoption of the contested measure.

III   The WTO and the elaboration of the precautionary principle

What will not yet be apparent from the above discussion, is the influence wielded by the WTO on the European courts' account of the precautionary principle. In *Pfizer*, to an extent at least, the CFI is open about this:

  '[...] it is for the Community institutions to define, observing the applicable rules of the international and Community legal orders, the political objectives which they intend to pursue within the parameters of the powers conferred on them by the Treaty. Thus within the World Trade Organisation ('the WTO') and, more specifically, in the Agreement on the Application of Sanitary and Phytosanitary Measures, which is set out in Annex 1A to the Agreement establishing the WTO, as approved by Council Decision 94/800/EC of 22 December 1994 [...] it is specifically provided that members of that organisation may determine the level of protection which they deem appropriate'.[71]

In other respects, the influence of the WTO is not explicitly acknowledged but may be inferred. Perhaps the clearest example in this respect – along with the heavy emphasis placed by the European courts upon the need for a risk assessment – is the prohibition upon seeking to guard against 'purely hypothetical risk'. In this respect the language of the CFI is strongly resonant of the case law of the WTO Appellate Body, particularly in its interpretation of the SPS Agreement.[72] The CFI reminds us that 'zero risk' does not exist, 'since it is not possible to prove scientifically that there is no current or future risk associated with the addition of antibiotics to feedingstuffs'.[73] The Appellate Body, similarly, advises that 'theoretical uncertainty' which arises due to the fact that 'science

---

[69] *Supra* n. 3, para. 469

[70] See *supra* n. 3, para. 472, where the CFI concludes that, as regards allegations of errors in cost-benefit analysis, 'there is nothing to suggest that the policy choice made by the institutions was unreasonable in that regard'.

[71] *Supra* n. 3, para. 150.

[72] SPS refers to the Agreement on Sanitary and Phytosanitary Measures contained in Annex 1A of the WTO Agreement.

[73] *Supra* n. 3, para. 145.

can *never* provide *absolute* certainty that a given substance will not *ever* have adverse health effects', is not the kind of risk, which is to be assessed. Uncertainty of this kind will not suffice to ground rationally a protective measure under the SPS Agreement.[74]

The strong – even decisive – impact of the WTO Agreement as regards the European courts' construction of the precautionary principle, raises a constitutional issue of great importance. As is well known, subject to certain exceptions, the European Court has denied the direct effect of the WTO Agreement.[75] Consequently, on the whole, this Agreement is not susceptible to direct judicial application in the Community legal order. It cannot be used as grounds to invalidate a Community act, or as a basis for illegality in the context of a direct action for judicial review. The position of the European Court on this question is controversial. It rests upon constitutional sensibilities:

'[...] to require the [European] judicial organs to refrain from applying the rules of domestic [i.e. European] law which are inconsistent with the WTO agreements would have the consequence of depriving the legislative or executive organs of the contracting parties of the possibility afforded by Article 22 of that memorandum of entering into negotiated agreements even on a temporary basis.'[76]

Thus, the European Court laid emphasis upon the nature of the WTO Agreement and upon the fact that it 'accords considerable importance to negotiation between the parties'.[77] Particularly important in this respect is the Dispute Settlement Understanding. Article 22 thereof – referred to by the European Court above – does not provide for the automatic withdrawal of measures found to be incompatible with WTO law, but also allows for the payment of 'mutually acceptable compensation'. While this is not 'preferred to full implementation' and may consequently be regarded as second best,[78] it is nonetheless a route which remains open to the offending WTO member. Thus, for the European courts to apply the WTO Agreement, even following condemnation at the hands of a panel, would be to deprive the political branch of its capacity to exercise the choices which it was so careful to preserve in the striking of so delicate a balance between the 'judicial' and the 'inter-governmental' in the WTO.

---

[74] *Hormones, supra* n. 52, para. 186.

[75] Case C-149/96 *Portugal* v. *Council* [1999] ECR I-8395.

[76] *Ibid*, para. 40. For an excellent discussion of this perspective, see F. Snyder, 'The Gatekeepers: the European Courts and WTO Law' (2003) 40 *CMLRev.* 313.

[77] *Ibid*, para. 36.

[78] See Article 22 DSU regarding suspension of concessions or other obligations in the event that a member fails to bring a measure into compliance with the covered agreements. Article 22.1 explicitly provides that neither compensation or suspension of concessions is to be preferred to full implementation.

This absence of direct effect is qualified in two respects. Where the Community legislature intended to implement a particular WTO obligation, or where the contested Community measure refers expressly to the precise provisions of the WTO Agreement, the European courts have exhibited willingness to review the legality of Community measures in the light of WTO rules.[79] More recently, the European Court implied that it would be willing to conduct a WTO-based check on legality (and entertain a related claim for damages) where, following a finding against the Community in the WTO, 'the Community had stated that it intended to comply with its WTO obligations' and where the reasonable period of time granted to it for so doing had expired.[80] Prior to the expiry of this deadline, no review on legality could be conducted 'without rendering ineffective the grant of a reasonable period for compliance with the DSB recommendations or decisions, as provided for in the dispute settlement system put in place by the WTO agreements'.[81] This is not the place for an analysis of the all-important *Biret* case. Nonetheless, this judgment may be regarded as a variant on the 'intention to implement' theme. By stating an intention[82] to comply with the specific findings of the dispute settlement bodies, the Community's political institutions may be thought to have elected to tie their own hands as regards compliance with the WTO Agreement.

The *Biret* case flows directly from the infamous *Hormones* dispute.[83] The *Pfizer* case raises some of the same issues, but in the context of an entirely different set of facts. The stated intention of the European Community to comply with *Hormones* entails an intention to comply with the specific recommendations of the panel (as re-written by the Appellate Body on appeal) *in that case*. It does not entail a commitment to adjust Community policy across the board, with a view to guaranteeing its conformity with the reasoning with underpinned the findings in that case. *Pfizer*, consequently, does not fall within the remit of the 'intention to implement' jurisprudence of the European Court. As such, in the context of this case, the WTO Agreement does not enjoy direct effect.

In the light of this, the impact of the WTO in the *Pfizer* case may seem surprising even though, formally, it is not out of synch with the jurisprudence discussed above. The WTO Agreement is not treated as directly effective in this case. Practically though, it might as well have been, in so far as the supposed autonomy of the Council is concerned. With little ado and less hesitation, the

---

[79] These are known as the 'implementation exceptions'. See also Snyder *supra* n. 76, pp. 342-347 who talks of the 'clear reference exception' and the 'transposition exception'. This was confirmed in *Council* v. *Portugal, supra* n. 75.

[80] Case C-93/02 P *Biret* v. *Council* judgment of 30 September 2003, para. 61.

[81] *Ibid*, para. 62.

[82] See Article 21.3 DSU which requires the offending party to inform the Dispute Settlement Body of its intentions with respect to implementation of its recommendations and rulings.

[83] *Supra* n. 52.

CFI did tie the hands of the Council with respect to the WTO, by *construing* the relevant Community principles to be in conformity with the jurisprudence of the WTO Appellate Body. As a matter of law, this is not strange. We already know that the doctrine of 'indirect effect' (consistent interpretation) applies generally with respect to the interpretation of Community law in the light of international agreements[84] and more specifically in relation to the WTO.[85] Indeed there are those who point out that 'the duty of consistent interpretation can do pretty much the same job [as direct effect], while sparing the Court intellectual acrobatics'.[86] As a matter of politics, however, the application and vigour of this doctrine in the context of the WTO seems not only strange, but intensely problematic.

The problem here is in part a familiar one. It is merely necessary to recall the consternation arising from the juxtaposition of 'no direct effect' but 'plenty of indirect effect' in the case of directives. The expedient incoherence of that position was readily exposed.[87] The language of incoherence has a pedantic ring, seeming to reflect the aesthetic sensibilities of the ivory tower academic. Objection to incoherence in the case of the WTO might be merely aesthetic had the arguments of the European Court in *Portugal* been less compelling, but these arguments are compelling. The European Court is quite right. The WTO Agreement is not typical in many respects. It represents a unique conflation in international law of the unusually ambitious and the characteristically reticent. For domestic courts to guarantee conformity – absent any clear intention on the part of the political institutions concerned – is to dismantle the 'safety valves' which inhere in this agreement, most notably in the functioning of its system for the settlement of disputes. *Pfizer* is an excellent illustration of this.

The readiness of the CFI to embrace the Appellate Body's findings in *Hormones* ignores the considerable uncertainty which continues to characterise WTO law in crucial, relevant, respects. *Hormones*, represents a first, but not final, step in the analysis and application of the precautionary principle in WTO law. To illustrate, the *Hormones* case did not call for an analysis of Article 5.7 of the SPS Agreement, accepted by most as constituting the most explicit

---

[84] *Gianni Bettati, supra* n. 1.

[85] See Case C-61/96 *Hermès International* v. *FHT Marketing Choice* [1998] ECR I-3606 and *Dior* v. *Tuk Consultancy* [2000] ECR I-11307

[86] A. Dashwood, quoted in *supra* n. 76, fn. 200. See Snyder, *supra* n., p. 363 for a discussion of the limitations of indirect effect in securing consistency: The relevant EC or national legislation must exist and be sufficiently flexible to be interpreted, there must not be a manifest conflict between WTO law and the legislation to be interpreted, case-by-case interpretation cannot resolve all problems, and consistent interpretation is less effect than direct effect in establishing legal certainty and hence creating confidence among the EU's trading partners.

[87] See P. Craig, 'Directive: Direct Effect, Indirect Effect and the Construction of National Legislation' (1997) ELRev. 519.

embodiment of the precautionary principle.[88] Article 5.7 is concerned with circumstances in which 'relevant scientific evidence is insufficient'. Thus, in so far as the Appellate Body constructed a threshold for risk regulation, it did so without recourse to the 'back-up' provided by Article 5.7; a provision about which we know practically nothing at this stage.[89] The basic point is this. We cannot even be sure that it would not, in certain circumstances, be open to the political institutions of the EU to take steps to guard against 'theoretical' or 'hypothetical' risk. We do not know where the threshold of 'scientific plausibility' will be set under Article 5.7 SPS. It is not at all unlikely that it will be the European Union which will test the limits in this respect; that is unless the European courts pre-empt it, by the adoption of an approach to risk regulation which turns out to be over-zealous, or misconceived, in its reading of the WTO.

Further, as I have argued previously, the bark of the Appellate Body in *Hormones* may be muted, but its bite is strong. It may not seem excessive to insist that members may not take steps to guard against 'theoretical' or 'hypothetical' risk. Surely, as Cass Sunstein remarks, there must exist a threshold of scientific plausibility in order to avoid 'palpable absurdity'.[90] So, the argument seems to go, the limitations imposed by the Appellate Body are so minimal and so eminently reasonable, that their application in the European Union must be beyond reproach. Without developing a theory of risk regulation, the only point to be made here is that it is not difficult to conceive of circumstances in which a regulator might wish to depart from the prescriptions of the Appellate Body. There may be (and indeed I would argue that there ought to be) situations in which it would be appropriate to take steps to guard against a risk which has been characterised as no more than hypothetical (that is to say a risk which arises because of the impossibility of proving a product safe for all time, but in relation to which there is no positive evidence of risk. This may reflect the difficulty of adducing specific evidence of low probability risk:

> '[...] *statistically convincing studies demonstrating the existence of a small health risk from hormone residues in meat are likely to be exceedingly difficult to generate. One can observe that the hormones in question are known carcinogens, and that some residue of these hormones exists in the meat. But it is likely impossible to know with any degree of statistical confidence whether these small residues, when added to the diets of people who are exposed to the same hormones from many other sources [...] do not cause a few more cases of cancer at the margin.'*

---

[88] *Hormones, supra* n. 52, para., where the AB found that Article 5.7 does not exhaust the relevance of the precautionary principle in the WTO Agreement.

[89] The only ruling of the AB on this provision was in WT/DS76/AB/R, *Japan – Measures Affecting Agricultural Products (Japan Varietals)*.

[90] Sunstein, *supra* n. 20, p. 13.

Consequently, the Appellate Body's insistence that Europe point to highly partic-
ularised studies showing a risk from hormone residues in meat likely presents
an insurmountable obstacle.[91]

Also and Cass Sunstein acknowledges this, though he does not grapple with
it, there may be circumstances in which public opposition to a given technology
is such that it makes sense for a government to take steps to guard against that
(hypothetical) risk. It may do so in the name of securing trust in government,
and in the interests of responsive government. It may well be that the regulation of genetically modified organisms – especially as regards the impact of GM
food on human health – will come to provide a classic case study in this respect.
As Sunstein concedes, 'public alarm, even if ill-formed, is itself a harm, and it
is likely to lead to additional harms, perhaps in the form of large-scale "ripple
effects". A sensible approach to risk will attempt to reduce public fear even if
it is baseless'.[92] This of course raises the immensely complex (and fascinating)
subject of public opinion in risk regulation (and public opinion in adjudication).
The point here is not to explore this, but merely to exemplify that risk regulation is contested all the way down. When you look behind the apparently banal
– it can never be lawful to guard against merely hypothetical risk for example
– there opens up a whole world of uncertainty and conflict. In such a setting
– above all in such a setting – the conclusions of the WTO's dispute settlement
bodies will never be less than controversial. As such, these conclusions should
never – by virtue of the principle of indirect effect – find automatic, uncritical,
acceptance in the European Union.

---

[91] 'Domestic Regulation, 'Sovereignty and Scientific Evidence Requirements: A Pessimistic View' (on file
with the author, p. 16).

[92] Sunstein, *supra* n. 20, p. 45 (footnotes excluded).

CHAPTER 5

European Environmental Law Principles in Belgian Jurisprudence

Luc Lavrysen

1 Introduction

A brief review of the Belgian environmental case law[1] revealed that in over 100 cases, there is reference to one or more of the environmental principles that are enshrined in the EC Treaty. The relatively common use of these principles in recent Belgian jurisprudence may be explained by the fact that these principles are also incorporated in national law, both at federal[2] level and at Flemish regional[3] level.[4] Given the significant number of cases where reference is made to these principles, it is impossible to give a complete overview of the case law. Therefore we will restrict ourselves to the leading cases for each of the relevant principles.

This chapter will examine the polluter pays principle, the precautionary principle, and the prevention at source principle. Although not specifically mentioned, in the EC Treaty, it might be of interest to also discuss the constitutional right to the protection of a healthy environment (Article 23 of the Belgian Constitution); the right to privacy (Article 22 of the Belgian Constitution); as well as the stand still principle, an environmental law principle of a general nature in the Flemish region, that is often invoked in conjunction with these constitutional rights.

---

[1] Only the case law of the highest courts is systematically reported. The case law of lower courts and tribunals is reported only fragmentarily. The archives of the *Tijdschrift voor Milieurecht* (Flemish Environmental Law Review) and the Databank Milieurechtspraak (http://allserv.rug.ac.be/~pbrewee/cgi-bin/dmr.cgi), however, contain an abundant collection of more than 9,000 environmental law cases.

[2] Act of 20 January 1999 for the protection of the marine environment in the marine areas that come under the jurisdiction of Belgium, *Moniteur belge*, 12 March 1999.

[3] Article 1.2.1., §2 of the Flemish Decree of 5 April 1995 laying down general provisions of environmental policy, Moniteur belge, 3 June 1995 (several times amended); Article 6 of the Flemish Decree of 18 July 2003 concerning integral water management.

[4] See on this issue: N. de Sadeleer, The Enforcement of the precautionary principle by German, French and Belgian Courts, *RECIEL*, 9(2) 2000, 149-150; N. de Sadeleer, *Environmental Principles: from Political Slogans to Legal Rules*, Oxford University Press, Oxford, (2002), pp. 32, 71, 135-136, 330-331, 332-333, 393-394; L. Lavrysen, The precautionary principle in Belgian Jurisprudence: Unknown, Unloved?, *European Environmental Law Review*, (1998), pp. 75-76; I. Larmuseau, The precautionary principle in Belgian Jurisprudence: So Many Men, So Many Minds?, in M. Sheridan and L. Lavrysen (eds), *Environmental Law Principles in Practice*, Bruylant, Brussels, (2002), pp. 173-179; I. Larmuseau, Beginselen van milieubeleid, in L. Lavrysen (ed), *Milieurechtspraak*, Kluwer uitgevers, Mechelen,(2002), pp. 281-326.

2 The polluter pays principle

2.1 The Court of Arbitration

The polluter pays principle is mainly[5] invoked before the Court of Arbitration. The Court of Arbitration is the Constitutional Court of Belgium; although it does not have the power to review compliance with the whole Constitution, only parts of it. The competence of the Court of Arbitration is twofold. Firstly, the Court oversees the division of powers between the federal legislator on the one hand and the legislators of the Communities and Regions on the other. In the area of environmental policy, the federal and regional legislators are the main actors involved. In practical terms, this means that the Court examines the conformity of statutes (from the federal legislator), decrees (Flemish and Walloon Regions) and ordinances (Brussels-Capital Region) with the rules determining the respective powers of the State, the Communities and the Regions. These rules are set out in the Constitution and in its special implementing acts, these include; the special Institutional Reform Act of 8th August 1980; the special Act of 12th January 1989 concerning the Brussels institutions and the special Act of 16th January 1989 concerning the funding of the Communities and Regions. Secondly, the Court since 1989 has had the power to review statutes, decrees and ordinances for compliance with the constitutional equality principle (Articles 10 and 11 of the Constitution) and with freedom and equality in respect of education guaranteed by the Constitution. In this regard, the Court took a broad view of its powers. It used the equality principle also to indirectly review these statutes, decrees and ordinances for compliance with rights and liberties that are guaranteed by other provisions of the Constitution, by the international human rights conventions and by Community law. Since the entry into force of the Special Act of 9th March 2003, the competencies of the Court have been extended to the direct review of legislation for compliance with all rights and liberties enshrined in the Constitution.[6]

The polluter pays principle has so far been applied in cases where taxpayers demanded the annulment of a particular environmental tax on the grounds of violation of the constitutional principle of equality and non-discrimination in conjunction with the polluter pays principle.[7] I have found over 30 judgments where this was the case. Hereafter, we will discuss the most important cases.

---

[5] We also found eight judgments of the Council of State were the polluter pays principle was invoked by the parties, but eventually the Council made no use of the principle in its final judgments, except in cases of local environmental taxes (*e.g.*: Council of State, n° 107.317, 4 June 2002).

[6] See: http://www.arbitrage.be/.

[7] N. de Sadeleer (2002) 333.

2.2 The *Flemish Wastewater Tax* case

In 1991, a company challenged the new wastewater tax legislation introduced in the Flemish Region that same year.[8] For the largest polluters, with a drinking water consumption of more than 500 m³ a year, the tax
is calculated on the basis of the volume of waste water and the concentration
of pollutants it contains (taking into account the following parameters: BOD,
COD, nitrogen, phosphates, heavy metals) discharged into sewers and surface
waters. The appellant was a surface water discharger, who complained about
the discriminatory treatment of surface water dischargers in relation to sewer
dischargers and the discriminatory treatment of some surface water dischargers
in relation to other surface water dischargers.

The appellant was of the opinion that, by imposing a tax for the year 1991
that was calculated on the basis of the water pollution caused in 1990 and by
not allowing the investments made in 1990 or in 1991 to limit this pollution to
be deducted for the purposes of this tax, the challenged provisions instituted a
difference in treatment between firms that made such investments and firms
that did not. This difference in treatment was thought not be in proportion to
the incentive function of the tax, referred to in the Recommendation of the
Council of the European Communities 75/436/EURATOM, EEC, ECSC, of 3rd
March 1975. The appellant therefore argued, that the challenged provisions
treated all firms that discharged into the surface waters in the same way, regardless of whether or not they carried out such investments.

In its answer to this argument, the Court referred to the parliamentary
preparation of the challenged provisions, revealing that the environmental tax
on water pollution was intended not only as a means to entirely, or partially, pay
for the collective measures to combat pollution, but also as a policy instrument
to influence polluters to limit the pollution they cause at source, applying the
polluter pays principle. The legislator therefore had a twofold objective in mind
when introducing the tax. While the aforementioned financing objective comes
first for the firms that discharge into the public sewers, the main objective, as
far as the firms that discharge into the surface waters are concerned, is to cause
as little pollution as possible. This distinction explains the differences between
the two categories of taxpayers in the calculation of the tax. The Court cited in
this respect some crucial passages of the Council Recommendation 75/436/EC,
namely:

'The tax is intended to incite the polluter to take the necessary measures at the
lowest cost in order to reduce the pollution it causes (incentive function) and/or to
let him bear his share of the costs of collective measures, such as the treatment costs

---

[8]   Court of Arbitration, n° 59/92, 8 October 1992, *n.v. Primeur* v. *Flemish Government*, www.arbitrage.be.

(redistributing function). The tax shall be withheld according to an effective proce-dure by the public authorities according to the degree of the pollution caused. The tax must be set in such a way that priority is given to the incentive function [...]

In order to prevent unfair competition that impairs trade and location of invest-ments in the Community, it will undoubtedly be necessary to arrive at ever-greater harmonisation at Community level of the various instruments that are applied in similar cases.

As long as this has not happened, the issue of the allocation of costs for combating pollution will not be fully settled at the Community level. The present communication of the Commission is therefore only a first step towards the application of the polluter pays principle. This first step should be followed as soon as possible by a harmonisa-tion within the Community of the instruments for the application of this principle when they are used is similar cases, which is also set out in the third indent of para-graph 8 of this document.'

As far as the first argument was concerned, the Court held finally:

'By referring to a recommendation that has been worded in this way, the legisla-tor definitely expressed the intention of taxing the discharges into the surface waters in such a way that they incite those firms to pollute as little as possible, but was not obliged to follow one particular method rather than another with a view to this. By introducing an important tax and by making the amount of the tax dependent not on the investments carried out during the tax year or the preceding year, but solely on the pollution actually caused in the preceding year, the legislator has adopted a measure that is in proportion to the objective that it has set itself.'

The appellant also criticised the transitional regime for surface water discharg-ers, contained in the so-called 'sanitation coefficients'. Under that system, applicable in the period 1991-1995, a year-to-year reduction (varying according to the sector concerned) of the wastewater tax was granted to some categories of surface water dischargers, specified in an annex of the challenged decree. The appellant argued that these coefficients in themselves instituted discrimina-tory treatment between the surface water dischargers. The Court considered that with those coefficients, a lower tax was, during the transitional period, introduced for surface water dischargers who were previously not liable for the tax. Those coefficients were determined in accordance with the sector specific wastewater discharge conditions. A reduction was allowed provided that those discharge conditions deviate more flexibly from the general discharge condi-tions. The Court accepted the basic idea of this remediation period, but annulled the system partially, because not all of the sectors that found themselves in the same situation were treated on an equal footing:

'The legislator is authorised to allow reductions, where appropriate, taking into account the wish to provide for a transitional arrangement and the observation that less stringent sectorial discharge conditions have been laid down for certain sectors, taking into consideration the developments in wastewater treatment technology.

However, where the legislator uses those criteria, he is obliged to apply those criteria equally to all sectors that are in an equivalent situation in regard to the measure under review and the objective aimed at. By allowing certain sectors to benefit from those remediation coefficients and excluding others, without any justification being offered or emerging from the answers to the questions put by the Court, the legislator introduced a distinction that is contrary to Articles [10] and [11] of the Constitution.'

2.3   The *Walloon Waste Tax* case

In 1991 the Walloon Region instituted a waste tax, in which the regime differed according to the type of waste. On non-domestic waste, a proportional tax of €125 per tonne was charged. Domestic waste was taxed on a flat-rate basis; the amount of the tax was fixed at €25 per building or part of a building that was used as private dwelling. A lower tax was charged for private dwellings occupied by fewer than 4 persons (€7.5, €15 or €22.5 respectively if the dwelling was occupied by 1, 2 or 3 persons). These provisions were challenged by some environmental NGOs and individuals[9], referring to the Opinion of the legislation section of the Council of State, given prior to the new regime being adopted by the Walloon Parliament. The legislative section of the Council of State, had raised objections to the flat-rate tax because although the decree cites the generation of waste as the circumstance giving rise to the tax, the challenged provisions rather assume that the tax is levied on the occupation of a property as a dwelling place; without the quantity of waste being generated, the type of waste and the method of disposal being taken into account, unlike in the rules that apply for non-domestic waste. The Council of State concluded in its opinion that such a regime cannot be allowed since it does not comply with the principles of community law on waste and was not in keeping with the polluter pays principle, since the dissuasive aspect of the tax is lacking. Furthermore it was contrary to the equality principle since, according to that principle, dissimilar situations should be treated distinctly.

The Court held that, where a waste tax is inspired by the polluter pays principle, it will only comply with the non-discrimination principle if it is levied on the polluters and if it takes into account the degree in which each taxpayer contributes to the pollution, against which the tax is directed. In accordance with this principle, the legislator has introduced a tax, which for non-domestic waste is determined according to the volume of waste produced by each taxpayer. On the

---

[9]   Court of Arbitration, n° 41/93, 3 June 1993, *A.-M. Begaux-Lateur e.a.* v. *Walloon Government*, www.arbitrage.be.

other hand, as far as domestic waste was concerned, the legislator concluded for different reasons that at that moment it was impossible to institute a proportional tax. By taxing households, the legislator reaches the polluters who produce domestic waste. By setting the tax at an amount that does not vary according to the volume of waste produced by each household, but according to the number of persons constituting the household; the legislator started from the assumption that the volume of waste produced differs according to the number of persons. It thus opted for a tax regime that, in theory, is based on an application of the polluter pays principle, although it does not fully attain this objective. It justified this choice by contending that the introduction of a proportional tax met with practical difficulties, which were considered insurmountable. The flat-rate taxation method introduced by the legislator does not have the dissuasive or incentive effect of a proportional tax because it does not take into account the efforts, which each household makes to limit its waste production. However, the Court concluded it is up to the legislator, to decide whether it was possible to introduce a proportional tax on domestic waste comparable to that levied on non-domestic waste. The Court dismissed the action on the following grounds:

'*By taxing all households at the same rate and by letting the amount of the tax vary according to the number of persons making up a household, the legislator treats persons in different situations in the same way, and adjusts the tax using a criterion that, for practical reasons, represents the real situation only approximately and in a simplified way. The practical reasons why the legislator refrained from introducing a proportional tax which would have made better allowance for the differences between taxpayers and the reimbursement to the municipalities and associations of municipalities of all or part of the tax, as allowed by Article 35, in order to stimulate their initiatives for waste disposal and recycling show, however, that the challenged measure, even if it is not perfectly adequate in regard to the objective pursued, is still sufficiently in keeping with it.*'

2.4   The *Flemish Cooling Water Tax* case

In 1992 the wastewater tax that was discussed earlier (2.1), was extended to the discharge of cooling waters. This extra tax was calculated only on the basis of the volume of discharged cooling water, not taking into account the temperature of it, nor the impact on the receiving surface waters. The main electricity producer of Belgium challenged the new tax.[10] The appellant criticised the challenged provisions first of all, for introducing an environmental tax without any technical or ecological justification; for being chargeable to dischargers of cooling water as well as dischargers of wastewater; for determining the calculation of the tax on the discharge of cooling water in a discriminatory

---

[10]   Court of Arbitration, n° 79/93, 9 November 1993, *Electrabel* v. *Flemish Government*, www.arbitrage.be.

way in comparison with the tax on the discharge of wastewater; and for introducing a tax which, as a result of this calculation method, is not in keeping with the function that is ascribed to it, namely to encourage industries and individuals to pollute less.

The Court rejected the arguments of the electricity producer. The Court considered that the challenged measures are aimed, on the one hand, at discouraging the discharge of cooling water on account of the adverse ecological effects of the thermal and chemical pollution on the receiving surface waters and on the other at the financing and division of the costs resulting from the pollution according to the polluter pays principle. The Court recalled that where a tax is inspired by the polluter pays principle, it will only comply with the non-discrimination principle if it is levied on the polluters and if it takes into account the degree in which each taxpayer contributes to the pollution against which the tax is directed. In accordance with this principle, the legislator had introduced a tax, which for the discharge of cooling water was determined according to the volume of cooling water produced by each taxpayer. The Court held:

'By fixing the tax base and the rate of the tax on the discharge of cooling water on a flat-rate basis until a less approximate calculation method can be worked out, the legislator was mindful of the technical difficulties and the costs that would accompany a system in which the real environmental impact of the cooling water discharges can be measured precisely in terms of oxygen level, flow intensity and difference in temperature between the water that is drawn and that which is discharged. Apart from the uniform reduction factors [...] which are not disputed, the calculation of the tax is not on a flat-rate basis insofar as it is in proportion to the discharged volume, an element which is easy to measure and of which the relevance is beyond dispute. Consequently, there are no obvious disproportionate effects between the challenged measure and the objectives of the legislator.*

The impossibility of deducting the volume of waste in the used surface water in the event that the wastewater derives wholly or partially from the use of surface water is inextricably linked to the choice made by the legislator in favour of a flat-rate base for charging the tax on the discharge of cooling water.

3   The precautionary principle

In 1998, I could have written, without violating the truth, that this principle wasn't known in Belgian jurisprudence, although one could find a hidden precautionary approach in some judgments.[11] Things have dramatically changed since then. Nowadays it is the most popular principle in environmental

---

[11]   L. Lavrysen, *op. cit.* note 4; N. de Sadeleer, *op. cit.* note 4 pp. 134-138.

jurisprudence and there is extensive commentary published on the subject.[12] The precautionary principle is particularly prevalent in case law on magnetic fields[13], although in other issues too, the principle is invoked.

3.1 The *Aubange-messancy Transmission Line* case

In July 1998, the CPTE-company applied for a permit to carry out technical works for installing a second, three-phase transmission line on the existing pylons in the municipalities of Aubange and Messancy. In its application, the company stated, 'the pylons of the high-voltage line already exist'; 'the installation of the 2nd three-phase transmission line will therefore in no way disrupt the developed and undeveloped sites'; 'there are neither schools or hospitals in the vicinity of the works' and 'the question of any nuisance is irrelevant'. The mayor and aldermen of Aubange and Messancy delivered favourable opinions on the project, "considering that, for economic reasons, there are no grounds for opposing this project" and in September 1998, the acting official granted the requested planning permissions.

Mrs. Nadine Venter brought an action for the suspension of these building permits before the Council of State, in June 1999.[14] The Administration Section of the Council of State has jurisdiction to handle applications for annulment of acts (*e.g.* decisions on environmental and other licences) and regulations of the different administrative authorities. The Council can annul these acts and regulations if they conflict with higher legal standards, if they violate the principles

---

[12] N. de Sadeleer, Het voorzorgsbeginsel: een stille revolutie, *Tijdschrift voor Milieurecht*, (1999) pp. 82-99; N. de Sadeleer, Reflexions sur le statut juridique de principe de precaution, in E. Zaccai and N. Missa (eds), *Le principe de precaution: significations et consequences*, Brussels, ULB, (2000), 117-142; N. de Sadeleer, Les avatars du principe de precaution en droit public: effet du mode ou revolution silenceuse? *Rev. Fr. Dr. Adm*, (2001), 547-562; N. de Sadeleer, The effect of uncertainty on the threshold levels to which the precautionary principle appears to be subject, in M. Sheridan and L. Lavrysen (eds), *Environmental Law Principles in Practice*, Brussels, Bruylant, (2002) 17-43; I. Larmuseau, Het voorzorgsbeginsel geïntroduceerd in der Belgische rechtspraak: zoveel hoofden, zoveel zinnen?, *Tijdschrift voor Milieurecht*, (2000), 24-32; I. Larmuseau, *op. cit.* note 4; L. Lavrysen/P. De Smedt, Over het success van mobieltjes en de emancipatie van het voorzorgsbeginsel. Een status questionis van de wetgeving en rechtspraak met betrekking tot de exploitatie van GSM-zendmasten, *Tijdschrift voor Milieurecht*, (2002), 470-485; L. Lenaerts, GSM-mast zorgt voor stralend recht. Noot bij arresten van de Rechtbank van Brugge van 21 december 2001 en 4 februari 2002, *Juristenkrant*, (2002) 6; D. Misonne, Het voorzorgsbeginsel, *Milieurecht Info*, (2001), p 71. We found eighteen cases in witch the Principle was invoked before the Council of State.

[13] See: L. Lavrysen/P. De Smedt, *op. cit.* note 12, pp. 475-484; M. Pâques, *Antennes GSM, urbanisme, préjudice et précaution dans la jurisprudence du Conseil d'état, Le Point sur lee droit des biens*, Edition Foramtion Permanente CUP, Novembre, (2002), Université de Liège, pp. 419-436.

[14] Council of State, n° 62.130, 20 August 1999, http://www.raadvst-consetat.be.

of proper government, or if they have been impaired by an abuse of discretion. The Council of State also provides for the possibility to demand the suspension of the challenged act or regulation in anticipation of a judgment on the merits. The conditions are that serious arguments must be adduced and that the immediate enforcement of the challenged act or regulation could cause serious detriment that is difficult to rectify.

The Council of State decided to suspend the building permits. The Council found that the applicant invoked serious arguments;

'Whereas in this case it emerges from the brief that the high-voltage line in question overhangs several houses, including that of the applicant; whereas it will appear later on, as we examine the risk of serious detriment that is difficult to rectify, the compatibility of a high-voltage line with a residential area is subject to discussion; whereas the presence of houses underneath the high-voltage lines should have been mentioned in order to draw the attention of the authorities to this matter; whereas in this connection the argument is serious'.

Furthermore, the Council took a precautionary approach in assessing the risk of serious harm;

'Whereas it emerges from the documents submitted in the proceedings that the effects of magnetic fields induced by a high-voltage line are the subject of debate in medical circles; whereas it is not up to the Council of State to settle such a debate; whereas the Council can merely note that there are elements that lead it reasonably to suspect a health risk, even if the relevant existing regulations are amply respected, as the intervening party points out; whereas if this risk cannot be established with certainty, as the respondent points out, it cannot be ruled out either; whereas for the Council of State to be able to suspend a challenged act, the detriment need not be certain; whereas it suffices for the risk of detriment to be plausible; whereas this applies in the present case; whereas the risk in question poses a threat to the right to the protection of health, guaranteed by Article 23, 3rd paragraph, 2°, of the Constitution, as well as the right to the safeguarding of a healthy environment, guaranteed by 3° of the same paragraph; whereas with respect to the basic rights, the detriment, of which the risk must be considered certain, is serious; whereas it is, by its very nature, difficult to rectify'.

3.2   The *Wilrijk Waste Incinerator* case

The President of the Tribunal of Antwerp, in a judgment of 2nd February 1999, on the grounds that the precautionary principle was breached, prohibited an incineration plant operated in Wilrijk by ISVAG, from starting up again.[15] The action had been brought by residents of the city of Antwerp and the

---

[15]   President of the Tribunal of First Instance of Antwerp, 2 February 1999, A.J.T., 1998-99, 809-811, with

municipality of Aartselaar on behalf of the city and municipality, under the Act of 12th January 1993 which grants a right of action in environmental matters, in conjunction with Article 271, §1 of the New Municipal Act.[16] The operation of the incineration plant in Wilrijk was licensed until 2012, however, the plant was shut down in November 1997 because it exceeded the dioxin emission standards imposed by Flemish Environmental Regulations (VLAREM II). With a view to reopening the plant, ISVAG carried out improvement works during the course of 1998, however it failed to perform the dioxin exposure survey that had been suggested by a committee of experts. Faced with the absence of this dioxin exposure survey and on the basis of a number of concrete facts in the case, the President of the Tribunal considered that there was no absolute certainty that the incineration plant would not pose any further health risks to the residents of the neighbourhood. According to the President, in such a case of uncertainty the precautionary principle says that damage can be avoided by not starting up high-risk activities. The President concluded the judgment with the striking words:

'whereas with regard to public health no compromises should be made, precisely because it is the future of the residents and their quality of life that are at stake; whereas this is a problem that concerns everyone and should not leave anyone unaffected'.

On appeal and after a third-party action was dismissed by the same President[17], the Antwerp Court of Appeal[18] held that the domestic waste incineration plant operated by ISVAG was built in accordance with the building permit and the operation of the plant had been licensed by the relevant authority; no action for annulment had been instituted against these licences before the Council of State. In accordance with Article 159 of the Constitution, the Court verified the internal and external legality of this building permit and environmental licence. The permits were issued in accordance with the forms and procedures prescribed by law and were found legal in that respect. At the moment when they were granted, the licensing decisions complied in terms of content with the legal limits within which the licensing authority was permitted to use its administrative discretionary authority and are therefore also found to be legal in that respect. The Court believed that the authority has given shape to the precautionary principle, by imposing on ISVAG the emission standards specified in

---

comment Larmuseau, 'Het voorzorgsbeginsel niet langer een papieren tijger'. An English translation of this judgment is published in: Sheridan/Lavrysen (2002) 193-200.

[16] I. Larmuseau, *op. cit.* note 12. pp. 182-186.

[17] President of the Tribunal of First Instance of Antwerp, 20 April 1999, also published in English: Sheridan/Lavrysen (2002), 200-203.

[18] Antwerp Court of Appeal, 11 October 1999, *cvba ISVAG v. G.A. and others – Flemish Region and OVAM.* See: Sheridan/Lavrysen (2002) 203-209.

the environmental licence (a dioxin emission limit value of 0.1 Ng TEQ/Nm3). Since the operation of the domestic waste incineration plant had already ceased before the action for cessation was instituted, there could, according to the Court, be no question of an obvious violation of one or several provisions of laws, decrees, orders, regulations or decisions relating to the protection of the environment, upon which an action for cessation may be based. What was at issue was the question of whether the start-up and resumption of operation of this incineration plant, even if in accordance with the licensing conditions, as such constituted a patent violation or posed a serious risk of violation of one or several of those provisions. Through the unanimous recommendation of the Experts Committee, ISVAG were considered in the opinion of the Court, to have made a reasonable case for the fact that the residual emission of dioxin would be so small and even barely measurable. The start-up of the plant, even with the accumulated pollution from the past, in the neighbourhoods concerned did not constitute a patent violation, or a serious risk of violation, of one or several provisions of laws, decrees, ordinances, regulations or decisions relating to the protection of the environment. The Court for these reasons lifted the suspension order issued by the President of the Tribunal.

3.3   The *Sint-Niklaas Waste Incinerator* case

In similar facts to the previous case, residents of the city of Sint-Niklaas brought an action before the President of the Tribunal of First Instance. The action, on the basis of the Act of 12th January 1993 concerning a right of action in matters of environmental protection in combination with Article 271 of the New Municipal Act, was to obtain the closure of a Waste Incinerator that was operated by MI-WA. On appeal, the Ghent Court of Appeal[19] held that an action for cessation might also be based on a violation of the precautionary principle and the principle of preventive action. The Court was of the opinion that citizens have the right to the greatest possible protection of their health. The non-application of the best available technologies to reduce air pollution (in this case the installation of a DENOX system), was in the view of the Court a violation of the aforementioned principles, the licensing conditions and constituted a threat within the meaning of Article 1 of the Act of 12th January 1993. The preventive effect of this Act permits a judicial supervision and judicial measures to prevent damage. Having regard to all the interests involved, the Court ordered MI-WA to cease by December 2002 the activities carried out at the plant, allowing the company in this way a period of a little more than one year to set up and implement a conversion plan.

---

[19]   Ghent Court of Appeal, 20 November 2001, *D.B.F. and c.s.* v. *Intercommunale Vereniging voor Huisvuilverwerking Midden-Waasland*, published in: L. Lavrysen/ P. De Smedt, *op. cit.* note 13, pp. 718-724.

4 The prevention at source principle

The prevention at source principle is less prevalent in Belgian litigation.[20] As the following case shows, it is nevertheless a Principle that could have a decisive impact on the outcome of some litigation. Following an Executive Order of the Flemish Minister of Agriculture and Environment of 21st January 2000, a licence to operate a dumping site for inert materials was refused to the Steenbakkerijen Floren. The company appealed against this decision with the Council of State[21] in order to demand by urgent necessity, the suspension of the enforcement of this decision. The appellant suggested that the Proximity Principle had been violated, arguing that the principle provides that waste must be disposed as close as possible to its place of production and that every province must provide sufficient dumping capacity in order to meet the local needs in terms of waste disposal. Particularly as, in this case, the dumping site was considered by the competent waste authority to be the only one in the province where waste could be dumped in an environmentally sound way. The Council of State rejected the demand, referring to the 'waste management hierarchy' of Directive 75/442/EEC (Article 3) that is also implemented in Flemish legislation. The Council noted that it follows from this provision that the dumping of waste should be prevented as much as possible, that dumping has the lowest priority of the various waste processing methods and that, if dumping has the lowest priority, it would on the face of it be obvious that the mere dumping of inert waste, without reuse or recycling, is discouraged. Furthermore, it is obviously not reasonable to create any new dumping sites, if there is still a lot of residual capacity. As far as the argument, derived from the violation of Article 174, is concerned, the Council held:

'[This provision] does not appear to have been violated, since the question as to where dumping sites are created would only appear to be relevant in the event that dumping sites are needed; whereas the first question with regard to waste management is whether and to what degree dumping is allowed and that only afterwards the question is relevant as to where dumping is allowed; whereas observance of the proximity principle appears to imply that, if waste has to be dumped, this happens as close as possible to the place where the waste is produced; whereas it does not seem to imply that new dumping sites have constantly to be opened if dumping has the lowest priority in waste processing and there is still sufficient dumping capacity.'

---

[20] We found only 4 Council of State judgments where the Principle or one of its variants (*e.g.* the Principle of Proximity) was invoked. The Principle was also discussed in the *Sint-Niklaas Waste Incinerator* case, in combination with the precautionary principle (see 3.3).

[21] Council of State, n° 85.462, 21 February 2000, *n.v. Steenbakkerijen Floren* v. *Flemish Region*, www.raadvst-consetat.be.

5   The constitutional rights on the protection of a healthy environment and of privacy – The stand still principle

5.1   The constitutional rights

The right to the protection of a healthy environment forms part of the economic, social and cultural rights that were incorporated in 1994 into the Belgian Constitution (Article 23, third paragraph, 4°). The concept of environment has a broad scope in this article of the Constitution.[22] Although the Belgian Council of State expressly denies direct effect to the economic and social rights enshrined in Article 23 of the Constitution, it has accepted the standstill action of the right to the protection of a healthy environment[23] and linked this to the standstill principle enshrined in Article 1.2.1, §2, of the Decree of 5th April 1995, establishing general provisions of environmental policy. The standstill principle of that Decree, in turn has a European background, derived from a series of European environmental directives that establish quality standards. In the Flemish Region, the principle has been upgraded to a general principle of environmental policy as such.

Article 22 of the Belgian Constitution concerns the right to respect for private and family life, which according to the Court of Arbitration should be given the same scope as Article 8 of the European Convention on Human Rights. In the case concerning the regional airport of Liège, this gave rise to the application of the case law of the European Court of Human Rights in the case of *Powell and Rayner* and of *Hatton I* v. *United Kingdom*[24], which itself builds on the judgments in the cases of *Lopez Ostra* and *Guerra*, among others.

---

[22]   J. Theunis, Milieubescherming en grondrechten, in L. Lavrysen (ed.), *Milieurechtspraak*, Kluwer Publishing, Mechelen, (2002), p 3; J. Theunis, Deel IV – Milieu en staatsrecht, in K. Deketelaere (ed.), Handboek milieurecht, Bruges, die Keure, (2001), pp. 355-362.

[23]   The issue also came up in the Court of Arbitration judgment no. 50/2003 of 30 April 2003. In this case, however, the Court did not have to rule on the question whether or not Article 23 of the Constitution concerning the right to the protection of a healthy environment implies a standstill obligation, because the challenged regulation on night flights did not involve a deterioration in relation to the previously existing situation. The Court has already accepted such a standstill effect in respect of the right to social security (Court of Arbitration, no. 169/2002, 27 November 2002).

[24]   The judgment of the Court of Arbitration was delivered after the *Hatton I* judgment of the European Court of Human Rights (E.C.H.R., 2 October 2001, *Hatton a.o.* v. *United Kingdom*, www.echr.coe.int) but before the *Hatton II* judgment delivered by the Grand Chamber (E.C.H.R., 8 July 2003, *Hatton a.o.* v. *United Kingdom*, www.echr.coe.int).

5.2 The *Zolder Race Circuit* case

In 1999, the Flemish Government relaxed the existing regulations for the operation of motor vehicle race circuits. Before that relaxation, competitions and practice runs were without noise restrictions and allowed only one out of two weekends, so that neighbours could enjoy peaceful weekends for half of the time. Following the relaxation, the organiser was restricted to only one weekend per month, in which he could not organise such races. A neighbour of the Zolder Race Circuit, the main circuit in Flanders, challenged this relaxation in the law, before the Council of State and asked for its suspension by way of urgent necessity.[25]

The Council of State accepted the appeal and suspended the new regulation. The Council held that the fundamental right to the protection of a healthy environment appears to imply, among other things, that relaxing the current environmental regulations can only be deemed compatible with Article 23 of the Constitution if there are compelling reasons for doing so. The standstill principle that emerges from this provision was laid down for the Flemish Region in the Decree of 5th April 1995, establishing general environmental policy principles. The Flemish Government must, according to the Council, bear those principles in mind when enacting environmental conditions that apply either generally or per category of establishment by virtue of Article 20 of the Environmental Licensing Decree. The new regulation for motor vehicle races could not be regarded as an equivalent alternative to the previous regulation. If it is true that the new regulation imposes stricter rules on events organised during the week, recreational activities usually take place at weekends, which is precisely the time of the week, which the interests of the neighbourhood prevail. So, the challenged regulation had the effect of diminishing the protection of man and the environment against the unpleasant effects of the organisation of motor vehicle races. The Council concluded that, neither the administrative case file, nor the defence set up by the Flemish Government had shown that there were compelling reasons to justify all this in the light of Article 23 of the Constitution.

5.3 The *Bierset Airport* case

The Walloon Government decided some years ago to transform an old military air base in Bierset, near Liège, into an airport specialising in cargo. The airport mainly operated cargo flights at night, because parcel express services like TNT (the main company operating from Bierset) operate mainly during the night. This business was rapidly growing. With a view to protecting the airport's neighbours against the noise, a Decree of the Walloon Parliament

---

[25] Council of State, n° 80.018, 29 April 1999, *Jacobs* v. *Flemish Region*, www.raadvst-consetat.be.

of 8th June 2001 (amended by a Decree of 25th October 2001) instituted different noise protection zones around the airport, depending on the expected noise
levels when the airport would be operated at maximum capacity. In the 'A-zone'
(with an average expected noise exposure level of 70 dB(A) or more, expressed
in LDN or day-night level), the owners have the right to force the government
to buy their houses so that they may relocate to another area. In the 'B-zone'
(with an average expected noise exposure level between 65 dB(A) and 70 dB(A)),
there were no such obligations, but the owners and occupiers of the houses in
that area could ask the government to bear the costs incurred for soundproofing. The residents association near the airport, found that the inhabitants of the
'B-zone' were discriminated against in their fundamental right to protection of
family life and privacy, when compared with the inhabitants of the 'A-zone' and
demanded the annulment of these provisions.

The Court of Arbitration[26] partially accepted their argument. The Court
was of the opinion that Article 22 of the Belgian Constitution must be interpreted in the light of Article 8 of the European Convention on the Protection of
Human Rights and Fundamental Freedoms (ECHR). The Court recalled that
the European Court of Human Rights had accepted that noise nuisance caused
by aircraft, where this is excessive, may impair the quality of the private lives
of the people living in the neighbourhood and that this noise nuisance may
be regarded either as a failure in the positive obligation of the States to take
adequate measures in order to protect the rights which the appellants draw from
Article 8, par. 1, of the ECHR, or as an interference by an authority which should
be justified according to the criteria enumerated in the second paragraph of that
article. In cases of this nature, account should, however, be taken of a balance
that needs to be achieved between the interests of the individual and those of
society as a whole. The State, in both cases, enjoys a margin of appreciation for
determining which measures have to be taken, in particular when a legitimate
aim is pursued with the operation of an airport and the negative effects thereof
on the environment cannot be entirely avoided. Inspired by this jurisprudence,
the Court held that it might be assumed that, where noise nuisance caused by
aircraft reaches an unbearable level, this nuisance may prejudice the rights,
which the neighbourhood of an airport derives from Article 22 of the Constitution.

The appellants submitted several noise research reports to the Court. A
report from the Brussels Institute of Environmental Management pointed
out that, as regards the noise measured on the outside of the homes, a noise
level between 65 and 70 dB(A) is unbearable and harmful to health and that
it is usually accepted that no person can live in an area exposed to aircraft
noise exceeding 65 dB(A). An impact study carried out by the firm POLY'ART

---

[26] Court of Arbitration, n° 51/2003, 30 April 2003, *Beckers e.a. and a.s.b.l. Net Sky v. Walloon Government*,
www.arbitrage.be.

indicated that the solution consisting of soundproofing the existing homes,
in order that the 45 dB(A) limit in the bedrooms is not exceeded, would oblige
the occupants to live in unbearable conditions. The same firm also stressed
that noise levels in excess of LDN = 66 dB(A) are not suitable for residential
areas. This viewpoint was also confirmed by the A-Tech (Acoustic Technologies) working group, which was set up by the Walloon Region, as well as by the
expert J.-S. Bradley, who was referred to in the parliamentary preparation of the
challenged decrees. The Court said that it could not give an assessment of the
conclusions of the various reports that had been written by the experts. The
Court observed, however, that none of those reports permitted it to conclude that
the people living near Bierset airport will be able to live in their homes without
their right to private life being inordinately affected as they are exposed to noise
levels between 65 and 70 dB(A). The Court added that the nuisance caused
to the residents living in Zone B could be justified by the technical possibility
of soundproofing their homes, whereas for noise levels above 70 dB(A) such
soundproofing would necessitate a structural reinforcement of the buildings. It
emerged from all the reports, however, that those soundproofing works would
make it possible to diminish the nuisance to such a degree that the health of
the neighbours is no longer threatened, on condition however that they keep all
their doors and windows closed. The Court concluded that the residents of zone
B, in terms of the right to respect for their private and family life, did not find
themselves in an essentially different situation from that of the residents of zone
A, which meant that the difference in treatment was not reasonably justified.
The Court annulled the difference in treatment between these two zones; the
decision was based on a violation of Articles 10 and 11, read in conjunction with
Article 22 of the Constitution.

5.4   The *Brussels National Airport Night Flights* case

A similar problem occurred at Brussels National Airport with
night flights, mainly due to the growing activities of the parcel express service
DHL, which has its European hub at that airport and mainly operates at night.
To reduce the number of people who suffered from aeroplane noise at night,
the government decided in 2002 to concentrate before the end of that year,
most of the outgoing flights above one area North of Brussels (the so-called
'Noordrand'), by using the 'stable concentrated runway use' model, instead
of the old system of overflying different areas according to the destination
of the outgoing flights. This decision was coupled with a decision to set up a
programme of financing acoustic insulation of the houses in that area. Some
residents and action committees from that area applied for an injunction on
the basis of Article 544 of the Civil Code (neighbourhood nuisance), Article 8.1
ECHR, Article 1 Additional Protocol ECHR and Article 1382 Civil Code (fault

liability). Their demand was dismissed in the first instance. On appeal, the Brussels Court of Appeal[27] upheld their claims.

The Court held that the absence, or at least the reduction, of excessive noise pollution must be seen as a right to health, as laid down in Article 23 of the Constitution, a right that is also enshrined in Article 8 ECHR and that must be guaranteed without discrimination. There was, on the basis of the material presented to the Court, no doubt that the new organisation of the night flights caused excessive noise pollution for the inhabitants of the area concerned, that the possible consequences and results of the soundproofing project had not been examined in depth beforehand and that there was no reference to WHO standards in terms of results to be achieved with that programme. The Court stated:

'Non discriminatory treatment in this respect implies that, taking into account reasonable policy considerations, the intensity of the nuisance – to be labelled as harmful – must be spread among all who live in areas above which safe flight routes can be followed in such a way that the subjective basic rights are restricted as little as possible.

The degree of concentration of the population in a given area can not be taken as a point of reference; on the other hand, the degree of exposure that is imposed can be'.

The Court ordered provisionally that no outgoing day and night flights should be organised, causing noise pollution in the area concerned, that exceeds the level of noise pollution that may be attained when; all available runways are used in relative equal proportion, all available flight routes are used, spread out as much as possible and that WHO noise standards must not be exceeded at any time. A two-month period, starting on the day of notification of the judgment, was given to the authorities to set up such a new model.

6   Conclusion

Belgian environmental case law increasingly makes reference to environmental principles and to the interpretation given by the European Court of Human Rights to Article 8 of the European Convention on Human Rights.

As far as the polluter pays principle is concerned, this principle was discussed in relation to environmental taxes that are justified by the legislators, with reference to this principle. The constitutional case law shows that the principle can indeed be used to justify such environmental taxes, provided that they

---

[27] Court of Appeal, Brussels, 10 June 2003, *C.T. ea.* v. *Belgian State, n.v. Brussels International Airport Company and Belgocontrol*, T.M.R., 2003, 632-640. There is an appeal against this judgment pending before the Court of Cassation (the Supreme Court).

are levied on the polluters and that they take into account the degree in which each taxpayer contributes to the pollution, against which the tax is directed. The principle, however, seems to have a great deal of discretion, because the legislator is free to choose the actual method of inciting polluters to pollute less (see 2.2.) and for reasons of practicality can justify a tax that does not apply the Principle in an optimal way (see 2.3 and 2.4).

The precautionary principle was applied in cases of uncertainty about health risks that could result from some activities. The first case (3.1) shows that, when there are serious indications that magnetic fields can cause negative health effects, this element cannot be overlooked completely in a licensing procedure. The problem must be discussed at least in the application for a permit, so that it comes to the attention of the licensing authorities and that those authorities can decide whether the risk can be taken or not. The second case (3.2) shows that courts can have entirely opposite views on the consequences of the application of the precautionary principle. Where the first court decided that, when there is no absolute certainty that the operation of an incineration plant will not pose any further risk for the residents of the neighbourhood, the principle commands that the risk can be avoided by not restarting high-risk activities, the second court, on the other hand, held the view that the very strict dioxin emission standard imposed on the facility could be seen as a correct application of the same principle. In the third case (3.3) the court held that the non-application of the best available technologies constituted a violation of the precautionary and prevention at source principles. The latter principle can justify a refusal of a permit for the opening of a dumping site that is believed not to be in keeping with the priority that must be given to prevention of waste (4).

Constitutional provisions can restrict the wide margin of discretion that authorities have, in developing policies that could harm the living conditions of people whose environment is seriously affected. The question that arises is of course, whether these developments in jurisprudence can be evaluated as positive or not. I believe I may conclude from my analysis, that it is a positive development. Let us, for the sake of argument, imagine that those principles or constitutional rights did not exist, would the courts have come to the same conclusions? Although the application of these principles and rights in case law is a very new trend and a lot of questions and uncertainties still remain, I believe that reference to those principles and rights has given a decisive edge to all the cases discussed. Where existing positive law does not offer a cut-and-dried solution to a particular dispute, the court has a discretionary power. The environmental principles urge the court to use this discretionary power in a way that is consistent with the basic options of common environmental policy. This seems to me, to be the essential contribution of those principles to jurisdiction.

CHAPTER 6

Implementation and Application of Environmental Principles in Danish Law

Peter Pagh

The environmental principles as expressed in the Rio Declaration or in EC
Treaty articles 2, 5 and 174 are in general, not directly implemented into Danish
environmental legislation. *'Sustainable development'* is the only principle which
can be found directly mentioned in some of the most important legislative environmental Acts; the Environmental Protection Act, the Nature Protection Act,
the Physical Planing Act, the Act on extractions of raw materials and the Act on
Protection of the Marine Environment.

The *'Principle of Prevention'* cannot be found, directly or indirectly, in any
Danish legislative Act, but is indirectly reflected in the proactive approach of the
environmental legislation. Industrial and certain other activities are subject to
various permitting schemes, operators and manufacturers are often obliged to
ensure that, no harm is caused by an activity or product. In court, the principle
seems to play an insignificant role.

The *'Principle of Integration'* is neither directly, nor indirectly expressed in
Danish legislation and it seems in Danish law to be considered a political principle which, is partly reflected in the legislative approach. It has not been possible
to find any court cases in which the principle has been applied.

The other environmental principles mentioned in Article 174 of the EC
Treaty have been indirectly implemented in some of the legislative Acts. They
are in this respect, to be considered so-called administrative principles, guiding
the administrative decisions under the Act. However, the legal implication of
this indirect codification differs substantially.

The *'Polluter Pays Principle'* is reflected in sections 4(3), 4(4) and 43 of
the Environmental Protection Act and in section 1(5) of the Act on Polluted
Land.[1] Although section 4(4) could be read as establishing a principle of strict
liability for environmental damage, this is not the case. The provision is only
establishing the intention. Legislators have however, reasoned that the polluter
pays principle establishes strict liability for environmental damage caused by
industrial activities listed under the Act on Environmental Damage from 1994.
Moreover, in 1999 legislators adopted the Act on Polluted Land, establishing a
sort of strict liability for cleaning up contaminated land, but this was restricted
to business and public activities and not applicable for past pollution (no retro-

---

[1] Section 4(3): 'Any party commencing or carrying out activities likely to cause pollution shall take
measures to prevent and combat pollution and design and operate the activities so as to cause the least
degree of pollution, cf. section 3 above. In the design and operation of the plant, including choice of
production processes, raw materials and auxiliary substances, measures shall be taken to minimize the
use of resources, pollution and generation of waste.'

Section 4(4): 'Any person giving rise to or causing risks of pollution of air, water, soil or subsoil, shall
take the measures required to effectively prevent or combat the impact of pollution. In addition, he shall
seek to restore the original state of the environment.'

Section 43: 'Anyone producing, storing, treating or disposing of waste is responsible that such activities
do not cause unhygienic conditions or pollution of air, water or soil.'

spective effect). In court cases, the polluter pays principle has been used as a defence by landowners, who deny being liable for environmental damage caused by previous landowners or others. In the Rockwool case, concerning pollution caused by redundant tanks for mineral oil, this position was upheld by the Danish Supreme Court.[2] Thus, in Danish jurisprudence 'the polluter' does not include the landowner. In criminal cases, the polluter pays principle has been used as a successful defence, precluding the current operator from liability for environmental damage caused by previous operators. In sum, the implications of the polluter pays principle in Danish law are threefold: (1) the polluter must pay for the required preventive measures to reduce pollution and nuisances; (2) the polluter pays principle restricts the physical and legal persons who may be held liable for civil and criminal environmental offences; and (3) the polluter pays principle suggests, but does not establish, strict liability for environmental damage.

The *'Precautionary Principle'* is indirectly reflected in section 3(2)(1) of the Environmental Protection Act; 'When determining the extent and nature of measures to prevent pollution consideration shall be given to: (1) the nature of the physical surroundings and the likely impact of pollution thereon.'

According to the preparatory work for this subsection, the intention is that the precautionary principle should only govern general regulation under the Environmental Protection Act. Moreover, the precautionary principle cannot even be found indirectly in any other Danish legislative Act. These legislative limitations are reflected in practice. Not one Danish court case has been published, in which one of the parties has based their argument on the precautionary principle. Only in very few cases on administrative appeal, has the precautionary principle been relied upon by private parties challenging the public authority for insufficient environmental protection. In one case concerning the clean up of contaminated land, the precautionary principle in combination with the polluter pays principle was used as a reason by the Environmental Appeal Board to require the clean-up of a sensitive area of land, irrespective of recent use.[3] In another case regarding the reintroduction of beaver (a non-native species in Denmark for more than 1000 years) and the potential conflict with other nature protection interests, the Nature Appeal Board restricted the reintroduction, based on the precautionary principle (unknown effect), although the Nature Protection Act does not provide any legal basis for applying the precautionary principle.[4] The restricted reintroduction of beaver was later overruled by the High Western Court, for it was held to be in conflict with EC Directive

---

[2] Supreme Court ruling of 18th June 1991. Published in the Danish Weekly Law Journal, *UfR* 1991. p. 674.

[3] Published in the magazine on administrative decision on real estate: *KFE* 1993. p. 293.

[4] Nature Appeal Board ruling of 22nd September 1999. Published in the quarterly magazine on environmental court rulings and administrative decisions: *MAD* 1999. p. 851.

92/43 on the conservation of natural habitats and of wild fauna and flora.[5] Thus, in Danish Law the precautionary principle is (with few exceptions) considered a political principle, not a legal principle.

The *'Principle of Rectifying Environmental Impairment at Source'* is indirectly reflected in the Environmental protection Act section 4(3) – see above under the polluter pays principle. Moreover, the principle is reflected in the Danish waste legislation which is based on a principle of self-sufficiency. However, in contrast to ECJ rulings, the principle of self-sufficiency is also applied to waste for recovery – but this application is highly disputed in several ongoing court cases.

As in other Member States, Danish environmental law includes other environmental principles, than those principles listed in the Treaty. It is not possible within this chapter to give an exhaustive explanation, but some of the most important principles are discussed below.

The *'BAT Principle'* has been reformulated as a principle of cleaner technology in section 3(1) of the Environmental Protection Act: 'In the administration of this Act weight shall be given to the results achievable by using the least polluting technology, including least polluting raw materials, processes and plants and the best practicable pollution control measures. In this evaluation special consideration shall be given to preventive measures in the form of cleaner technology.' The principle of cleaner technology has until now not in itself been grounds to bring a case to court, nor has it been interpreted by any court. It has, however, been applied in many administrative appeals regarding technical preventive measures the operator must take.

The *'Cradle to Grave Principle'* or the principle of sustainable use of natural resources (minimizing waste generation) is reflected in section 3(19(2) of the Environmental Protection Act; 'When determining the extent and nature of measures to prevent pollution consideration shall be given to [..] (2) the whole cycle of substances and materials, with a view to minimizing wastage of resources.' The legal implications of this, however, remain rather uncertain.

The *'Principle of Substitution'* provides that a potentially dangerous product can be restricted or prohibited, if it can be replaced by a less dangerous product with proportional costs for producers and consumers. It has been adopted as section 30c of the Act on Chemicals and Chemical Products.[6] It follows from the

---

[5]   Western High Court ruling of 13th November 2003. Published in the Danish Weekly Law Journal, *UfR* 2004, p. 622.

[6]   Section 31 c: '[1] For reasons of environmental protection in general, the Minister for Environment and Energy can, even if the provisions of section 30 are not fulfilled, decide or lay down rules on restrictions or ban on sale or use of the substances, products or goods specified in section 30 above. [2] Restrictions on sale or use under subsection (1) above can be laid down if the substances, products or goods involved can be replaced by other substances, products, goods or methods with the same field of application, which result in significantly less pollution in connection with production, use or disposal of the substances, products or goods involved or which otherwise significantly increase the possible

text of section 30c that the principle widens the discretion of the Government to restrict the use of dangerous chemicals. As a result of exhaustive EC legislation on chemicals, this discretion can only be used for a few chemicals. In practice, the principle of substitution has only been applied by the authorities in a very few cases and none of these cases have gone to court.

---

applications of cleaner technology. [3] Restrictions on sale or use under subsection (1) above can only be laid down if replacement of substances, products or goods referred to in subsection (2) above can take place without significant overall additional costs to the enterprises and the consumers.'

CHAPTER 7

Principles into Practice – The German Case

Bernhard W. Wegener[*]

Introduction

Although there is no disagreement about the general legal value of environmental principles in German law, there is nevertheless some speculation about their exact legal nature, more precisely the legal nature of principles in general. A good number of authors[1] follow the distinction made by the leading German authority on the application of principles, Robert Alexy. He distinguishes between directly applicable rules on one hand and principles on the other. In this view the latter are to be regarded not as strict rules but as *'Optimierungsgebote'* (an obligation to optimise, to reach a goal as far as possible).[2] Their scope of application, their significance and their legally binding quality have to be determined with a view to realities and to conflicting principles.[3]

Of these *'Optimierungsgeboten'* there is quite a number that play a role – sometimes a concurring and a limiting one – in German environmental law. So far no unanimously accepted classification of the principles has emerged.

---

[*]   I am grateful for the help and advice offered by Prof. Dr. Gerhard Roller, on whose earlier and excellent examination of the role of environmental law principles in the jurisprudence of German courts this text is mainly based, see G. Roller, Environmental Law Principles in the Jurisprudence of German Administrative Courts, in: M. Sheridan/L. Lavrysen (eds.), *Environmental Law Principles in Practice*, Brussels 2002, p. 157 *et seq*. All omissions and faults are of course my responsibility.

[1]   See – in the context of environmental law – for example R. Sparwasser/R. Engel/A. Voßkuhle, *Umweltrecht*, 5th ed. 2003, p. 67 *et seq.*; E. Rehbinder, Nachhaltigkeit als Prinzip des Umweltrechts, in: *Gesellschaft für Umweltrecht* (Society for Environmental Law), Umweltrecht im Wandel, Berlin, 2001, p. 721 (722 *et seq.*), Rehbinder offers a comprehensive overview about the differing qualities principles of (environmental) law can have.

[2]   Note that this understanding differs substantially from the ideas that Ronald Dworkin developed on principles. In his view principles should be understood to only contain individual rights. They should be distinguished from collective goals. Such goals are pursued, he says, not by principles but rather by policies. 'Arguments of principle are arguments intended to establish an individual right; arguments of policy are arguments intended to establish a collective goal. Principles are propositions that describe rights; policies are propositions that describe goals', see R. Dworkin, *Taking Rights Seriously*, Harvard UP, Cambridge Mass, 1977, p. 90. For Dworkin the difference between principles and rules is a matter of generality and hierarchy: principles are more general than rules and they have the power to direct their application. See for the differences and the importance of the debate for our topic: G. Winter, *Principles of Environmental Protection*, Paper presented to the avosetta-group, October 11, 2002, www.avosetta.org.

[3]   For the distinction between rules and principles see R. Alexy, *Theorie der Grundrechte*, Baden-Baden, 1985, p. 75 *et seq.*; R. Alexy, *Recht, Vernunft, Diskurs*, Frankfurt a.M, 1995, p. 177 (182 *et seq.*); see also M. Borowski, *Grundrechte als Prinzipien*, Baden-Baden, 1998, S. 76 f.

The number of principles that different authors consider as 'main' environmental law principles tends to vary.[4] Nevertheless, there is belief, that three of them – the so called *'Prinzipientrias'* of the precautionary principle, the polluter-pays or causation/perpetrator principle, and the cooperation principle, should be treated as paramount guidelines.[5] It should be noted, that the integration principle, which is of such great importance in EU environmental law, the principle of sustainable development, which plays a leading role in the policy of international environmental law, and the principle or rectification of damage at source, which is contained in Article 174 EC, are not among those main principles. The principle of integration is hardly ever discussed in German environmental law. Nevertheless, its central meaning, the integration of environmental considerations and policies into the design and development of other policy areas, can be interpreted to be part of the obligation embedded in Article 20a of the German constitution, the *'Grundgesetz'* (to protect and preserve the environment).[6] The principle of sustainable development on the other hand has received some interest,[7] but is considered still too 'political' and vague to be listed among the most important of the principles of environmental law. The principle of rectification of damage at source has only been considered in connection with the well-known judgments of the European Court of Justice on the treatment and shipment of waste.[8] The three leading principles, however, are explicitly defined in the proposal for a unified environmental code (*'Umweltgesetzbuch'*)[9] and were

---

[4] While M. Kloepfer mentions a triad of principles in his textbook on environmental law, (*Umweltrecht*, 2nd ed. Munich, 1998, p. 163); R. Sparwasser/R. Engel/A. Voßkuhle identify no less than five main 'material' and four main 'procedural' principles of environmental law, see Sparwasser et al., *Umweltrecht*, 5th ed. 2003, p. 67 *et seq.*

[5] See *e.g.* Rehbinder, (*op. cit.* 2), p. 721.

[6] See H. Schulze-Fielitz, in: H. Dreier, *Kommentar zum Grundgesetz*, Vol. II, Tübingen, 1998, Article 20a, para 22. The constitutional mandate to protect the environment reads as follows: 'The State, bearing responsibility for future generations as well, protects the natural bases of life within the existing constitutional order through legislation and, pursuant to statute law and justice, through its executive power and the judiciary.'; translation taken by Roller, (*op. cit.* 1). Apart from the idea of integration also the precautionary principle and the prevention principle are regarded as coming within the purview of this provision, see D. Murswiek, Article 20a, in: Sachs (ed.), *Grundgesetz*, 3rd ed. Munich, 2002; R. Scholz, Article 20a, in: Maunz/Dürig, *Grundgesetzkommentar* (loose-leaf), Munich, June 2002, para 11.

[7] See E. Rehbinder, (*op. cit.* 2), p. 721 *et seq.*

[8] See e. g. BVerwG, Neue Zeitschrift für Verwaltungsrecht (*NVwZ*), 1999, p. 1228 (1230).

[9] For the proposal to codify the precautionary, polluter-pays, and the cooperation principle see M. Kloepfer/E. Rehbinder/E. Schmidt-Assmann/Kunig, *Umweltgesetzbuch, Allgemeiner Teil*, Berichte [reports] 7/90 of the Umweltbundesamt (Federal Environmental Agency) Berlin 1990 at 40 and 138. See the latest version: Bundesumweltministerium, Umweltgesetzbuch (UGB-KomE), Berlin 1998. An English translation is also available: Ministry for the Environment, Nature Conservation and Nuclear Safety, Environmental Code (draft), Berlin 1998:

expressly recognized as such in Article 16(1)(2) of the *'Staatsvertrag'* and in Article 34(1) of the *'Einigungsvertrag'* (Reunification Treaty)[10] of 1990.[11] It is mainly because of the explicit mention of these main principles in German law, that German courts rarely feel the need to refer to them as principles of European law.

I The precautionary principle

The *'Vorsorgeprinzip'* (precautionary principle)[12] is surely the most prominent and probably the most important of the three main environmental law principles in German law. It has rightly been called the *'Leitprinzip des Umweltstaates'* ('leading principle of the environmental state').[13] The German *'Vorsorgeprinzip'* is said to be the source of origin for the precautionary principle in international environmental law[14] and has thereby also influenced its formulation in Article 174 EC. It has been introduced at the international level by the

---

'Article 5 – Precautionary Principle (*Vorsorgeprinzip*)

(1) Risks for the environment or for people shall, especially through anticipating planning and suitable technical measures, be excluded as far as possible or shall be diminished (...)

Article 6 – Perpetrator Principle (*Verursacherprinzip*)

(1) He who causes considerable adverse effects, dangers or risks for the environment or for the people, will be responsible (...)

Article 7 – Cooperation Principle (*Kooperationsprinzip*)

The protection of the environment is a task for citizens and the state. Competent authorities and citizens concerned will co-operate when fulfilling the tasks and duties that stem from environmental legal rules. For that purpose there will be rules on participation of the general public and on access to environmental information.'

[10] Vertrag zwischen der Bundesrepublik Deutschland und der Deutschen Demokratischen Republik über die Herstellung der Einheit Deutschlands – Einigungsvertrag – Vom 31. August 1990 (BGBl. II p. 889 [Federal Statutes of Germany, part II], modified with the agreement of 18.9.1990, BGBl. II p. 1239).

[11] It was the latter provision that subsequently gave rise, in 1994, to the constitutional amendment that mandates the State, in Article 20a of the Grundgesetz to protect the environment.

[12] See R. Schmidt, Der Staat der Umweltvorsorge, *DÖV* 1994, p. 749 (752 *et seq.*); W. Köck, Risikovorsorge als Staatsaufgabe, *AöR* 121 (1996), p. 1 *et seq.*; U. di Fabio, Voraussetzungen und Grenzen des umweltrechtlichen Vorsorgeprinzips, *Festschrift Ritter*, 1997, p. 807 *et seq.*

[13] C. Calliess, *Rechtsstaat und Umweltstaat*, Tübingen, 2001, p. 153 *et seq.*

[14] See *e.g.* W. T. Douma, The Precautionary Principle, *Úlfljótur* (Icelandic Legal Journal) 1996, p. 417 *et seq.*; (also under www.eel.nl/virtue/precprin.htm); more cautious for the origins of the precautionary principle in EU-environmental law L. Krämer, *EC Environmental Law*, London,5 2003, p. 21: 'origin and content of the precautionary principle are unclear'.

German government at the so-called North-Sea conferences held in Bremen (1984), London (1987), The Hague (1990) and Esbjerg (1995).[15] The *'Vorsorge-prinzip'* gains some of its importance from its 'catch all' qualities: questions which could be discussed under the heading of other principles (such as the question of the non-liquet situation with respect to the possible dangers of new technologies,[16] which also could be discussed as a problem of the perpetrator-principle) are regularly considered to be questions of a precautionary approach.

A. Precaution in the field of air quality protection and emission control

To understand the special importance of the precautionary principle in German environmental law, one must take into account some more general aspects of the legislation on air quality protection. Air quality control and protection in Germany follows a double approach: Secondary legislation,[17] especially the *'TA-Luft'* (short for: *Technische Anleitung Luft* – Technical Instruction Air), an administrative guideline that gives an authoritative interpretation of general clauses and terms of environmental law, provides both emission control standards and ambient air quality standards. All industrial plant requiring prior authorisation under the provisions of the *'4. BimSchVO'* (short for: *Vierte Verordnung zur Umsetzung des Bundesimmissionsschutzgesetzes* – Fourth Regulation to Implement the Federal Emission Control Act) have to conform to the emission control standards. Moreover, where the authorisation of a new installation would lead to ambient air quality threshold values being exceeded, no further authorisations can be issued even when the individual installation itself is not exceeding the emission control standards. In practice, because of the rather limited restrictions the quality standards offer, the emission control standards play the more relevant role in the process of licensing of new installations.

---

[15] See Mitteilung der Kommission über die Anwendbarkeit des Vorsorgeprinzips of 2.2.2000, KOM 2000 (1), reprinted in Neue Zeitschrift für Verwaltungsrecht (*NVwZ*), supplement IV/2001 to vol. 4/2001, p. IV/13; for a critical analysis of this communication see H.-W. Rengeling, Bedeutung und Anwendbarkeit des Vorsorgeprinzips im europäischen Umweltrecht, Deutsches Verwaltungsblatt (*DVBl.*), 2000, p. 1473 *et seq.*

[16] See Calliess, (*op. cit.* 14), p. 226 *et seq.*

[17] For examples as the 'Großfeuerungsanlagenverordnung' see E. Kutscheidt, Anmerkungen zum Vorsorgegrundsatz, in: Gesellschaft für Umweltrecht (Society for Environmental Law), *Umweltrecht im Wandel*, Berlin, 2001, p. 437 (441 *et seq.*).

1   Precaution under the *'Bundesimmissionsschutzgesetz'*

Originally developed and used as a political guideline,[18] Parliament laid down the precautionary principle, already in 1976 in § 5(1) of the *BImSchG* (short for: *Bundes-Immissionsschutzgesetz* – Federal Emissions Control Act,[19] the federal air protection legislation). § 5(1) of the BImSchG lays down the mandatory conditions a plant operator has to comply with, in order to be granted an operating licence.[20] It differentiates between *'Gefahrenabwehr'* (prevention) in § 5(1)(1) and *'Vorsorge'* (precaution) in § 5(1)(2).[21] Section (1) provides, *inter alia*, that an installation which is subject to licensing shall be built and operated in such a way that

1) 'no detrimental environmental effects or other hazards' (*'Gefahren'* in the above mentioned sense of *'Gefahrenabwehr'* = prevention), 'noticeable adverse effects and nuisance to the public and the neighbourhood are caused', and that

2) 'precaution is taken to prevent detrimental environmental effects [...], in particular through measures corresponding to state of the art technology'[22].

2   The precautionary principle and the question of standing

Interpreting the differentiation provided for in § 5(1) BImSchG, the administrative courts have construed the ambient air quality standards (*'Immissionswerte'*) as interpreting § 5(1)(1) of the act, hence the prevention principle, while the more important emission control standards (*'Emissionswerte'*), on the other hand, have been interpreted as rules emanating from § 5(1)(2)

---

[18]   See the Environmental Program of the Federal Government (Umweltprogramm der Bundesregierung) of 1971, BT-Drs. 6/2710, (= Papers of the Sixth Bundestag no. 2710) para 9 *et seq.*; Environmental Report (Umweltbericht) 1976, BT-Drs. 7/5684, p. 8 *et seq.*, para 4 *et seq.*; see also M. Kloepfer, *Umweltrecht*, 2nd ed. Munich, 1998, p. 163.

[19]   Official titel: Gesetz zum Schutz vor schädlichen Umwelteinwirkungen durch Luftverunreinigungen, Geräusche, Erschütterungen und ähnliche Vorgänge, see the consolidated version of september 26, 2002 (BGBl. I p. 3830).

[20]   See on this: J. Jahns-Böhm, From Combating Air Pollution to an Integrated Pollution Prevention, in: B. Gebers/Robesin, *Licensing Procedures for Industrial Plants and the Influence of EC-Directives*, ELNI-Studies no. 3, Frankfurt a.M. 1993, p. 81 *et seq.*

[21]   The differentiation became less clear with the latest adjustments to EC environmental law, namely to the IPPC-Directive. § 5(1)(2) refers now not any more exclusively to emission control measures and also mentions dangers as an object of precaution. The described differentiation made by the administrative courts has nevertheless not been altered by the changes, see Kutscheidt, (*op. cit.* 18), p. 438.

[22]   Translation taken by Roller, (*op. cit.* 1), p. 162 and adjusted to the changes in law mentioned above in note 22.

of the act. This difference in interpretation, attributing ambient air quality to prevention while viewing emission control as an element of precaution, has had far-reaching consequences for the question of standing, (*locus standi*) for neighbours of industrial installations. Since the late 1970s the courts ruled, that only those plaintiffs had standing when alleging a violation of the (less relevant) ambient air quality standards and thereby of the prevention principle. When alleging a violation of the (more important) emission control standards and thereby the precautionary principle, the plaintiffs were informed they had insufficient standing.

The reason for this is to be found in § 42(2) of the *'VwGO'* (short for: *Verwaltungsgerichtsordnung*, Administrative Courts Procedure Act), which reads as follows:

'Unless otherwise determined by law the suit is admissible only if the plaintiff claims to be violated in his rights by the administrative act or its denial or omission'.[23]

Disregarding ever-growing criticism in the literature,[24] the courts and especially the Federal Administrative Court,[25] interpreted this section of the Procedure Act quite restrictively. To be 'violated in his rights', the plaintiff has to show that his rights are impinged in a legally relevant way. He therefore has to claim an infringement of legal provisions, issued to protect him individually and not only general or common interests. The main function of this restrictive interpretation is to rule out any public interest litigation or class action.[26] The implementation of rules, emanated in the public interest, is left to the public administration alone. Their enforcement is said not to be the business of individual plaintiffs or the administrative courts. In the view of the Federal Administrative Court, the

---

[23] Translation taken by Th. Ormond, Environmental Group Actions in West Germany, in: M. Führ/G. Roller, *Participation and Litigation Rights of Environmental Associations in Europe*, ELNI Studies no. 1 Frankfurt a.M. 1991, p. 81.

[24] See for example Roller, (*op. cit.* 1), p. 165; R. Wahl/Schütz, in: F. Schoch/E. Schmidt-Aßmann/Pietzner, *VwGO*, Munich, § 42 II para 151 *et seq.*; Sparwasser/Engel/Voßkuhle, (*op. cit.* 2), p. 237 *et seq.*

[25] See BVerwGE 61, 256 (267) [*i.e.* Federal Administrative Court Reports, vol. 61 at p. 256/267]; 65, 313 (320); note that (mainly because of the potentially high dangers of nuclear energy production) in nuclear energy law, the sophisticated and somewhat arbitrary dichotomy of preventive and precautionary standards does not exist, see BVerwGE 72, 300 (319) – *Wyhl*. For the nevertheless existing limits of locus standi in nuclear energy law see OVG Schleswig-Holstein, 3.11.1999, Recht der Energiewirtschaft (RdE), 2000, p. 146 *et seq.* For a discussion about the existence or non-existence of the differentiation in genetic engineering law and of the limits of the relevant jurisdiction concerning the material aspects of administrative risk-assessment and risk-evaluation see Roller, (*op. cit.* 1); for (limited) specialities of the concept of precaution under the law of environmental assessment see Schmidt, (*op. cit.* 13), p. 754 *et seq.*

[26] See B. W. Wegener, *Rechte des Einzelnen – Die Interessentenklage im europäischen Umweltrecht*, Baden-Baden, 1998, p. 100 *et seq.*

provisions providing the more important emission control standards are set to
implement the precautionary approach of § 5(1)(2) BimSchG. They are therefore, contrary to the ambient air quality standards established under § 5(1)(1)
BimSchG, established not in an individual, but in a common interest alone and
cannot be invoked by individuals who are, as neighbours for example, interested
in their effective enforcement.[27] The only emission control standards that are
positively actionable before the administrative courts, are those that concern
carcinogenic or highly toxic substances. In those cases, the standards are
deemed to be emanations of the concept of prevention because of the high level
of risk inherent in the use and emission of these substances.[28]

3   Precaution and the justification of environmental protection

The administrative courts' interpretation of the precautionary
principle on the one hand, has limited the rights of concerned third parties to
invoke emission standards before the courts, it has on the other hand widened
the possibilities of the law-maker and the administration to justify their general
environmental policies and decisions. The main effect of the concept of precaution is to give the authorities some margin of appreciation to decide whether
a certain environmental protection measure is truly needed (and thus a legitimate restriction of the freedom of the potential polluter) or not. This margin
of appreciation is not limited to combating risks arising from gaps in scientific
knowledge and the resultant impossibility of proving empirically certain causal
links that scientific hypotheses suggest, may nevertheless exist. According to
the jurisdiction of the Federal Administrative Court, precaution can go further
than this: 'Precaution, understood as proactive environmental protection, aims
beyond concrete detrimental threshold levels and, hence, justifies prevention
efforts vis-à-vis detrimental air pollutants that are taken with a view to achiev-
ing, or preserving, on a longer-term basis air quality standards which are
sufficiently removed from any situation suggesting the concrete presence of
adverse environmental effects or justifying an apprehension as to their develop-

---

[27] See on this: Ormond (*op. cit.* 24) p. 81 *et seq.*

[28] VGH (Verwaltungsgerichtshof) Mannheim, Neue Zeitschrift für Verwaltungsrecht – Rechtsprechung-
sreport (NVwZ-RR) 1995, p. 639 (644); Neue Zeitschrift für Verwaltungsrecht (*NVwZ*) 1996, p. 300.
For an extension of this approach to other standards (*e.g.* to those of the 17. BImSchVO, Siebzehnte
Verordnung zur Umsetzung des Bundesimmissionsschutzgesetzes, 17th regulation to implement the
Federal Emissions Control Act, dealing especially with standards concerning the incineration of waste)
see G. Lübbe-Wolff, Sind die Grenzwerte der 17. BImSchV für krebserzeugende Stoffe drittschützend?,
Natur und Recht (*NuR*) 2000, p. 19.

[29] BVerwG, Umwelt- und Planungsrecht (*UPR*) 1995, p. 196 *et seq.*; translation taken by Roller, (*op. cit.* 1).

ment.'[29] Some fear that this understanding of the precautionary principle has the potential to give *carte blanche* to the authorities and call for the development of limitations of the precautionary approach.[30] The general position is, that precaution must not be taken *'ins Blaue hinein,'* that is to say not without a hint, or a defined suggestion, that a specific environmental problem might arise in connection with the activity in question.[31] So far, the courts have been reluctant to stop environmental policies, as long as they have taken the form of an overall *programme* that aims at reducing emissions across the board. These kinds of general programmes have been said to be in conformity with the so-called requirement of 'global' or overall proportionality.[32] They can be legitimised, not only with reference to possible detrimental effects of the emissions in question, but also with a concept which is designed to leave room for further industrial developments in the future (*'Freiraumkonzept'*).[33] Against such general emission control schemes individual plant operators cannot dispute the economic difficulties, which arise from their implementation. The chances of operators successfully challenging authoritative restrictions are higher, however, where those restrictions are not of a general nature, but are individually defined for the installation in question. The proportionality of such individual restrictions has to be individually assessed.[34]

B.   Precaution as a constitutional obligation

Although, as we have seen, the concept of precaution is thoroughly embedded in the federal ambient air quality protection legislation and in other related areas of the law, it should not be forgotten that there is also a (limited) constitutional dimension to precaution. According to the jurisdiction of the Federal Constitutional Court, Article 2 of the *'Grundgesetz'* (which guarantees the right to life and physical integrity), obliges the legislator to provide sufficient

---

[30]   See *e.g.* di Fabio, (*op. cit.* 13).

[31]   See Kutscheidt, (*op. cit.* 18), p. 439; H. D. Jarass, *Bundesimmissionsschutzgesetz*, 4th ed., Munich, § 5 para 46 *et seq.* For a slightly differing view on the precautionary principle of EC environmental law see Krämer (*op. cit.* 15), p. 22: according to Krämer the argument that the adoption of the precautionary principle requires a scientific assessment of risks stems from political efforts to limit the field of application of the principle and finds no basis in the text of Article 174 EC.

[32]   BVerwGE 69, 37 *et seq.* – *Heidelberger Heizkraftwerk*. See also: S. Rose-Ackerman, *Controlling Environmental Policy*, 1995, p. 77.

[33]   See Kutscheidt, (*op. cit.* 18), p. 440.

[34]   BVerwG, Zeitschrift für Umweltrecht (*ZUR*) 1997, p. 158 *et seq.*; the case concerned an industrial operator who, without success, challenged a new and stricter individual standard setting for threshold values for dioxin and furan by the authorities for his older installation. For the emissions in question, at the time no regulation existed that set a general emission standard.

protection against the possible detrimental effects of the private use of eventually dangerous technologies.[35]

From this reading of Article 2 of the *'Grundgesetz'* it follows that the state is constitutionally obliged to provide for a mechanism of prior authorisation for high risk installations. Where protection against foreseeable dangers is technically impossible, the operation of the respective installations must not be allowed. This feature of the jurisdiction, regarding the precautionary principle, has recently given rise to the question of the acceptability of the operation of nuclear power plants under the threat of terror attacks such as those of 9-11.

However, with respect to the principle of the separation of powers and the competences of Parliament, the courts have been reluctant to substantially limit the legislator's margin of appreciation while dealing with the risks of potentially dangerous technologies.[36] In its interpretation by the Federal Constitutional Court the *'Grundgesetz'* does not call for a no-risk policy.[37] On the contrary, certain "socially adequate" risks and risks which are said to lie *'jenseits der Grenzen praktischer Vernunft'* (beyond the limits of practical reasoning) may be defined as risks, that have to be borne collectively by the entire citizenry.[38] In addition, the constitutional duty to provide for a measure of statutory precaution against risks does not entail a requirement to prescribe minimum threshold values for the emission of potentially dangerous substances, that is to say to set standards that ensure that the best available techniques are applied actually and in all possible situations.[39] Finally, limits to precaution, as a constitutional obligation also exists, where a dangerous conduct of the past leads to actual risks. In a case concerning sites contaminated during the production of nuclear energy for the former GDR, the Federal Constitutional Court decided, that the precautionary standards for radiation set in the respective regulation do not have to be applied.[40]

---

[35] BVerfGE 39, 88, 203 [Federal Constitutional Court Reports, vol. 39 at p. 88, 203]; 49, 89 – *Kalkar I*; 53, 30 – *Mülheim-Kärlich*; 77, 170 – *Fischbach*; Hess.VGH, Deutsches Verwaltungsblatt (*DVBl.*) 1990, p. 63 *et seq.*; Neue Juristische Wochenschrift (*NJW*) 1990, p. 336 *et seq.*

[36] BVerfG, Natur und Recht (*NuR*) 1997, 394 (395); BVerfGE 56, 54 (81); 77, 381 (405); 79, 174 (202); 85, 191 (212 *et seq.*); 92, 26 (46).

[37] BVerfGE 49, 89 – *Kalkar I*; see also BVerfGE 53, 30 – *Mülheim-Kärlich*; OVG Lüneburg, 5.2.1981, Deutsches Verwaltungsblatt (*DVBl.*) 1982, p. 32 (33) – *Grohnde*.

[38] BVerfGE 49, 89 – *Kalkar I*.

[39] BVerwG, Zeitschrift für Umweltrecht (*ZUR*) 1999, p. 112; in the case concerned the plaintiffs called – without success – for the individual definition of a cadmium-emission standard in the permit authorising a waste incineration plant, which they claimed could (with a view to the future enhancement of technical possibilities) be set much lower than the general standard set in the 17th regulation to implement the Federal Emission Control Act. As the Federal Administrative Court makes clear, however, Parliament retains unfettered discretion to prescribe minimization standards.

[40] BVerfG, Neue Zeitschrift für Verwaltungsrecht (*NVwZ*) 2000, p. 309 (312), refering to the report of the Sachverständigenrat für Umweltfragen (Federal Council of Experts in Environmental Matters) 1990, BT-Drs. 11/6191, p. 118.

II The polluter pays principle

The polluter pays principle[41] has its roots in the general concept of causation in law. In German public law it is of special importance for the law governing policing, where it is embedded in the method of just allocation of responsibilities for (potentially) dangerous conduct, or for a (potentially) dangerous object such as a contaminated site. It is of importance also for the law relating to public charges and contributions, for example the definition of prices charged for public services, such as the collection and the treatment of waste.[42] For the principle in this wider sense, the number of court decisions, which reflect its application, is too high to give even an overview of the general character of the case law. One should note, however, the following aspects of the use of the polluter pays principle in German administrative law.

Firstly the polluter pays principle in German environmental law, differs from the understanding of the polluter pays principle in EU environmental law,[43] it is nowadays generally understood to be more than an instrument for the allocation of costs. The so-called 'Verursacherprinzip' ('principle of causation' or 'perpetrator-principle'), is also of importance for any form of conduct-obligations.[44]

Secondly, this time a very similar interpretation to that of the polluter pays principle in EU law, the 'Verursacherprinzip' is understood to be a guideline mainly for the legislature. As a guideline it is of an especially limited and vague nature. The lawmaker is generally free to allocate costs and other responsibilities to the perpetrator or to the public. The latter approach is sometimes given the name 'Gemeinlastprinzip.' The term is misleading as the allocation of costs to the general public is surely not a principle in the sense of Alexy's aforementioned definition (no 'Optimierungsgebot').

Thirdly the 'Verursacherprinzip' should be understood as a principle that calls only for the allocation of costs to the perpetrator. Non-perpetrators who face an unjust obligation regarding environmental costs, for which they are not liable, should seek relief not by invoking the 'Verursacherprinzip', but by invoking principles like that of proportionality.[45]

---

[41] For an early study on the principle see E. Rehbinder, *Politische und rechtliche Probleme des Verursacherprinzips*, Berlin, 1973. For a more recent publication on the principle see W. Frenz, *Das Verursacherprinzip im öffentlichen Recht*, Berlin, 1997.

[42] For attempts by and obligations of the local authorities to define the 'right prices' for the environmental services they provide see G. Lübbe-Wolff/B. W. Wegener (ed.), *Umweltschutz durch kommunales Satzungsrecht*, 2nd ed., 2003.

[43] The English version (like the others) of Article 174 EC Treaty only states 'the polluter should pay'. It is only the German text, that talks of the principle of 'causation', see Krämer, (*op. cit.* 15), p. 25; see also L. Krämer, *The Genesis of EC Environmental Principles*, College of Europe, Research Papers in Law, 7/2003, p. 14, www.coleurop.be.

[44] W. Frenz (*op. cit.* 42), 39.

[45] See for this argument Roller, (*op. cit.* 1), who rightly interprets this to be the proper understanding of the ECJ Judgment in the *Standley* case C-293/97, 29 April 1999.

III   The cooperation principle

The third of the main principles of German environmental law is the cooperation principle. It is noteworthy that this principle is not, at least not explicitly, mentioned in the EC Treaty and thus rarely discussed as a principle of EC environmental law.[46] Even in German environmental law it has traditionally played only a limited and more political role. This changed to a somewhat limited and doubtful extent in 1998, when the cooperation principle became the subject of two highly controversial decisions of the constitutional court. Both decisions deal with economic instruments for environmental regulation. One case concerns a local tax on non-recyclable packaging, the other a *'Länder'* (provincial state) tax on dangerous industrial wastes. The Federal Constitutional Court declared both the municipal ordinance and the provincial state statute levying these taxes as unconstitutional and hence null and void.

·   According to the Court's reasoning in both cases,[47] the federal German waste legislation is based on the cooperation principle. Following this principle, in the Court's view, the legislature had practised restraint in order to promote voluntary schemes and a system of 'open choices' for preventing the generation of and for dealing with waste. The Court believed a local tax on non-recyclable packaging as well as a provincial state tax on dangerous waste contradicted this 'cooperative' concept. The Federal Constitutional Court's principal argument was that the taxes were intended to promote and reward a certain kind of behaviour, namely restraint on the part of the consumer with respect to buying goods using non-recyclable packaging or on the part of industrial entrepreneurs with respect to the production of dangerous waste. This, according to the Court, conflicts with the cooperative approach of the federal law which, in the Courts view, only stipulates objectives but leaves the means to attain them to the 'cooperating' partners.

The much-criticised point of the judgments is not so much the outcome, but the reasoning employed by the Court. It is said to give the rather vague concept of cooperation, which is not expressly mentioned in the federal statutes at issue, a much greater importance than was intended by the legislator. It is also said to ignore the fact, that the federal as well as the local or state law in question, have the same objective – waste prevention – and that they complement rather than impinge on one another.[48] According to *Gerhard Roller,* the decisions serve as

---

[46] See *e.g.* Krämer, *EC Environmental Law,* (*op. cit.* 15).

[47] BVerfG (Bundesverfassungsgericht Federal Constitutional Court), judgment of 7 May 1998, repr. in Umwelt- und Planungsrecht (*UPR*) 1998, p. 261. BVerfG, Umwelt- und Planungsrecht (*UPR*) 1998, p. 265. For a critical analysis of the latter decision see M. Führ, Widerspruchsfreies Recht im uniformen Bundesstaat?, Kritische Justiz (*KJ*) 4/1998, p. 503.

[48] For a supportive discussion of the courts ruling see: U. di Fabio, Das Kooperationsprinzip ein allgemeiner Rechtsgrundsatz des Umweltrechts, Neue Zeitschrift für Verwaltungsrecht (*NVwZ*) 1999,

a reminder of the 'interpretative pitfalls' of 'deliberating on abstract principles that have been artificially severed from the specific legislative context in which they were first adopted.'[49]

p. 1153 (1156 *et seq.*); for the predominant critical view, see: H.-J. Koch, Das Kooperationsprinzip im Umweltrecht, Natur und Recht (*NuR*) 2001, p. 541 *et seq.*; H. D. Jarass, Bemerkenswertes aus Karlsruhe: Kooperation im Immissionsschutzrecht und vergleichende Analyse von Umweltschutzinstrumenten, Umwelt- und Planungsrecht (*UPR*) 2001, p. 5 *et seq.*; H. Sendler, Grundrecht auf Widerspruchsfreiheit der Rechtsordnung? – Eine Reise nach Absurdistan, Neue Juristische Wochenschrift (*NJW*) 1998, 2875. See also S. Deimann, The Federal Administrative Court Upholds the Right of German Cities to Tax One-Way Non-Reusable Packaging, elni-Newsletter 2/1995, p. 31.

[49] Roller, (*op. cit.* 1).

CHAPTER 8

The Environmental Principles of the EC Treaty as a Legal Basis for Judicial Decisions in the Italian Case Law

Stefano Grassi

1 Introductory remarks

In order to ascertain to what extent Italian courts have been
faced with decisions involving the core environmental principles of the EC
Treaty and to understand the effects of these principles on the actual outcomes
of judicial decisions, it is important to remember that the principles stated
in Article 174(2) EC Treaty reflect in their structural and logical progression
two general and well-established patterns of legal and judicial protection, the
preventive and the compensative functions of legal and judicial decisions.[1]
Referring to the principle of preventive protection, I will examine the case law
concerning the precautionary principle and the principle that preventive action
should be taken. I will consider the precautionary principle in detail, for today in
Italy; some of the most complex cases arise from the widely invoked need for a
precautionary approach in the interpretation of environmental law. In relation to
compensative remedies, I will also discuss the case law concerning the polluter
pays principle.

The Italian Parliament is currently debating a governmental draft for a
primary law, which empowers the Government to integrate and complement
a wide range of environmental rules.[2] According to Article 76 of the Italian
Constitution, the delegation of the Legislative power should mention the principles and criteria guiding the exercise of the conferred power. Article 1.8. (f) of
the governmental draft provides as general guiding principles, the precautionary
principle, the principle that preventive action should be taken and that environmental damage, should as a priority be rectified at source and the principle that
the polluter should pay.[3]

---

[1] See on the ways and means of environmental protection, S. Grassi, Ambiente e diritti dei cittadini, in
Scritti in onore di Giuseppe Guarino, Cedam, 1998, II, 499; A. Gragnani, *Principi e modelli argomentativi
nel diritto ambientale: l'esempio del principio di precauzione*, paper presented in Pisa, April 2003, at the
meeting on The patterns of judicial reasoning, in printing with plus.

[2] See Senato, draft no. 1753 – B, XIV Legislatura, Article 1.8. f), in www. parlamentoitaliano.it.

[3] See on the environmental principles, S. Grassi, Costituzioni e tutela dell'ambiente, in S. Scamuzzi,
Costituzioni, razionalità, ambiente, Bollati Boringhieri, 1994, p. 389; see also in S. Grassi, M. Cecchetti,
A. Andronio, *Ambiente e diritto*, Olshki, 1999; S. Grassi, *Introduzione*, p. 7 and B. Caravita di Toritto,
Costituzione, principi costituzionali e tecniche di normazione per la tutela dell'ambiente, p. 175; M.
Cecchetti, *Principi costituzionali per la tutela dell'ambiente*, Giuffrè, 2000.

2.1 The need for precautionary protection in the case law of the Constitutional Court

The precautionary principle[4] has been introduced into the Italian legal system via EC law and it may be considered a necessary instrument for an adequate and effective protection of rights and interests threatened by technological risks. Sometimes it is expressly incorporated in the law, (*e.g. legge* 22 February 2001, no. 36, on protection from exposure to electric, magnetic and electromagnetic fields; *legge* 5 March 2001, no. 57 concerning consumer protection); more often it is only implied, (*legge* 28 December 1993, no. 459 concerning prevention of ozone layer depletion; *legge* 19 January 2001, no. 3, on risks related to bovine spongiform encephalopathy and the variant Creutzfeldt-Jacob disease). In any case, the precautionary principle has been increasingly invoked and sometimes applied as a legal basis for judicial decisions.

The precautionary approach reflects the awareness that some rights and interests, in order to achieve effective protection, need something different than compensatory remedies and something more than preventive action in the strict sense of the word. The question is to what extent the need for protection is a reasonable cause for abridging other rights and freedoms of individuals and industry. In our constitutional law system, where no act contrary to the Constitution is valid, the answer is not a strict political question, although the choice of adequate precautionary measures is an eminently political responsibility. The Constitutional Court has made an important contribution to the development of a precautionary approach in the field of health and environmental protection.

The following principles, developed by the Constitutional Court, suggest how the precautionary standard of protection might be implemented and could help us to find out whether a precautionary approach is required by our Constitution to ensure the effective protection of the rights of individuals.

1) Precautionary measures shall be adopted after a full evaluation of risks, based on available scientific data, has been made. A law, which establishes precautionary measures, without a full evaluation of scientific data, is therefore unconstitutional (cf. *Corte costituzionale*, decision 26th June 2002, no. 282[5], about a regional law which had temporarily forbidden electroshock treatment).

---

4   See in the italian literature, M. C. Tallacchini, Ambiente e diritto della scienza incerta, in S. Grassi, M. Cecchetti, A. Andronio, p. 57; D. Amirante, Il principio precauzionale fra scienza e diritto, in *Diritto e gestione dell'ambiente*, 2001, p. 17; S. Grassi, Prime osservazioni sul 'principio di precauzione' come norma di diritto positivo, in *Diritto e gestione dell'ambiente*, 2001, p. 37; A. Gragnani, Il principio di precauzione come modello di tutela dell'ambiente dell'uomo, delle generazioni future, in *Riv. dir. civile*, 2003, II, p. 9.

5   See *Corte costituzionale*, 26 June 2002, no. 282, in Foro it., 2003, p. 395 and A. Gragnani, Principio di precauzione, libertà terapeutica e ripartizione di competenze tra Stato e regioni, 2003, Foro it. p. 406.

2) Article 32 of the Constitution recognises the right to health in absolute terms. Consequently:

(a) affirmative actions for the implementation of the right to health should be undertaken in a non-discriminatory way, even when there is no conclusive evidence that they might be effective to save life, (for example, *Corte costituzionale*, decision no. 185, 26th May 1998[6], concerning a new cancer-fighting therapy; decision 14th November 2003, no. 338, about a regional law which had temporarily forbidden electroshock treatment).

(b) It is implied that protection afforded by Article 32 of the Constitution covers potentially dangerous effects on health, even though available scientific data remains uncertain, cf. decision no. 399, 20 December 1996, concerning passive smoking. In this decision the Court said that Article 32 requires preventive measures in order to exclude unintentional exposure to risks for health.

3) Article 32 of the Constitution produces direct effects between the State and individuals and amongst individuals; therefore, it may be invoked before a court in order to decide a particular case, c.f. *Corte costituzionale*, decision 26th July 1979, no. 88.[7]

4) Local authorities may choose their own standard of precautionary protection as long as it does not affect the objectives of health and environmental protection, or any other objective pursued by the central Government within its constitutional competences, cf. *Corte costituzionale*, decision 7th October 1999, no. 382 on electromagnetic pollution; decision 26th July 2002, no. 407 concerning a regional law on dangerous activities; decision 20th December 2002, no. 536 concerning a regional law on hunting decision; decision 1st October 2003 no. 303 and decision 7th October 2003 no. 307 on electromagnetic pollution.[8]

It is important to point out, that in decision 407/2002; 536/2002; 303/2003 and 307/2003 the Court has given a landmark interpretation of the revised Article 117 of our Constitution. The Court has suggested that environmental protection is a constitutional value and not just a strictly defined sector of competence. Consequently, the objective of environmental protection may be pursued by the central Government also in spheres of regional competence and vice-versa. In addition, the Regions may pursue objectives relating to environmental protection within the limits of their powers, although according to Article 117, environmental protection is an exclusive responsibility of the central State.

In my opinion, in relation to this question of division of powers, it is essential that both central government and regional governments identify common law-making techniques, especially in framing technical regulations. They must avoid entering into conflict with one another and should strive to harmonise their procedures for drafting legislation and their enforcement of environmental protection.

---

[6] See *Corte costituzionale*, no. 185, 26 May 1998, in www.cortecostituzionale.it.

[7] See *Corte costituzionale*, 26 July 1979, no. 88, in Giur. cost., 1979, p. 657.

[8] See *Corte costituzionale*, 382/1999; 407/2002 e 536/2002; 303/2003 and 307/2003.

2.2 The enforcement of the precautionary principle in civil case law

In cases before the civil courts, the precautionary approach has been frequently invoked, either as a result of its express or implied incorporation in national laws or on the basis of Article 32 of the Constitution. In civil case law it is controversial as to whether Article 32 affords protection against potential risks for health, or whether it requires the scientific evidence of an actual danger. In this regard, it is important to underline the conceptual distinction between risk and danger, as in this context it has many implications.

Following the first construction, the constitutional guarantee of the right to health precludes the application of the law, which authorises activities causing unintentional exposure to the risk of irreparable health damage. Such a law would be indeed unconstitutional. Therefore, judges should not apply it, or they should promote a judicial review of legislation before the Constitutional Court. This depends on whether the rule is established by an administrative authority, an Act of Parliament or in an Act of Government based on Articles 76 and 77 of the Constitution.

Nevertheless, the uncertainty of scientific knowledge makes it hard to prove the existence of reasonable risks of irreparable health damage that the Legislative and the Executive have failed to take into due account. It is indeed hard to define what due account is; therefore, the ambit of judicial review of laws providing technical rules is actually quite narrow. Among the situations in which a precautionary approach may be claimed, it is important to mention the cases where the risk is due to the particular conditions of individuals, (for example hypersensitivity, conditions of ill-health) or groups (for example children), whose protection actually requires a higher standard of precautionary safety. The following decisions on risks related to electromagnetic fields, relied on the aforementioned construction:

- *Corte di cassazione*, III, decision no. 9893, 27th July 2000;[9]
- *Tribunale di Milano*, 7th October 1999;[10]
- *Tribunale di Como*, 22nd gennaio 2002;[11]
- *Tribunale di Milano*, 23rd October 2002, recognised economic damage as a consequence of a health risk related to the installation of a mobile telephone mast on a roof-top;[12]
- *Tribunale di Verona*, 28th March 2001, insisted on the need to take into account the circumstances of each particular case, such as the one in

---

[9] See *Corte di cassazione*, III, decision no. 9893, 27 July 2000, in Foro it., 2001, p. 141; in Urbanistica e appalti, 2001, p. 161.

[10] See *Tribunale di Milano*, 7 October 1999, in Foro it., 2001, p. 141.

[11] *Tribunale di Como*, 22 January 2002, in www.elettrosmog.com.it.

[12] See *Tribunale di Milano*, 23 October 2002, in www.elettrosmog.com.

which a building's inhabitants were subjected to higher and long-term
exposure, when a mobile telephone mast was positioned on/near their
property;[13]
· *Tribunale di Reggio Calabria*, 30th January 2001;[14]
· *Tribunale di Como*, 30th November 2001, emphasised the need for a
precautionary approach whenever the circumstances demand it in order
to achieve effective protection of the right to health. The case also stressed
the concept of scientific evidence in face of reasonable risk;[15]
· *Tribunale di Milano*, 7th October 1999[16], took into account stress caused by
exposure to an electromagnetic field as a potential breach of the right to
health. In this regard see also *Corte di cassazione, Sezioni unite civili*, decision no. 2515, 21st February 2002, on damages related to loss of amenities
of life (lifestyle amenities) as a consequence of an environmental crime;[17]
· *Pretura di Pietrasanta*, 8th November 1986[18], is one of the first decisions
based on a precautionary argument.

On the other hand, under the opposite interpretation of Article 32, precautionary protection is not required by the Constitution. Consequently the need for a
precautionary approach is justifiable as long as it is provided for or implied in
the law. The following decisions relied on this interpretation:
· *Tribunale di Catanzaro*, 30th May 2001, affirmed that the time set by law
36/2001 in order to comply with the precautionary standards established
by the *decreto del Presidente del Consiglio dei Ministri or d.P.C.M.* (President of the Central Government) 23rd April 1992 is binding for the court;
therefore the request for an immediate correction should be refused.[19]
· *Tribunale di Udine*, Palmanova, 8th January 2001[20], affirmed that protection of the right to health could be afforded only on the basis of scientific
evidence of an actual danger.

One further remark should be made. In civil case law, precautionary protection has often been claimed in proceedings for interim relief. Some courts say
that the lack of scientific certainty precludes the possibility of an interlocutory
judgment. As it is well known, in our legal system the distinction between

---

[13] See *Tribunale di Verona*, 28 March 2001, in Giur. it., 2001, p. 2063.

[14] See *Tribunale di Reggio Calabria*, 30 January 2001, in Rass. giur. en. elettrica, 2001, p. 279.

[15] See *Tribunale di Como*, 30 November 2001, in www geocities.com.

[16] See *Tribunale di Milano*, 7 October 1999, in Rassegna giuridica en. elettrica, 2000, p. 114.

[17] See *Corte di cassazione, Sezioni unite civili*, decision no. 2515, 21 February 2002, in Ambiente, 2002, p.
     775.

[18] See *Pretura di Pietrasanta*, in Foro it., 1987, I, p. 3372.

[19] See *Tribunale di Catanzaro*, 30 May 2001, in Rass. giur. energia elettrica, 2001, p. 268.

[20] See *Tribunale di Udine*, Palmanova, 8 January 2001, in www.elettrosmog. com.

interlocutory and final judgment finds its mainstay in the distinction between 'cognizione sommaria' and 'cognizione piena', that is to say, respectively, 'a superficial and partial [perception]' and 'a full one'. According to the aforementioned proceedings, a full [understanding] of the facts is required in order to depart from safety standards established by the Legislative and the Executive, (see for example, *Tribunale di Milano*, 20th May 2000[21]).

In my opinion, since laws providing for safety standards are supposed to be adopted in full understanding of the facts, this argument is worth considering in order to draw the limits of a judicial review concerning technical rules.

In any case, the opposite construction prevails, (see for example, *Tribunale di Verona*, 28th March 2001[22]).

2.3 The precautionary approach in administrative case law

The precautionary principle has been frequently invoked before administrative courts, in cases concerning breaches of Article 32 of the Constitution and in cases concerning division of powers. Also, in administrative case law, both the aforementioned constructions of Article 32 can be found. I will cite some cases about risks posed by electromagnetic fields. The following decisions affirmed that Article 32 affords protection against potential health risk.

Expressly in these terms, *Consiglio di Stato*, VI, 28th September 2000, no. 4959.[23]

Consiglio di Stato, IV, 16th September 1997, no. 1708, stated that it is not reasonable to use pass devices generating electromagnetic fields for monitoring the observance of working hours, because of the inherent health risk[24]. Moreover, it is worth mentioning *T.a.r. Puglia*, sez. I, Lecce, 6th February 2002[25], which considered stress resulting from fear of exposure to electromagnetic fields, as a breach of the right to health.

As a consequence of the above-mentioned construction, Article 32 of the Constitution precludes the application of laws that provide inadequate safety standards. In this regard a significant decision is *T.a.r. Veneto*, 29th July 1999, no. 927.[26] It is important at this point, to underline that this is a typical example where the Judiciary risks exceeding the parameters of its discretion.

---

[21] See Tribunale di Milano, 20 May 2000, in Rassegna giuridica en. elettrica, 2000, p. 114.

[22] See Tribunale di Verona, 28 March 2001, in Giur. it., 2001, p. 2063.

[23] See *Consiglio di Stato*, VI, 28 September 2000, no. 4959, in *Consiglio di Stato*, 2000, I, p. 2092.

[24] See *Consiglio di Stato*, IV, 16 September 1997, no. 1708, in www.giustizia-amministrativa.it.

[25] See T.a.r. Puglia, Lecce, 6 February 2002, in www.giustizia-amministrativa.it.

[26] See T.a.r. Veneto, ordinanza 29 luglio 1999, no. 927, in Riv. giur. amb., 2000, p. 119.

On the other hand, *T.a.r. Sicilia*, Palermo, sez. II,14th November 2000[27], demonstrates that, protection afforded on the basis of Article 32, requires scientific evidence of an actual danger of irreparable damage.

Furthermore, some key principles concerning the scope of judicial review emerge from administrative case law. Firstly, precautionary measures interfering with constitutional rights, such as freedom of enterprise, require a strong objective justification for the interference according to the principle of proportionality. Therefore, the breach of constitutional rights must be the minimum that is necessary. In this regard see *Consiglio di Stato*, 160/2003[28] on waste, which stressed the need to employ the least restrictive means possible to reach the same aim.

Secondly, the choice of precautionary action should obviously comply with the rules relating to division of powers, between local authorities and the central Government. On that basis, administrative case law has largely affirmed that Municipalities may not establish a higher precautionary standard as a general derogation to that one fixed by central authorities. Particular derogations are allowed, but they must be in accordance with the law, which provides Municipalities with the power to adopt precautionary measures in order to minimise risks posed by electromagnetic fields, (Article 8, law 36/2001). In this regard a significant decision is *Consiglio di Stato*, sez. VI, 3 June 2002, no. 3098.

Thirdly, whenever taking a precautionary measure, public authorities should adopt the policy that is best suited to the merits of particular cases[29]; otherwise the discretionary decision would be unreasonable and therefore unlawful. It is easy to affirm this principle; however, when considered in the context of scientific uncertainty, it might be very hard to turn it into practice. In this regard, see *T.a.r. Veneto*, sez. II, 13th February 2001. In this decision the court struck down the administrative acts locating an elementary school near an electroduct. According to *T.a.r. Veneto*, the public authorities failed evaluate the higher health risk, which threatens children exposed to electromagnetic fields.

2.4   The precautionary principle in criminal case law

I wish to make just a few general remarks concerning the precautionary approach before criminal courts. I believe that in this context the precautionary principle is a very dangerous one. It has been said; criminal law should aim 'to protect the victims as well as the innocent'.[30] The precautionary principle could protect potential victims, but may also punish innocent people in

---

[27] See *T.a.r. Sicilia, Palermo, sez. II*, 14 November 2000, in www.giustizia.amministrativa.it.

[28] See *Consiglio di Stato*, 160/2003, in www.giustizia amministrativa.it.

[29] See T. Dalla Massara, Due pronunce in tema di elettrosmog: ovvero dei ragionevoli limiti di un approccio generalizzante di fronte alla specificità del caso concreto, in Giur. it., 2001, p. 2063.

[30] F. Stella, Giustizia e modernità – La protezione dell'innocente e la tutela delle vittime, Giuffrè, 2001.

vain. Therefore, in my opinion the precautionary principle is not helpful for the purpose of interpreting criminal environmental law. In this sense see, *Corte di Cassazione* 27th February 2002, no. 352 on questions relating to electromagnetic flow.[31] The Supreme Court excluded in such cases the application of Article 674 of the criminal code. However, in the case, *Pretura di Rimini* 14th May 1999, the court applied Article 590 of the criminal code. In this case, concerning negligent personal injury, the court concluded it was due to the presence of an electromagnetic field, despite the lack of scientific evidence.[32]

2.5 The principle that preventive action should be taken in Italian case law

In our legal system the principle of preventive action against actual dangers for rights and freedoms is a well-established pattern of protection. Therefore its application in judicial decisions, as a result of national law incorporating the EC policy, has not raised the same questions as those raised by the implementation of the precautionary principle. Although the principle that 'preventive action should be taken' already existed in our legal system, its explicit statement in Article 174 EC Treaty is not devoid of legal significance. According to the Italian supreme administrative court, *Consiglio di Stato*, the principle that preventive action should be taken produces direct effects and precludes therefore, the application of any conflicting measure of national law. See in this sense *Consiglio di Stato*, VI, 5thDecember 2002, no. 6657 on waste, which says that D.l. 8th March 1996, no. 113 is not compatible 'with the principle that preventive action should be taken [...] consequently its application is precluded'.[33]

When considering the principle of preventive action, it is also important to mention a decision of the Italian Constitutional Court, 16th March 1990, no. 127.[34] The Court recognizes the right to health in absolute terms. According to the Court, no criteria of economic containment are admissible in cases where there is an actual danger to health, due to environmental pollution. In such cases the best available technology should be adopted. The criterion of cost containment may be chosen, only in order to achieve a further reduction of environmental pollution and to reach this objective in a reasonable period of time.

---

[31] See *Corte di Cassazione* 27 February 2002, no. 352, in Rass. giur. en. elettrica, 2002, p. 145.

[32] See Pretura di Rimini 14 May 1999, in Guida al diritto, 1999, p. 37.

[33] See, *Consiglio di Stato*, VI, 5, December 2002, no. 6657, in www.giustizia_amministrativa.it; see on this matter, P. Giampietro, La nozione autentica di rifiuto: dalla incostituzionalità della *legge* alla sua disapplicazione, in Ambiente, 2002, p. 1133.

[34] See Constitutional Court, 16 March 1990, no. 127, in Foro it., 1991, I, p. 36.

3 The principle that the polluter should pay in Italian case law

The polluter pays principle has been incorporated explicitly
or by implication in several laws relating to environmental protection. See for
example Law 349/1986 on liability for environmental damage[35] and D.Lgs. 5th
February 1997, no. 22 on land reclamation.[36] As an example of judicial application of this principle it is important to mention *Consiglio di Stato*, V, 28th June
2002 regarding a call for bids concerning separate collection and transport of
waste.[37] In that decision the supreme administrative court stated that, according
to the polluter pays principle, the Public Administration had fairly established
as a binding criterion of the bids, the assessment of the best environmentally
compatible technical devices.

The polluter pays principle is also applied by criminal courts as an aid to
interpretation, in decisions relating to criminal liability for waste management,
see for example *Corte di cassazione*, III, 11th July 1997.[38]

4 The integration principle and the division of powers in a federal state

The integration principle is implied in the decisions of the
Constitutional Court 407/2002 and 536/2002, regarding a question of the
division of powers, between central and regional authorities. Article 117 of the
Italian Constitution indicates environmental protection as an exclusive competence of the central Government and recognizes the regional legislative powers
in other spheres of competence, such as health, energy and agriculture, which
are inextricably related to environmental matters. According to the Constitutional Court environmental protection is a value and not just an exactly defined
sector of competence. Consequently, the exclusive power of the State concerning
environmental protection pervades all the related sectors of competence of the
regions. I believe this is a way of integrating environmental protection into any
other public policy.[39]

---

[35] See F. Giampietro, Evoluzione della disciplina sul danno ambientale, in *Ambiente*, 2002, p. 833.

[36] See D. Rottingen, Spese di bonifica: potere discrezionale della P. A. nella richiesta di rimborso?, in
Ambiente, 2002, p. 428.

[37] See *Consiglio di Stato*, V, 28 June 2002, in www.giustizia_amministrativa.it.

[38] See Corte di cassazione, III, 11 July 1997, in Diritto e giurisprudenza agraria e dell'ambiente, 1997, 134.

[39] See on the integration principle, S. Grassi, La Carta dei diritti e la tutela dell'ambiente, in *Carta europea
e diritto dei privati, a cura di G. Vettori*, Cedam, 2002, p. 227.

5 The direct effects of EC environmental principles in Italian case law

In Italian case law it is still controversial as to whether, the principles stated in Article 174 of the EC Treaty produce direct effects, therefore precluding the application of any conflicting measure of national law.[40] See in the negative; *T.a.r. Emilia-Romagna, sez. I*, 5th April 2001, no. 300 referring to 'the polluter pays principle'; or in the affirmative the above-mentioned *Consiglio di Stato*, VI, 5th December 2002, no. 6657 which says that 'd.l. 8th March 1996, no. 113 is not compatible with the precautionary principle and with the principle that preventive action should be taken [...] consequently its application is precluded'; *Corte cass., III*, 4th February 1993, referring to the principle that 'preventive action should be taken' and to 'the polluter pays principle'. See also *Corte cassazione*, 19th March 1999, no. 494, which mentions the 'legal duty to fulfil a high level of environmental protection' and stresses the structural and logical progression, which distinguishes each principle considered as a peculiar pattern of protection.[41]

---

[40] See on EC law, G. Gaja, *Protecting the environment in conformity with scientific and technical knowledge under EC law*; S. Grassi, *The precautionary principle in a written constitutional system*, London meeting, 18 October 2002; in the German literature see in the negative, H. W. Rengeling, Bedeutung und Andwendbarkeit des Vorsorgeprinzips im europäischen Umweltrecht, in *DVBl.*, 2000, p. 1473.

[41] T.a.r. Emilia-Romagna, sez. I, 5 April 2001, no. 300, in Trib. amm. reg., 2001, I, p. 1751; Corte Cass., III, 4-2-1993, in Dir. e giur. agr. e dell'ambiente, 1994, p. 292; *Consiglio di Stato*, 5 December 2002, no. 6657, in www.ambientediritto.it.

Further Observations on the Application of EC Environmental Principles before Italian National Courts

Massimiliano Montini*

With regard to the application of the EC environmental law principles before
national Courts of the Member States there are still some basic issues, which
have not yet been solved at European level by the ECJ, although some have been
addressed before national courts, including Italy. These include the following
open questions; what is the legal nature of EC environmental principles? Do
these constitute binding principles or merely guidelines? Are they directed to
EC institutions only or also to national institutions of the Member States? Is it
possible to invoke them before national courts, to declare a national legal act
void or are they simply interpretative tools? In this paper I cannot provide a
comprehensive answer to all these issues, but I will try to comment on these
questions after considering the findings of the most relevant case-law decided
by Italian courts with specific reference to the application of the polluter pays
principle and the precautionary principle.[42]

The polluter pays principle, for instance, was considered as a mere guideline, which could inspire the legislative activity of both the EC and the Italian
national authorities in *Corte di Cassazione*; a case in which the Supreme Civil
Court was asked to determine whether the payment of a certain sum imposed
on industrial waste water discharges by a national law was considered to be a
tax. In this case the Court found, after considering the polluter pays principle,
which was inserted into Italian law through Article 130R (now 174) EC Treaty,
that the sum in question did not amount to a tax, but should be considered a sort
"partial indemnification" of the environmental damage caused to the waters by
the industrial discharges in question.[43]

On the same line of reasoning, the polluter pays principle was invoked
several times before lower administrative courts. For instance, the principle
came into play in various decisions of lower administrative courts, such as *T.a.r.
Lombardia* 267/1994, *T.a.r. Lombardia* 602/1994 and *T.a.r. Emilia-Romagna*
300/2001, in which it was relied upon by the courts in order to determine the
lawfulness of the actual determination of the amount of the waste collection and
disposal tax to be paid by different categories of waste producers.

In *T.a.r. Lombardia* 267/1994, the administrative court stated that 'the
polluter pays principle has a fundamental importance not only for EC Environmental law, but also for EC environmental tax law', insofar as it represents one

---

[*] Addendum to Stefano Grassi's paper.

[42] See on EC environmental law principles in the Italian literature: G. Gaja, Protecting the environment in
conformity with scientific and technical knowledge under EC law, in A. Biondi, M. Cecchetti, S. Grassi,
and M. Lee (eds) *Protecting Scientific Evidence in European Environmental Rule-Making*, (The Hague,
2003), Kluwer, p. 41; M. Montini, Unione Europea e Ambiente, in S. Nespor and A.L. de Cesaris (eds)
Codice dell'Ambiente, II edition, (Milano, 2003), Giuffré, p. 44; M. Cecchetti, *Principi costituzionali per la
tutela dell'ambiente*, (Milano, 2003), Giuffré.

[43] See Italian Supreme Civil Court, 9 Marzo 1992, Corte di Cassazione, I, [1992] no 2801, in Il Corriere
Giuridico, 1992, p. 416.

of the leading criteria to be used by the European and Italian authorities in the application of the legislation on waste disposal and recovery. The Court held that the importance of the polluter pays principle was not limited to the contribution it may give to the prevention of pollution and the correspondent increase in the protection of the environment, but it extends to the role it may play as an 'economic instrument' in the promotion of an European industrial development in the sector of waste recovery.[44]

Similarly, in *T.a.r. Lombardia* 602/1994, the administrative court argued that priority had to be given to EC law over the conflicting provisions of Italian law. More interestingly, by referring to a previous statement of the *Corte di Cassazione* 3148/1993, which explicitly states that the polluter pays principle, having been introduced into the Italian legal system by way of the EC Single European Act of 1987, binds Italy to the European Community and must be directly applied by Italian Courts.[45]

With reference to the precautionary principle and with the principle that preventive action should be taken, it is worth mentioning *Consiglio di Stato* 6657/2002, in which the supreme administrative court implicitly held that these EC environmental principles are directly binding for the Italian legislative and administrative authorities and can be directly applied by national courts when judging on the legality of a certain national measure. The Court, in fact, affirms here that a national decree, which authorised the performance of activities potentially dangerous for the environment, is to be considered unlawful insofar as it runs contrary to the prevention and the precautionary principles, as enshrined in Article 174 of the EC Treaty. The Court stated that, on the basis of the principle of the supremacy of EC legislation over conflicting national legislation, the application of the national decree under scrutiny must be suspended in this case.[46]

A different approach was taken in *T.a.r. Emilia-Romagna* 300/2001, where the administrative court refused to apply the polluter pays principle, as well excluding the direct applicability of the provisions of Article 130R (now 174) of the EC Treaty before national courts to judge on the legality of national legislative or administrative measures. To use the Court's own words: "the polluter pays principle, which informs all EC environmental policy, has merely a programmatic nature and needs a further intervention of the legislature in order to become fully operative. Therefore, the principle, as such, cannot be considered directly applicable, and can be relied upon under national law only as an interpretative means, but not for the creation of a specific rule for the solution

---

[44] See Italian Administrative Court, 5 April 1994, T.a.r. Lombardia, Milano, I, [1994] n. 267, in *Rivista Giuridica dell'Ambiente*, 1995, p. 347.

[45] See Italian Administrative Court, 16 June 1994, T.a.r. Lombardia, Milano, I, n. 602, in *Rivista Giuridica dell'Ambiente*, 1995, p. 499.

[46] See *Consiglio di Stato*, VI, 5 December 2002, no. 6657, in www.ambientediritto.it.

of an unregulated circumstance by a Court." The Court also considered that
the polluter pays principle, represents a basis for the European environmental
policy, but not for the correspondent environmental policy of the Member States,
which can be bound to its requirements only if the principle is incorporated in
binding legal provisions of secondary EC legislation.[47]

Finally, an interesting view from the Italian Courts on the respective role
of EC environmental principles in light of the overall objective of EC environmental policy to ensure a 'high level of environmental protection', can be found
in *Corte di Cassazione* 494/1999.[48] In this case the Court, with reference to the
application of the relevant EC and national provisions on waste disposal and
on the incineration of waste, affirmed that the EC and the national provisions
at stake must be interpreted and applied in an integrated way and that account
must be taken of the relevant EC environmental principles. With regard to the
EC environmental principles in particular, the Court stated that: "The legal
obligation to ensure a 'high level of environmental protection', with the adoption of the best available technologies tends to shift the focus of the European
legal system from the prevention and reparation of the damage ('polluter pays
principle'), to the prevention as such (mostly with the EIA, Environmental
Impact Assessment), to the rectification of environmental damage at source, to
the precautionary approach with the integration of legal, technical, economic
and political instruments for a development which is really sustainable, and for,
social development, which guarantees the quality of life and the environment as
a fundamental human value of every person and of the society as a whole (information, participation and access to justice)."

---

[47] See T.a.r. Emilia-Romagna, I, 5 April 2001, n. 300, in Trib. amm. reg., 2001, I, p. 1751.

[48] See Corte di Cassazione, III, 19 March 1999, no. 494, in www.tuttoambiente.it.

CHAPTER 9

European Environmental Principles in Dutch Case Law

Liselotte Smorenburg-van Middelkoop

This chapter[1] highlights to what extent Dutch courts have been faced with decisions involving European environmental principles: the polluter pays principle, the precautionary principle, and the rectification at source principle. The chapter also considers the effect of the integration principle, ex Article 6 EC in Dutch environmental case law. Finally, it will identify some similar environmental principles that play a role in Dutch case law: the alara principle, the stand still principle and the substitution principle. I shall, however, provide a short introduction on how legal principles are handled by the Dutch courts and on the provenance of the European environmental principles in the Netherlands.

1 Introduction

1.1 Legal principles and Dutch courts

In principle the Dutch system of law is a codified system, including several legal principles, such as the general principles of sound administration (*algemene beginselen van behoorlijk bestuur*), which in most administrative cases play a role. These general principles of sound administration include the general duty of care (*zorgvuldigheidsbeginsel*) in Article 3:2 in the general administrative act (*Algemene wet bestuursrecht*)[2], (hereafter Awb) and the justification principle (*motiveringsbeginsel*) in Article 3:46 Awb.[3] Both provisions relate to administrative decisions, for example to grant a permit. These two principles are often the basis of court decisions, when in fact environmental principles, such as the precautionary principle, are implicitly applied.

Non-codified legal principles also play an important guiding role in Dutch courts. They provide consistency and coherence in case law. Examples of two important, non-codified legal principles, present in many of cases, are the principles of reasonableness and fairness (*redelijkheid en billijkheid*). These principles have been codified though for civil cases in the Dutch Civil Code.

---

[1] This chapter is based on reported case law in key law reports, including those on computer data bases, and on the website www.rechtspraak.nl, which were searched with free word searches covering the principles, such as *voorzorgsbeginsel* (precautionary principle) and *voorzorg* (precaution).

[2] This requires that, when preparing decisions, the administrative authorities gather the necessary information concerning the relevant facts and the interests to be weighed.

[3] This requires that decisions are based on proper reasons and that these reasons are stated in the decision.

1.2 The provenance of European environmental principles in the Netherlands

1.2.1 The polluter pays principle (*het beginsel de vervuiler betaalt*)

Although the polluter pays principle is not explicitly recorded in Dutch legislation, the principle underlies several provisions in Dutch legislation. Examples are provisions regarding liability for damages in the Environmental Management Act (*Wet milieubeheer*) (hereafter EMA)[4]; strict liability provisions in the Dutch Civil Code[5], and soil protection in the Soil Protection Act.[6] Furthermore, several (fiscal) levies based on environmental laws are considered to put the polluter pays principle into practice.[7] Legislation containing financial security also further shapes the principle.[8] Examples of subordinate legislation are municipal rules on waste levies.[9]

The polluter pays principle has been one of the leading principles of Dutch environmental policy.[10] It has been part of the National Environmental Policy Plans (*Nationale Milieubeleidsplannen*) since the late nineteen eighties. It has also been one of the leading principles of the policy on water quality[11] and it is often referred to in parliamentary documents.

---

[4] Article 15.20 and 15.21 EMA. According to these Articles damages due to or costs based on new environmental measures, for example an EMA-permit, will only be compensated if these damages or costs "in reason should not of not entirely be chargeable to the one at whom these measures are directed". This is based on the polluter pays principle. (J. E. Hoitink, Het beginsel de vervuiler betaalt: revival van een milieubeginsel, Tijdschrift voor Milieu & Recht, (2000),2, 34)

[5] Such as the strict liability for damages caused by hazardous substances, landfill and mining sites (Article 6:175-177 of the Dutch Civil Code).

[6] The principle also underlied the former Interim Soil Clean-up Act, of 1982, which was incorporated in the Soil Protection Act in 1994. Article 75 of the current Soil Protection Act incorporates the principle. This stipulates in short that the State is entitled to recover the costs of soil surveys and clean ups from the person whose wrongful act(s) caused the pollution of the soil and who is (non contractually) liable for it to the State under civil law (Article 75, par. 1). And when there is no wrongful act, the costs can be recovered in the circumstances stipulated in Article 75, par 6 of the Soil Protection Act.

[7] Examples are the Pollution of Surface Waters Act (*Wet verontreiniging oppervlaktewateren*) and the Taxes on Environmental Basis Act (*Wet belastingen op milieugrondslag*). See Ch. W. Backes, C. J. Bastemeijer, A. A. Freriks, R. A. J. van Gestel and J. M. Verschuuren, Codificatie van milieurechtelijke beginselen in de Wet milieubeheer, Boom Juridische Uitgevers, (2002) 105-106.

[8] Such as the recent Decree on Financial Security Environmental Management (*Besluit financiële zekerheid milieubeheer*). See www.vrom.nl/pagina.html?id=10544.

[9] See note 4, p. 32.

[10] See note 4, pp. 30.

[11] See note 7, p. 105.

1.2.2   The precautionary principle (*het voorzorgsbeginsel*)

The precautionary principle can only very rarely be found explicitly in Dutch environmental law.[12] The two acts (or provisions therein) where this has occurred have not yet entered into force: the Nature Protection Act 1998 (*Natuurbeschermingswet*)[13] and the Antarctica Protection Act (*Wet bescherming Antarctica*)[14]. It is argued that the EMA leaves room for the application of the precautionary principle by incorporating possible consequences into the framework for assessing permits.[15] Furthermore, the principle is often referred to in the explanation of laws and orders in council (*AmvB's*) and the parliamentary proceedings of legislative proposals.[16]

One could also argue that the precautionary principle has very implicitly been the basis of the recent ministerial circular Required Information on Chemical Substances (*Circulaire benodigde gegevens van chemische stoffen*)[17], which provides guidelines for a considered decision making process concerning permits based on the EMA and the Pollution of Surface Waters Act. This circular was issued, following two cases heard on 29th January 2003 by the Administrative Law Division of the Council of State (*Afdeling Bestuursrechtspraak van de Raad van State*), regarding the production of the substance FR-720.[18]

---

[12]   Furthermore Article 1.1 EMA is considered by some to express the precautionary principle (M. Faure and E. Vos, Juridische afbakening van het voorzorgsbeginsel: mogelijkheden en grenzen, nr. A03/03, (2003) 188). Others consider it to be an expression of the Prevention principle (see note 7, p. 87). It stipulates: '1. Everyone has to observe sufficient care for the environment. 2. This care [...] means at least that everyone who knows or in reason can assume that his actions or omissions can cause adverse effects for the environmental, is obligated to, as far as reasonably can be expected, omit such actions; take measures to prevent these effects or in case they can not be prevented, to limit or remedy these effects as much as possible (Article 1.1.a, par 2).'

[13]   Article 16, par. 3 of the Nature Protection Act, stipulates in short that a permit sees to acts 'which can have significant effects for the natural beauty (*natuurschoon*), the scientific meaning or for animals or plants in a protected nature reserve, this permit will only be granted if it is certain (*met zekerheid vaststaat*) that these acts will not affect the national characteristics of the protected nature reserve, unless important public interests compel the granting of a permit.' See note 7, p. 69.

[14]   See Article 15, b, under 1 and 3 and, c, under 3 of the Antarctica Protection Act, which requires that precautionary measures be taken. See note 7, p. 69.

[15]   See note 7, p. 70. They refer to Article 8.8, par. 1, sub b, which would require a principle conform interpretation of the EMA.

[16]   See note 7, pp. 70-71.

[17]   Staatscourant 2003, 197, p. 15.

[18]   ABRvS 29 January 2003, no. 200200255/2 and 200200259/2, *Vereniging Zeeuwse Milieufederatie and Stichting Greenpeace Nederland v. the Provincial Executive of Zeeland*, www.raadvanstate.nl and www.rechtspraak.nl LJN AF3545 and AF3544. This will be discussed further on.

The precautionary principle is also included in subordinate legislation and policies, such as the Key Physical Planning Decision on the Wadden Sea (*Planologische Kernbeslissing Waddenzee*), hereafter Key Physical Planning Decision, where the principle is explicitly included[19], the National Environmental Policy of 2001 (*NMP4*) and the Third Policy Document on Water Management (*Derde Nota waterhuishouding*), hereafter Third Policy Document.[20]

1.2.3 The rectification at source principle (*het bronbeginsel*)

Although the rectification at source principle is also not explicitly part of Dutch environmental law, it has already extensively been used as a starting point for Dutch legislation and policies. For instance, the rules based on the Air Pollution Act and the emissions or discharges, in permit or in general rules based on the EMA or the Pollution of Surface Waters Act. Another example is the policy to control noise pollution, based on the Noise Pollution Act.[21]

1.2.4 The integration principle (*het integratiebeginsel*)

The integration principle has not been explicitly incorporated into Dutch legislation, however, some consider Article 21 of the Constitution as a call for external integration of environmental interests, similar to that in

---

[19] It is included in the criteria to consider when assessing new activities or extension or revision of existing activities in the Wadden Sea. 'When, at the assessment on basis of the best available information, there is clear doubt (duidelijke twijfel) about the non-occurrence of possible important negative consequences for the eco-system, the benefit of the doubt will go in the direction of the conservation of the Wadden Sea.' (Planologische Kernbeslissing Waddenzee, deel 3: Kabinetsstandpunt). The Third Policy Document Wadden Sea will replace the Key Physical Planning Decision as of 2004. There the precautionary principle is defined as: 'Approval of an activity can only be granted after the guarantee (zekerheid) had been provided that the activity will not affect the essential characteristics or values of the Wadden Sea. The precautionary principle implies that deterioration of essential characteristics or values and the most far-reaching effects for the Wadden Sea are assumed when there is doubt.'

[20] See note 7, pp. 71-73. The Third Policy Document states that the first starting point for discharges is reduction of the pollution, at which for almost all pollution a emission approach is the main thing, which according to the text is comparable to the precautionary principle as agreed upon during the second Ministerial North Sea Conference (ABRvS 12 May 2000, no. E03.96.0055, *Landelijke Vereniging tot Behoud van de Waddenzee and Aramid Products v.o.f.* v. *Minster of Transport, Public Works and Water Management*, Tijdschrift voor Milieu & Recht 2000/9, no. 94 and AB 2000/394, in par. 2.11.). Currently there is the Fourth Policy Document on Water Management. Other policies are the Policy Document Biotechnology and the Strategy Document Handling Substances (See note 12, pp. 190-205, also on *NMP4*).

[21] See note 7, p. 122.

Article 6 EC.[22] More explicitly, it is given shape in the environmental test in the ministerial circular – Instructions for the Regulatory Measures (*Circulaire van de Minister President (Aanwijzingen voor de Regelgeving)*)[23]. It is also implicitly part of the Pesticides Act (*Bestrijdingsmiddelenwet 1962*), the Fisheries Act (*Visserijwet 1963*)[24] and the tax system. The integration principle has been part of policies since the mid-eighties and 'It has been referred to in the third National Environmental Policy Plan as one of the most important starting points for the realization of environmental policy.'[25] This pursuit has been elaborated in the Environmental Program 2000-2003, through the division of competences and responsibilities of ministers.[26]

1.2.5   Codification of the principles

In conclusion, none of the European environmental principles have been explicitly codified in Dutch legislation (of the central government).[27] There is however, a legislative proposal on environmental principles being drafted[28]. It is likely that the proposal will codify the most important environmental principles, including the precautionary principle, in the EMA, which is the Dutch environmental framework Act.[29]

2   The European environmental principles in Dutch case law

2.1   The polluter pays principle

Overall, there is little case law where the polluter pays principle plays a role. In only but a few cases, has the court referred to the polluter pays principle. Sometimes one of the parties raises the principle, but the court fails to

---

[22] Article 21 of the Constitution stipulates that 'the care of the government is aimed at the liveability of the country and the protection and improvement of the living environment (*leefmilieu*)'.

[23] In Instruction 256 of this circular (Staatscourant 2002, 97 of 22 May 2002).

[24] Respectively Article 3 and 4. Article 3 of the Pesticides Act stipulates that a pesticide can only be admitted if it has no unacceptable effects for the environment. (N. Dhondt and R. Uylenburg, Het beginsel van externe integratie, (2000), 5, Tijdschrift voor Milieu & Recht, 126). The principle is part of the Fisheries Act since 12 July 2002. Article 4, par. 1, of this Act stipulates that 'the interests of nature conservation can also be taken into account when measures are adopted'.

[25] See note 7, pp. 118-120.

[26] See note 7, pp. 118-120.

[27] With the exception of the precautionary principle, see notes 13 and 14.

[28] Ministry of Housing, Spatial Planning and the Environment (2003) 28.

[29] Ministry of Housing, Spatial Planning and the Environment (2001) 58. See on codification also note 12, pp. 190, 203 and 216-220, which refers to Backes (2002).

consider it.[30] In other cases the principle has been mentioned in the conclusion of the Advocate-General to the Supreme Court, but this did not reappear in the final judgment.

2.1.1 Is the polluter pays principle a general principle of law?

It is also noteworthy that Dutch courts do not always consider the polluter pays principle as a general principle of law with legal consequences. In the Court of Appeal at Den Bosch on 22nd February 1995[31] and the Court of Appeal at Arnhem on 20th February 2001[32], the Tax Chamber of these courts rejected recourse to the polluter pays principle and considered 'furthermore this saying does not constitute a general principle of law'.[33] Because there are only a few (tax) cases where the status of the polluter pays principle has been discussed, a definite conclusion that it is not a principle of law seems unjustified, however, the exact meaning of the principle in case law remains unclear.

2.1.2 In the context of which issues is the polluter pays principle referred to?

The majority of cases in which the principle was referred to related to tax issues, such as waste or discharge levies, handled by the Tax Chambers of the courts. The few administrative and civil cases where the principle is mentioned by the court concerned discharge and soil cases, regarding the Discharge Decree (*Lozingbesluit open teelt en veehouderij*)[34], Pollution of Surface Waters Act[35], and wrongful acts (based on liabilities) under the Dutch Civil Code.[36]

---

[30] For example in ARRvS 25 February 1992, no. R01.91.1789/Q01, *T.D.F. Tiofine B.V. and R.M.F. van Loon v. Minister of Transport, Public Works and Water Management*, AB 1992/ 491; HR 27 October 1993 no. 1161, *The Municipality of Rotterdam v. A.P.H. Henket and I. Van den Boorgert*, NJ 1994/703; HR 21 June 2000 no. 33816, www.rechtspraak.nl LJN AA6253 (regarding tax for dogs in the Municipality of Hellendoorn) en HR 25 October 2002, no. C01/145HR, *Total Nederland N.V. and TotalFinaelf Nederland N.V.* v. *Staat der Nederlanden*, www.rechtspraak.nl AE8451.

[31] Gh. Den Bosch 22 February 1995, no. 0519/93EV, Belastingblad 1995/707 (regarding a waste levy of the Municipality of Eindhoven

[32] Gh. Arnhem 20 February 2001, no. 98/03631, www.rechtspraak.nl. LJN AB0441 (regarding a tax of the Municipality of Gorssel)

[33] In Dutch: '*Bovendien houdt dit gezegde geen algemeen rechtsbeginsel in.*'

[34] Rb. Den Haag 20 March 2002, no. 00/1511, *Vereniging voor Nederlandse Landbouwluchtvaartbedrijven and others* v. *Staat der Nederlanden*, www.rechtspraak.nl LJN EA7271

[35] HR 26 January 1990, no. 13 724, *De Staat der Nederlanden* v. *Windmill Holland B.V.*, NJ 1991/393

[36] Rb. Amsterdam 31 October 1990, no. H88.0088, *L.P. Broekveldt* v. *Van Houten B.V. and E.H. Swaab*, BR 1991/293 (also regarding the Interim Soil Protection Act).

When the principle does occur in case law, it is mostly referred to in the context of national laws or policies incorporating them. In these cases the courts do not substantively test the principle.

It may also be noted, that in cases regarding tax issues, the polluter pays principle is often used in a negative way, for example when a appellant tries to argue that his tax levy should be less, based on the polluter pays principle[37], or that the norms for the tax levy are based on this principle, without taking into account the special circumstances of the case.[38]

2.1.3 Case law regarding the polluter pays principle in the context of Article 174(2) EC

There has only been one reported case that of 27th March 2002[39], where the Administrative Law Division referred to the polluter pays principle explicitly in the context of Article 174(2) EC. This case concerned an appeal by environmental groups against decisions to permit cockle fishing in the Wadden Sea on the basis of the Nature Protection Act, because these decisions were in breach with the Habitats Directive (92/43/EEC). It gave rise to a preliminary reference[40]. According to the preliminary opinion of the court, Article 174(2) EC, including the polluter pays principle, can play a role in determining whether 'appropriate steps' or an 'appropriate approach', as mentioned in Article 6, paragraphs 2 and 3, of the Habitats Directive, have been taken. The court asked the European Court of Justice, in a preliminary question to determine whether this assumption is correct.[41] This case will be discussed in more detail in the context of the precautionary principle, for the court specifically focused on that principle.

---

[37] For example in Gh. Den Bosch 9 November 2000, no. 98/00634, *R. B.V. v. the tax assessment official of the municipality V.*, www.rechtspraak.nl LJN AA8459.

[38] Koninklijk Besluit of 11 March 1978, no. 61, *C. Kleinepier v. the Provincial Executive of Zeeland*, AB 1978/336.

[39] ABRvS 27 March 2002, no 200000690/1 and 200101670/1, *Landelijke Vereniging tot Behoud van de Waddenzee also on behalf of the Nederlandse Vereniging tot Bescherming van Vogels v. State Secretary of Agriculture, Nature Management and Fisheries*, www.rechtspraak.nl LJN AE0731.

[40] Case C-127/02, OJ 2002, C 156/4, still pending.

[41] Literally in Dutch *'Hebben de begrippen "passende maatregelen", respectievelijk "passende beoordeling" een zelfstandige betekenis of dient bij het oordeel daarover ook rekening te worden gehouden met artikel 174, tweede lid, van het EG-Verdrag en met name het in dat artikellid genoemde voorzorgsbeginsel'.*

2.1.4   Is the polluter pays principle applied *ex officio?*

In the majority of (tax) cases it is the appellant who raises the principle. The court seems to have *ex officio* referred to the polluter pays principle, and the other principles, as mentioned in Article 174(2) EC, in the case of 27 March 2002 mentioned above.

2.2   The precautionary principle

Contrary to the position in respect of the polluter pays principle, the precautionary principle is, after some reluctance in earlier case law[42] increasingly used by Dutch courts when reviewing plans or decisions of the authorities.

'no support exists in general under Article 13 and 17 of the Nuisance Act [Hinderwet] for the argument that a permit cannot be granted as long as no clarity exists regarding the influence of the declining rainfall on the vegetation in the Deurnse Peel'.[43]

It is, however, possible to derive from recent case law that the precautionary principle has to be applied. For example in 1999[44] the Administrative Law Division concluded that the authorities had granted an EMA permit for a motor club in the nature reserve Centraal Veluwe:

'While lacking insight into the consequences of the operation of the establishment, for the nature, scientific and ecological values of the location. The appealed decision (is in so far) in violation of Article 3:2 Awb.'[45]

---

[42] ABRvS 30 September 1996, no. E03.94.0576, *Stichting Werkgroep Behoud de Peel* v. *Burgomaster and Aldermen of Deurne*, Tijdschrift voor Milieu & Recht 1997/6, 76. The Nuisance Act has been replaced by the Environmental Protection Act 1994.

[43] In Dutch: '*Voor de stelling dat geen vergunning zou mogen worden verleend, zolang geen duidelijkheid bestaat omtrent de invloed van verminderde inzijging van regenwater op de vegetaties in de Deurnse Peel, bestaat ... in zijn algemeenheid geen steun in de Article 13 en 17 van de Hinderwet.*'

[44] ABRvS 28 January 1999, no. E03.97.1803, *Stichtingen Milieuwerkgroepen Ede and others* v. *Burgomaster and Aldermen of Ede*, Tijdschrift voor Milieu & Recht 1999/7-8, 65.

[45] In Dutch: '*...hebben verweerders de vergunning verleend, zonder over inzicht te beschikking in de gevolgen van het in werking zijn van de inrichting voor de natuurwetenschappelijke en ecologische waarden ter plaatse. Het bestreden besluit is in zoverre in strijd met Article 3:2 Awb [...] .*'
The court annulled the appealed decision, because the degree of these consequences is essential for the question whether the establishment can be operative within the limits of the interest of the protection of the environment (Article 8. 10, par 1 EMA).

Overall the precautionary principle affects Dutch case law rarely as part of European law and not yet as part of International law, but mostly as part of Dutch policy or through Article 3:2 (the general duty of care) and, sometimes Article 3: 46 Awb (the justification principle).[46]

The precautionary principle has lead to the annulment of appealed decisions by the courts, mostly implicitly through Article 3:2 Awb (the general duty of care).[47] Examples can be found in the two Administrative Law Division cases of 29th January 2003[48], regarding temporary permits based on Article 8.17 EMA[49] (concerning the production of the substance FR-720 and the discharge of waste-water thereof). The court concluded that:

'in this case there is a lack of information about the accurate qualities of a new substance to be produced in an establishment, which would end up in the environment through emissions into the air and against which a strong assumption exists that it will have very negative consequences for the environment.'[50]

After considering the other circumstances of the case[51], the court concluded that:

---

[46] Parties sometimes try to raise the precautionary principle included in international law, for instance in ABRvS 16 November 2000, no. E03.97.0883, *Akzo Nobel Chemicals B.V. and others v. Minister of Transport, Public Works and Water Management*, Tijdschrift voor Milieu & Recht 2001/9, 91 and ABRvS 25 August 2000, No. E03.99.0202-0204, *Stichting Natuur en Milieu and others v. the Provincial Executive of Noord-Brabant and others*, BR 2000/946 and AB 2000/455. Only in Gh. Den Haag 21 October 1999, no. 98/144, *Stichting Zuidhollandse Milieufederatie and Stichting Natuur en Milieu v. Staat der Nederlanden*, Tijdschrift voor Milieu & Recht 2000/1, 2, the court implicitly paid attention to international law, after environmental groups referred to a breach of a Decree with general environmental principles, such as the precautionary principle, especially the principles 11 and 15 of the Rio convention and Article 130 R EC (old). The court stated that Articles 8.8, par 1, and 8:40 EMA comply with these principles.

[47] See for example the case of ABRvS 28 January 1999, no. E03.97.1803, in note 44.

[48] ABRvS 29 January 2003, no. 200200255/2 and 200200259/2, note 18.

[49] According to Article 8.17, par, 1, introduction and sub a, EMA, it can be decided in a permit that the permit is only valid for a certain period of time, with a maximum of five years, if this is necessary because of the development of better insight into the consequences of the establishment for the environment.

[50] In Dutch: *'In het onderhavige geval is sprake van een gebrek aan informatie over de exacte eigenschappen van een nieuwe in een inrichting te produceren, en via emissie naar de lucht in het milieu terechtkomende stof, waarvan het ernstige vermoeden bestaat dat deze zeer nadelige gevolgen voor het milieu heeft.'*

[51] Namely the expressed intention of the Minister of Housing, Spatial Planning and the Environment to ban FR-720 because a serious and motivated assumption exists of the dangers posed by FR-720 for humans and the environment. In view thereof the Inspector of the Environmental Health Department advised not to grant the permits. The expert's report showed that it is defensible to regard FR-720 as a potentially hazardous substance, until research, amongst others on the chronic effects of the substance, proves the contrary.

'in view of these [...] circumstances [...] this is not a situation where a temporary permit can be granted, following a better insight into the consequences for the environment. As further research prior to the decision was omitted, the decision was also taken in violation of Article 3:2 Algemene wet bestuursrecht [...]'.[52]

The precautionary principle as such was not mentioned. The court annulled the decisions.

2.2.1 A test against the precautionary principle: In the context of legislation, policy or autonomously?

Whilst it has been argued that there is case law which implies that there is room to explicitly test decisions autonomously against the precautionary principle, outside the scope of legislation and policies which mention the principle[53]; it seems that most of the case law indicates that the role of the precautionary principle in present legal practice is especially determined by the fact whether is part of legislation or policy (documents).[54]

The latter is also the position in the cases regarding the Wadden Sea. They refer in principle to policies or subordinate legislation, in which the precautionary principle is incorporated, more specifically the Key Physical Planning Decision and the Third Policy Document. This case law will be discussed later.

Contrary to the case law on the principle in policies regarding the Wadden Sea, the Administrative Law Division concluded on 12th May 2000[55] that the precautionary principle did not apply in a case regarding an EMA permit for the increase of production of polymer in Delfzijl because:

'the precautionary principle is [...] not a principle codified in the EMA and furthermore, not a principle which has been included by the defendants in their assessment rules in the context of their discretionary powers.'[56]

---

[52] In Dutch: *'De Afdeling is ... gelet op de hiervoor gegeven omstandigheden ... van oordeel dat geen sprake is van een situatie waarin een tijdelijke vergunning kan worden verleend in verband met het ontwikkelen van een beter inzicht in de gevolgen van de inrichting voor het milieu. Nu nader onderzoek voorafgaande aan het bestreden besluit achterwege is gelaten, is het besluit tevens genomen in strijd met artikel 3:2 van de Algemene wet bestuursrecht ...'.*

[53] W. Th. Douma, The Precautionary Principle, (2003) 412.

[54] See note 12, p. 215.

[55] ABRvS 12 May 2000, no. E03.96.0068, *Landelijke Vereniging tot Behoud van de Waddenzee v. the Provincial Executive of Groningen*, Tijdschrift voor Milieu & Recht 2000/9, no. 93 and AB 2000/395. The decision was finally annulled on another ground.

[56] In Dutch: *'Het voorzorgsbeginsel is ... geen in de Wm gecodificeerd beginsel en evenmin een beginsel dat verweerders in het kader van hun beoordelingsvrijheid hebben opgenomen in hun beoordelingsregels.'*

This conclusion seems to suggest that the Dutch courts are reluctant to 'explicitly' apply the precautionary principle when it is not included in legislation, rules or policies on which an appealed decision is (or should be) based.

The Administrative Law Division seemed to leave this question open in the next case, 25th August 2000[57], where the appellants requested for the application of the precautionary principle as laid down in various international documents, including the Rio Declaration and the EC Treaty. There the Administrative Law Division noted that where a test against this principle was concerned,

'that, apart from the fact whether the appealed decisions should be tested against the precautionary principle other than within the framework of the legislation applicable at the time when the decisions were taken, a test against this principle only could come up if there is insufficient insight into the environmental protection effects of a certain act. This has to be reviewed.'[58]

2.2.2 The precautionary principle and Article 3:2 Awb (the general duty of care) or 3:46 Awb (the justification principle)

There have been cases where the court was prepared to test the precautionary principle, even when it was not referred to in the applicable laws and policies. In these cases the test was implicit, through the application of Article 3:2 Awb (the general duty of care). For example in the case of 28th January 1999[59], regarding an EMA permit for a motor cycle club with circuit in the nature reserve of Centraal Veluwe, the Administrative Law Division concluded that in light of the circumstances the:

---

[57] ABRvS 25 August-2000, no. E03.99.0202-0204, in note 46. See also A.A. Freriks in a case note at ABRvS 12 May 2000, no. E03.96.0068, in note 55.

[58] In Dutch: *'dat, daargelaten of de bestreden besluiten aan het voorzorgsbeginsel dienen te worden getoetst anders dan in het kader van de ten tijde van het nemen van de bestreden besluiten geldende wetgeving, een toets aan dit beginsel eerst aan de orde zou kunnen komen indien er onvoldoende inzicht bestaat in de milieuhygiënische gevolgen van een bepaalde handeling. Dit moet eerst bezien worden.'*

[59] ABRvS 28 January 1999, no. E03.97.1803, *De Stichting Milieuwerkgroepen Ede v. Burgomaster and Aldermen of Ede*, AB 1999/177. Other examples are Pres. Rb. Leeuwarden 21 October 1997, no. 97/1246 WET, *De Landelijke Vereniging tot Behoud van de Waddenzee and others v. Minister of Economic Affairs*, KG 1997/379 and ABRvS 23 July 1999, no. E03.95.1762, *Zuidhollandse Milieufederatie v. Burgomaster and Aldermen of Naaldwijk*, Tijdschrift voor Milieu & Recht 2000/1, 5. See also A.A. Freriks in a case note at ABRvS 12 May 2000, no. E03.96.0068, in note 55.

'defendants had granted the permit, lacking insight as to the consequences of the operation of this installation for the natural science and ecological values. The appealed decision was in violation of Article 3:2 Awb'.[60]

The Administrative Law Division annulled the entire decision on appeal.[61] This particular application of Article 3:2 Awb (the general duty of care), seems to go beyond the standard due care obligation of this Article to gather all available information by actually adding a precautionary element.[62] However, this extensive interpretation of Article 3:2 Awb (the general duty of care) is not standard. In most cases the court will simply, sometimes even without implicitly referring to the precautionary principle, annul the pending decision because the authorities had not gathered all necessary information concerning the relevant facts and the interests to be weighed.[63]

2.2.3 Administrative case law regarding the precautionary principle and the Wadden Sea

Overall, most cases where the precautionary principle is explicitly,[64]or implicitly, referred to, concern the Wadden Sea (a nature reserve).[65] This administrative case law on the Wadden Sea is ambiguous. Not only does

---

[60] In Dutch: *Gelet op het vorenstaande 'hebben verweerders de vergunning verleend, zonder over inzicht te beschikken in de gevolgen van het in werking zijn van de inrichting voor de natuurwetenschappelijke en ecologische waarden ter plaatse. Het bestreden besluit is in zoverre in strijd met Article 3:2 Awb.'*

[61] 'Because the extent in which the values are affected by the operation of the establishment is an aspect which is of essential importance for the question whether the establishment can operate within the limits of the importance of the protection of the environment'. This refers to Article 8.10, par 1, EMA.

[62] In this case the boundaries of Article 3:2 Awb are stretched beyond the obligation to collect all information (see note 7, page 78).

[63] This is a regular application of Article 3:2 Awb. Another Article used by the courts in these cases is Article 3:46 Awb because the decision was not sufficiently motivated. When these two Articles are strictly applied, without referring to the precautionary principle explicitly, it can be argued that the final effect of the precautionary principle will be limited on these cases, because the authorities are able to mend these flaws in the appealed decisions rather easily.

[64] According to Ch. W. Backes and others the Dutch courts have also applied the precautionary principle on the basis of the directly applicable Birds and Habitats Directive in nature conservation cases. However no cases are mentioned, besides cases of the ECJ (note 7, p. 71).

[65] Such as in VzABRvS 30 August 2000, no. 200003692/1, *Cooperatieve Producentenorganisatie van de Nederlandse Kokkelvisserij v. State Secretary of Agriculture, Nature Management and Fisheries*, Tijdschrift voor Milieu & Recht 2001/4, 39; ABRvS 30 June 2000, no. E03.96.1555, *Waddenvereniging and others v. Minister of Transport, Public Works and Water Management*, Tijdschrift voor Milieu & Recht 2001/5, 67; ABRvS 16 November 2000, no. E03.97.0883, note 46; ABRvS 12 May 2000, no. E03.96.0068, note 55 and ABRvS 12 May 2000, no. E03.96.0055, note 20.

the definition of the precautionary principle in the policies and subordinate leg-islation differ[66], the courts are also not always consistent in applying and citing the precautionary principle in these documents. Therefore, no definite conclu-sion can be drawn as to how the Dutch judiciary would define the principle.[67]

Some cases are noteworthy, such as the interim decision of 21st December 1999[68], regarding a refusal to grant an exemption from the Nature Protection Act to allow the collection of mussels in the Wadden Sea. The President of the Administrative Law Division concluded that for the application of the precau-tionary principle (the authority in question sought to harmonise its policy the precautionary principle described in the Key Physical Planning Decision) it was of no importance that this principle already existed in 1996 when the previous exemption was granted.

A further example is the case of 26th April 2001[69], regarding a clearance permit granted to gather shells (cockles) in the Wadden Sea. This case also referred to the precautionary principle as included in the Key Physical Planning Decision. The decision seems to suggest that the Administrative Law Division puts the burden of proof of the precautionary principle, included in the Key Physical Planning Decision and the Third Policy Document, on the authorities. The court concluded that the authorities have to provide sufficient evidence, that the permitted activities will not cause damage.[70]

The court, however, seemed to conclude the opposite in the case of Admin-istrative Law Division of 12th May 2000[71], concerning an appeal against a permit granted under the Pollution of Waters Protection Act to discharge in the Zeehavenkanaal, near the Wadden Sea (Delfzijl). In this case the appellant, an environmental organisation trying to invoke the principle, had to prove the the view of the authorities was incorrect:

'because of a lack of adequate research methods, the [...] research on teratogenic, mutagenic, carcinogenic effect and endocrine disruption could not be prescribed. The defendant had negatively answered the question whether the effects, which resulted from this, regarding which the Commission for Environmental Impact Assessments

---

[66] See notes 19 and 20.

[67] See note 53, page 427.

[68] VzABRvS 21 December 1999, no. 199903191/1, *V.O.F. de Kokkelvisser v. State Secretary of Agriculture,* Nature Management and Fisheries, KG 2000/49.

[69] ABRvS 26 April 2001, no E01.99.0192-197, *Van der Endt-Lauwerse B.V. and others v. State Secretary of Transport, Public Works and Water Management,* Tijdschrift voor Milieu & Recht 2001/9, 92, with case note by J. Verschuuren.

[70] Literal in Dutch: *'In dit verband heeft verweerder onvoldoende aannemelijk gemaakt dat de vergunningen niet zullen leiden tot intering op de fossiele voorraad van kokkels.'*

[71] ABRvS 12 May 2000, no. E03.96.0055, note 20.

had noted lacunas, are enough to obstruct the granting of permits. It has been demonstrated insufficiently by the appellant ... that this view of the defendant is incorrect.'[72]

The court concluded that it should be regarded that the precautionary principle was met 'in so far as the assessment of the permit application is bound by this principle'.

Another interesting case regarding the Wadden Sea, is the Administrative Law Division case of 27th March 2002[73], already mentioned under the polluter pays principle. The case addressed the role of Article 174(2) EC in the application of Article 6, paragraphs 2 and 3, of the Habitats Directive. The court concluded in this case that the authorities 'were allowed to assume that the permits were not [...] in breach with the precautionary principle in the Key Physical Planning Decision – Wadden Sea', because

'there was no reason why the authorities could not have assumed that on basis of the best available information there was no clear doubt about the non-occurrence of possible important negative effects of mechanical cockle fishing for the geomorphology, flora and fauna of the bottom of the Wadden Sea.'[74]

The court determined this on the basis of the expert's report, which concluded that 'there are gaps in knowledge and that the majority of research results which were consulted and available did not unambiguously point at important negative (irreversible) consequences for the ecosystem.'[75]

---

[72] In Dutch: *'dat bij gebrek aan adequate onderzoeksmethoden, het voorschrijven van onderzoek naar teratogene, mutagene, carcinogene werking en endocriene verstoring niet kon worden voorgeschreven. De vraag of de effecten die het gevolg zijn van de verschijnselen, ten aanzien waarvan de commissie voor de Milieu-effectrapportage lacunes in kennis heeft geconstateerd, zodanig zijn dat die lacunes in de weg staan aan vergunningverlening, is door verweerder ontkennend beantwoord. Door appellante [...] is onvoldoende aannemelijk gemaakt dat dit standpunt onjuist is.'*

[73] ABRvS 27 March 2002, no. 200000690/1 en 200101670/1, note 39.

[74] In Dutch: de Afdeling zag *'geen grond voor het oordeel dat verweerder niet heeft kunnen aannemen dat op basis van de best beschikbare informatie geen sprake is van duidelijke twijfel over het achterwege blijven van mogelijke belangrijke negatieve gevolgen van de mechanische kokkelvisserij voor de geomorfologie en de flora en fauna van de bodem van de Waddenzee."* "*Derhalve is zij van oordeel dat verweerder ervan mocht uitgaan dat de vergunningen op deze punten niet in strijd zijn met het voorzorgsbeginsel in de PKB-waddenzee.'*

[75] In Dutch: *'De conclusie van het deskundigenbericht omtrent de literatuurstudie is dan ook dat uit dit onderzoek vooral blijkt dat er leemten in kennis zijn en dat het merendeel van de wel geraadpleegde en beschikbare onderzoeksresultaten niet eenduidig wijzen op belangrijke negatieve (onomkeerbare) gevolgen voor het ecosysteem.'*

2.2.4 Case law regarding the precautionary principle in the context of Article 174(2) EC

The interesting part of the aforementioned case of 27th March 2002, is that it can be argued[76] that the court has started to question the correctness of the interpretation of the precautionary principle as included in the Key Physical Planning Decision and as used in earlier case law.[77] Especially as the court in this context also specifically refers to the principle as a European principle of Article 174(2) EC. In this case the court also asked the ECJ to interpret the precautionary principle. Does it mean that a potentially harmful activity may be allowed only if it is established with certainty that there are no harmful consequences or is the threshold lower; there is no reasonable doubt that there are no harmful consequences.

The first interpretation was based on the Key Physical Planning Decision and the second was the view of the appellants. Case C-127/02[78] is still pending before the ECJ.

It should be noted that the Administrative Law Division case of 27th March 2002 is one of the few cases, besides two civil cases[79], where the precautionary principle is explicitly referred to as a European environmental principle.

2.2.5 Case law regarding the precautionary principle in the context of Articles 28-30 EC

The precautionary principle has also been explicitly referred to in the context of Articles 28-30 EC, in an appeal case by the Administrative Law Division of 26th February 2003.[80] In this case a permit, based on the Nature

---

[76] This is argued by J. Verschuuren in the footnote to ABRvS 20 March 2002, no. 200003711/1, *Nederlandse Aardolie Maatschappij B.V.* v. *State Secretary of Agriculture, Nature Management and Fisheries*, Tijdschrift voor Milieu & Recht 2002/7-8, 84.

[77] In ABRvS 20 March 2002, no. 200003711/1, note 75, regarding refused permits for drilling for gas at locations near the Wadden Sea, the court concluded that the authorities in reason could have taken the position that there exists reasonable doubt about the non occurrence of possible significant consequences for the eco system of the Wadden Sea. According to the court the authorities had not incorrectly interpreted the precautionary principle, as included in the PKB. Another example is ABRvS 26 April 2001, no E01.99.0192-197, note 69. The precautionary principle was decisive in these cases.

[78] Case C-127/02, in note 40.

[79] Rb. Den Haag 24 November 1999, no. 98/1396, *Stichting Waterpakt and others* v. *Staat der Nederlanden*, Tijdschrift voor Milieu & Recht 2000/3, 24 and Gh. Den Haag 21 October 1999, no. 98/144, in note 46 and mentioned hereafter.

[80] ABRvS 26 February, 2003, 200105644/1, appeal against decision of Rb. Middelburg of 9 October 2001 in the case between *Delisea B.V.* v. *State Secretary of Agriculture, Nature Management and Fisheries*, www.rechtspraak.nl, LJN AF5007.

Protection Act, was refused for planting oysters and mussels from Ireland in the Oosterschelde. According to the appellant, the Dutch legislation and the policy, used as the basis of the refusal, constituted a violation of Article 28 in conjunction with Article 30 EC. The State Secretary of Agriculture, Nature Management and Fisheries used the precautionary principle for the justification of a breach of Article 28 EC. The District court, at first instance, accepted this[81] and rejected the appeal. However, the Administrative Law Division reversed this judgment, stating that '[...] with the [...] very general formulated appeal to the precautionary principle the State Secretary had insufficiently taken into consideration [...] the [...] conditions under which such a justification could be accepted.'[82] In this case no research results were presented, no additional research was done and there had been no contact with the Irish authorities on possible risks of the import of mussels from the Irish Sea. According to the Administrative Law Division this very general foundation cannot serve as a justification for Article 30 EC. The Administrative Law Division concluded that the District court had failed to annul the appealed decision on the basis of violation of Article 3:2 and 3:46 Awb (the general duty of care and the justification principle) and finally annulled this decision.

2.2.6   Civil courts and the precautionary principle

Although parties sometimes try to raise the precautionary principle, civil courts, even more so than administrative courts, seem to be reluctant to apply it. This is evident from two civil cases where environmental groups tried to raise the precautionary principle as included in Article 174(2) EC.

In a wrongful act case of 21st October 1999[83], the court simply stated that 'in the light of the nature of these principles: fundamental principles to which

---

[81]   Rb. Middelburg 9 October 2001, no. Awb 00/469, *Delisea B.V. v. State Secretary of Agriculture, Nature Management and Fisheries*, www.rechtspraak.nl LJN AD9224. The Adm. Law Div. summarised the courts consideration as follows: 'The court concluded that the legislation was necessary and proportional in light of the uncertainties (*onduidelijkheden*) about the potential risks and the irreversible effects which could occur if there are harmful effects. Regarding the appeal of the State Secretary to the precautionary principle, the courts furthermore considered that he could in reason have taken the position that to prevent an irreversible situation relatively drastic measures were necessary during a certain period in anticipation of the development of knowledge.'

[82]   In Dutch: 'dat de staatssecretaris met het ... zeer algemeen geformuleerde beroep op het voorzorgsbeginsel onvoldoende rekening heeft gehouden met voornoemde voorwaarden waaronder een dergelijke rechtvaardigingsgrond aanvaard zou kunnen worden.'

[83]   Gh. Den Haag 21 October 1999, no. 98/144, note 46.

environmental law has to comply, the review of the civil court can only be very marginal.'[84] The court continued:

'According to the court of appeal, the Article 8:8, par 1, and 8:40 of the Act meet these principles. Because it furthermore [...] appears that the court of appeal does not find a violation of these provisions, it follows that there is also not a violation of these principles.'[85]

The review was even more limited in the civil case of 24th November 1999[86] regarding the Nitrate directive (91/676/EEC), where the District court dismissed the appeal of violation of the precautionary principle as mentioned in Article 174 EC because:

'the precautionary principle included in Article 130 R EC Treaty (now Article 174) is one of the objectives of the environmental policy of the European Communities and is not a norm directed at the member states'.[87]

It should be noted however that the precautionary principle does – implicitly – affect civil wrongful act cases ex Article 6:612 of the Dutch Civil Code. These are cases where the court requires parties, who create dangerous situations, to take preventive measures.[88]

2.2.7   The precautionary principle applied *ex officio?*

When the precautionary principles is not referred to explicitly, but seems to be applied implicitly under Articles 3:2 and 3:46 Awb, it may be argued that the court has applied it *ex officio*. This position is contrary to the cases where the precautionary principle is referred to explicitly. In many of the latter cases the parties seem to refer to the principles. One of the few exceptions might be the case of 27th March 2002[89], regarding Article 174(2) EC, where

---

[84] In Dutch: *'Gelet op de aard van deze beginselen: grondbeginselen waaraan milieuwetgeving dient te voldoen kan de toetsing door de burgerlijke rechter slechts zeer marginaal zijn.'*

[85] In Dutch: *'Naar het oordeel van het hof is met de artikelen 8:8 eerste lid en 8:40 van de Wet voldaan aan deze beginselen. Nu bovendien ... blijkt dat het hof geen strijd aanwezig acht met deze bepalingen volgt daaruit dat van strijd met deze beginselen evenmin sprake is.'* With the Act is referred to the EMA.

[86] Rb. Den Haag 24 November 1999, no. 98/1396, note 80.

[87] In Dutch: *'Het in Article 130R EG-verdrag (thans Article 174) opgenomen voorzorgsbeginsel houdt één van de doeleinden van het milieubeleid van de Europese Gemeenschappen in en is geen norm die zich richt tot de lid-staten.'*

[88] Note 7, page 76-77.

[89] ABRvS 27 March 2002, no. 200000690/1 en 200101670/1, note 39.

the Administrative Law Division seems to refer *ex officio* to this article and the principles therein.

2.3 Rectification at source (*het bronbeginsel*)

The European rectification at source principle is rarely referred to explicitly in Dutch case law. There have, however, been cases where the principle is implicitly referred to, within the context of the Dutch legislation and policies. This has occurred, when decisions were reviewed for compatibility with legal provisions[90], which are implicitly or indirectly based on the rectification at source principle.[91] An example[92] is the case of Administrative Law Division of 20th November 2002[93], regarding an (revision) EMA permit for an offal processing installation. An appellant did not agree with the prescribed emission limits. The court considered that the authorities (defendants)

'based the emission limits for the separate scent sources on the total expected scent emission of the establishment. The defendants had insufficiently researched each individual emission source if and the extent that these emission limits could be met.'[94]

Therefore the appealed decision was in violation of Article 3:2 Awb (the general duty of care) and the provisions in the permit regarding the emission limits for scent were annulled.

---

[90] Examples of these legal provisions can be found in the Air pollution act, the Aviation act, the Noise hindrance act, the WVO and the EMA.

[91] Note 7, page 122.

[92] Another example might be ABRvS 15 January 2003, no. 200200707/1, *X and others* v. *Burgomaster and Aldermen of Rucphen*, www.rechtspraak.nl LJN AF289, regarding a (revision) EMA permit based for a metal workshop working with explosives. The appeal was amongst other things directed against the reported distance, in the request for the permit, of 75 meters between the establishment and the nearest house. This distance was incorrect. According the authorities this was, if indeed true, irrelevant because the environmental burden on a house is set on the basis of the distance between the emission sources up to the house. The court concluded that it could not be deduced from the documents and the hearing that incorrect distances between the emission sources up to the houses were used when deciding on the permit request. The appeal failed.

[93] ABRvS 20 November 2002, no. 200101216/2, *X B.V.* v. *the Provincial Executive of Gelderland*, www.rechtspraak.nl LJN AF0802.

[94] In Dutch: *'bij het vaststellen van de emissiegrenswaarden voor de aparte geurbronnen zijn uitgegaan van de verwachte totale geuremissie vanwege de inrichting zoals die is weergegeven in de bij de aanvraag gevoegde geurrapporten. Verweerders hebben onvoldoende onderzocht of en in hoeverre per afzonderlijke emissiebron aan de hiervoor gestelde emissiegrenswaarde kan worden voldaan.'*

2.3.1 Case law regarding the rectification at source principle in the context of Article 174(2) EC

In the few cases the rectification at source principle has been referred to explicitly, it has been in the context of Article 174(2) EC.

An example can be found in a judgment of the Administrative Law Division regarding an appeal by Chemische Afvalstoffen Dusseldorp B.V. against decisions of the Ministry of Housing, Spatial Planning and the Environment, to object to the appellant's intention to export oil filters and other waste to Germany.[95] According to the appellant this objection was in violation of the free movement of goods. The court considered that the Long-term Plan on Removal of Dangerous Wastes constituted an export prohibition for lower quality or equal processing of waste in foreign countries and it appeared in this case to constitute a quantitative export restriction or a measure having equivalent effect. Following this consideration the court expressed:

'it is however not clear to the Division which meaning has to be attached in this context to the consideration 34 through 36 of [...] case C-2/90. In these considerations the Court indicates that when judging the question whether there is a discriminating trade barrier the special nature of waste has to be taken into account and that the aim included in Article 130R, par 2, EC-treaty, that the damages to the environment should by priority be rectified at the source is in conformity with the proximity and self-sufficiency principles in the Treaty of Basel of 22nd March 1989.'[96]

Unfortunately the court's uncertainty was not referred as a preliminary question and the ECJ did not consider it in its preliminary ruling upon C-203/96 (*Dusseldorp*) of 25th June 1998.[97] It also failed to reappear in the case of 28th January 1999,[98] where the procedure of 23rd April 1996 was continued.[99] It seems that

---

[95] ABRvS 23 April 1996, no. E03.95.0106, *Chemische Afvalstoffen Dusseldorp B.V. v. Minister of Housing, Spatial Planning and the Environment*, AB 1996/306.

[96] In Dutch: *'Het is de Afdeling evenwel niet duidelijk welke betekenis in dit verband moet worden gehecht aan r.o. 34 t/m 36 van ... zaak C-2/90. In deze overwegingen geeft het Hof aan dat bij de beoordeling van de vraag of er sprake is van een discriminerende handelsbelemmering rekening moet worden gehouden met de bijzondere aard van afvalstoffen en dat het in Article 130R tweede lid EG-Verdrag vervatte streven dat milieuaantastingen bij voorrang aan de bron moeten worden bestreden in overeenstemming is met de in het Verdrag van Basel van 22 maart 1989 neergelegde beginselen van zelfvoorziening en nabijheid.'*

[97] Case C-203/96 of 25 June 1998, *Chemische Afvalstoffen Dusseldorp and others v. Minister for Housing Town and Country Planning and Conservation*, AB 1998/340 and (1998) OJ C 278/5.

[98] ABRvS 28 January 1999, no. E03.95.0106-A, Chemische Afvalstoffen Dusseldorp and others v. Minister of Housing, Spatial Planning and the Environment, AB 1999/154.

[99] The Court concluded that the policy of the Minister was in violation of Article 34 EC and that the appeal decision was in violation of Regulation 259/93/EEC.

the court referred *ex officio* to the rectification at source principle in the case of 23rd April 1996.

In another case, it was not the Administrative Law Division, but the Minister of Housing, Spatial Planning and the Environment, who explicitly referred to the Source principle in the EC Treaty. In this case of 8th August 2000[100] the Minister had objected to the shipment of fly ash to Germany by NV Slibverwerking Noord-Brabant and others. According to the Minister this decision was not a breach of the free movement of goods and he had correctly applied the self-sufficiency principle. He relied on:

'Article 174(2) EC, which amongst other things stipulates that damages to the environment should by priority be rectified at the source, on the Treaty of Basel of 22nd March 1989 [...], which includes the principle of self sufficiency [...]'.

The Administrative Law Division mentioned the self-sufficiency principle, without referring even implicitly, to Article 174(2) EC. It merely posed preliminary questions regarding the principle of self-sufficiency in EEC Regulation 259/93 (on the transboundary movement of waste), without referring to the Rectification at source principle in Article 174(2) EC. Article 174(2), EC was not referred to in the Order of 27th February 2003 by the ECJ, regarding this Dutch case.[101]

No other cases were found where one of the parties or the court referred explicitly to the Source principle, in or outside the context of Article 174(2) EC.

2.3.2 Case law on the proximity and self-sufficiency principle within the scope of Regulation 259/93

There have been other administrative[102] and criminal[103] cases where the rectification at source principle is not mentioned, but merely the proximity and self-sufficiency principle within the scope of EEC Regulation 259/93. Although these principles are related to the rectification at source principle,

---

[100] ABRvS 8 August 2000, no. 199901635/2, *NV Slibverwerking Noord-Brabant and Glückauf Sondershausen Entwicklungs- und Sicherungsgesellschaft mbH* v. *Minister of Housing, Spatial Planning and the Environment*, AB 2000/414.

[101] Order of Joined cases C-307/00 to C-311/00 of 27 February 2003, *Oliehandel Koeweit B.V. and others* v. *Minister van Volkshuisvesting, Ruimtelijke Ordening en Milieubeheer*, [2003] ECR I-1821, which refers, in short, to Case C-6/00 of 27-02-2002, *Abfall Service AG (ASA)* v. *Bundesminister für Umwelt, Jugend und Familie* [2002] ECR I-1961. In the introduction of the case the ECJ only repeated the aforementioned argument of the Minister.

[102] Besides ABRvS 28 January 1999, no. E03.95.0106-A, note 97 and ABRvS 23 April 1996 no. E03.95.0106, note 94, other examples are ABRvS 24 December 1998 no. E03.96.1394, *Icova B.V.* v. *the Provincial Executive of North Holland*, AB 1999/153 and VzABRvS 31 March 1995, no. F03.94.1206, *Verol Recycling Limburg B.V. and others* v. *Minister of Environment*, AB 1996/25.

[103] HR 13 February 2001, no. 00800/99E, www.rechtspraak.nl LJN AB0076 (regarding a criminal case).

in view of the two cases mentioned above, these cases have not been reviewed further.

2.3.3   The rectification at source principle applied *ex officio?*

With the exception of the cases of 23rd April 1996 and possibly 27th March 2002, both regarding the principle in the context of Article 174(2), the courts appeared not to apply the principle *ex officio.*

2.4   The integration principle

With the exception of the following case, the integration principle is not explicitly[104] referred to in other environmental cases. A case in the District Court of Den Haag on 2nd May 2001 concerned a wrongful act action by environmental agencies, including Greenpeace, against the policy of the Dutch government concerning the extraction of gas.[105] According to the plaintiffs this policy violates the sustainability principle in the EC Treaty, including Article 6 EC. The court considered the plaintiff's argument in the context of the EC Treaty Articles 2, 6, 10 and 174(1) EC; 'The State pleaded that these provisions do not have direct effect, because they specify which goals should be pursued through European policy and therefore do not contain obligations for the individual Member States.' The court accepted the State's arguments and considered that; 'according to their text, the Articles[106] [...] and 174(1) of the EC Treaty are directed at the European Community and its organs; they do thus not contain statutory obligations for the State.'[107]

---

[104] There is case law on Article 21 of the Constitution, which is interpreted in literature as a call for external integration of environmental interests, which appears quite similar to that in Article 6 EC (Note 7, p. 118). The court appears to be very reluctant to derive obligations for the authorities from Article 21 of the Constitution and applies a limitative test. Example are ABRvS 27 March 2002, no. 20003011/2 and 200103587/1, *L.G. and others* v. *Burgomaster and Aldermen of Dordrecht*, www.rechtspraak.nl LJN AE0729 and BR 2002/509 and ABRvS 04 December 2002, no. 200201931/1, appeal against a decision of Rb. Dordrecht of 22 February 2002 in case between *X and others* v. *Burgomaster and Aldermen of Dordrecht*, www.rechtspraak.nl LJN AF1475.

[105] Rb. Den Haag 2 May 2001, no. 99/1493, *Nationale Jongerenraad voor Milieu en Ontwikkeling and Greenpeace Nederland* v. *Staat der Nederlanden*, www.rechtspraak.nl LJN AB1369 and Tijdschrift voor Milieu & Recht 2001/9, 83.

[106] This consideration also included the Articles 2 and 6 EC.

[107] In Dutch: *'Blijkens hun tekst richten de artikelen ... en 174, eerste lid, van het EG-verdrag zich op de Europese Gemeenschap en haar organen; zij houden derhalve geen wettelijke verplichtingen voor de Staat in.'* In contrast the court concluded that Article 10 EC is directed at the State, but because the plaintiffs had not intimated why the State was negligent in complying with its obligations based on Article 10 EC by pursuing its policy, this argument was left aside.

2.4.1 Article 21 of the Constitution, does it contain the integration principle?

In the introduction it is mentioned that some consider Article 21 of the Constitution to contain the integration principle, but this has not been confirmed in case law. Article 21 of the Constitution stipulates that 'the care of the government is aimed at the livability of the country and the protection and improvement of the living environment.'[108]Dutch courts have been very reluctant to derive obligations for the authorities from Article 21 of the Constitution and apply a limited test regarding this Article.[109] This seems to also be the case in the aforementioned case of 2nd May 2001, where the court concluded that the government has a wide discretionary power when carrying out its constitutional task on the basis of Article 21 of the Constitution

3 Similar principles that have emerged in the Netherlands

Several environmental principles have emerged in the Netherlands, including the alara principle; the standstill principle and the substitution principle. All of which, have similarities with the prevention principle.

3.1 The 'alara' ("as low as reasonably achievable") principle

The alara principle was derived from Article 6 of the Euratom Directive (80/836/Euratom). It has been codified, more restrictively in the Dutch EMA. Article 8.11(3) EMA, which stipulates that provisions should be attached to the EMA permit that provide the largest possible protection against environmental harmful consequences, unless this cannot reasonably

---

[108] In Dutch: *'De zorg van de overheid is gericht op de bewoonbaarheid van het land en de bescherming en verbetering van het leefmilieu.'*

[109] Examples are Rb. Almelo 6 December 1995, *Almelose Woningstichting "Beter Wonen"* v. *Municipality of Almelo*, NJ 1996/723, where the court considered that Article 21 of the Constitution 'does not directly create a duty of care for the municipal authorities' to ensure there is an acceptable ground water level in urban areas. 'But it does incite authorities to recognize the problem of the ground water level in urban areas … and subsequently to be able to consider adequate measures …' and ABRvS 27 March 2002, no. 200030II/2 and 200103587/I, note 105, which concerned the decision adapting the EMA permit for a food depot, where the court concluded that
'there exists extensive legislation regarding the object of care of the authorities in Article 21 of the Constitution. The Environmental Protection Act it part thereof. There were no special circumstances which would lead to the conclusion that the opposed decisions, in addition to the test against the Environmental Protection Act, qualify for direct assessment against Article 21 of the Constitution.'

be required. There is a lot of case law where the alara principle, as included in Article 8.11(3) EMA, is referred to.[110]

It has been argued that the alara principle is subordinate to the precautionary principle, because it is only applied if an adequate protection of the environment does mean that a permit should be refused.[111] When applied, the alara principle can have effect on the outcome of the case, directly or indirectly through Article 3:2 and 3:46[112] Awb (the general duty of care or the justification principle). Contrary to the administrative courts, the civil courts apply a very marginal test of the alara principle.[113]

3.2   The stand still principle

The stand still principle states that the environmental quality in any specific area may not worsen. Some authors do not perceive it as an autonomous principle, but as being related to other principles such as the prevention principle.[114] The stand still principle has been codified in Article 5.2, par 3, EMA and it is also included in subordinate legislation.

Most of the limited case law regarding this principle, has concerned the Dutch policy on water extraction[115], such as the Third Policy Document[116]. In

---

[110] The Administrative Law Division has in the past also referred to the principle directly in the context of Article 6 of Directive 80/836/Euratom, regarding a nuclear permit. The court concluded that review of the alara principle lacked and found the appealed decision in breach of the due care principle. At that time the principle was not yet part of the Dutch nuclear law. (Note 7, pages 81-82, which refers to AGRvS 17 March 1989, *R. Blom-de Ridder* v. *Minister of Housing, Spatial Planning and the Environment*, Tijdschrift voor Milieu & Recht 1989/12, 87.)

[111] Van den Biesen (1999) 83.

[112] VzABRvS 26 November 1999, no. 199901788/1, *Stichting Greenpeace Nederland and Burgomaster and Aldermen of Zijpe* v. *Minister of Housing, Spatial Planning and the Environment*, Tijdschrift voor Milieu & Recht 2000/2, 25K. It is worth noting that in this case, similar to the case of ABRvS 25 August 2000, no. E03.99.0202-0204, note 46, the foundation of the permit application was abandoned, but the case had a different outcome.

[113] Gh. Den Haag 21 September 1999, no. 98/1414, *Stichting Zuidhollandse Milieufederatie and Stichting Natuur en Milieu* v. *the State of the Netherlands*, Tijdschrift voor Milieu & Recht 2000/1, 2.

[114] Note 7, page 95.

[115] For example ABRvS 11 December 1995, no. E03.95.0372, *J.H.M. Hermanussen and E.J.M. Hermanussen-Thijssen* v. *the Provincial Executive*, AB 1996/138; ABRvS 3 September 1998, no. E03.95.1756, *H.H. van den Nieuwenaar* v. *the Provincial Executive of Noord-Brabant*, Tijdschrift voor Milieu & Recht 1999/7-8, 67 and ABRvS 29 September 1998, no. E03.97.1308, *Burgomaster and Aldermen of Landerd* v. *the Provincial Executive of Noord-Brabant*, AB 1998/414.

[116] The Stand still principle, as mentioned in the Third Policy Document, stipulates that emissions of black listed substances, calculated over a particular controlled area may not increase.

the majority of cases, the court has failed to touch upon the interpretation of the stand still principle itself. [117]

3.3   The substitution principle

The substitution principle, also known as the alternatives principle, is particularly relevant to pesticides.[118] It means that if less environmentally damaging substances or methods are available, these should be used. There is little case law regarding this principle. The Trade and Industry Appeal Tribunal (CBB) once recognised it, but this case was decided prior to the amendment of the Pesticides Act in 1993.[119] In that year, the principle was added to the admission requirement of the Pesticides Act, but was removed before it could be invoked, because Directive 91/414/EEC did not leave room for this criterion.[120] The President of the CBB concluded in 1999, that in the current Dutch legal system there is no room for an alternatives test.[121] There has not yet been a full court decision on this matter.[122]

---

[117] Exceptions are ABRvS 24 February 2000, no. E03.97.1261, *E. Brouwer and J. Borst v. Chairman and Members of the Higher Water Board of Rijnland*, Tijdschrift voor Milieu & Recht 2000/10, 108, regarding a permit based on the Pollution of Surface Waters Act of 1997.

[118] Alternatives also appear to play a small role in the recovery of clean up costs of soil pollution by the State ex Article 75, par 6 b under 1, of the Soil Protection Act (HR 20 April 2001, no. C99/173, *Akzo Nobel Chemicals B.V. v. the State of the Netherlands*, www.rechtspraak.nl, LJN AB 1202) as well as in the former Key Physical Planning Decision on Schiphol and surroundings, that included the aim to substitute part of the aviation traffic into rail traffic. (TK 2000-2001, 27 603, no. 6, page 98)

[119] CBB 6 December 1994, no. 93/0076/060/029, *Hoechst Schering Agro Nederland B.V. and B.V. Chemische Pharmaceutische Industrie Luxan v. Minister of Agriculture, Nature Management and Fisheries*, not published. According to the CBB the availability of alternatives attributed to the 'non acceptability' element in the criteria in the Pesticides Act. It should be noted that the current Pesticides Act includes a comparable element ('unacceptable effect'). However it has not been recognised by the court as having the same meaning.

[120] Cf. E.M. Vogelezang-Stoute, Bestrijdingsmiddelenrecht (2004) at chapter 11.2.

[121] Pres. CBB 5 November 1999, no. AWB 99/755, *International Paint (Nederland) B.V. and others v. Minister of Housing, Spatial Planning and the Environment*, Tijdschrift voor Milieu & Recht 2000/2, no. 24K. This conclusion is however based on information provided by E.M. Vogelezang-Stoute.

[122] Environmental groups have argued that the alternative test should be applied – either because Directive 91/414/EEC leaves room for it or on the basis of Article 3:2 Awb – but the CBB has not yet gone into this argument (CBB 29 January 1999, no. E03.95.1446, *ARCO Chemie Nederland Ltd v. Minister of Housing, Spatial Planning and the Environment*, AB 1998/111 respectively Pres. CBB 11 December 1998, no. AWB 98/1021, *Stichting Natuur en Milieu v. State Secretary of Health, Welfare and Sports*, KG 1999/94).

4 Conclusions

With the exception of the polluter pays principle, the Administrative Law Division handles most cases in which the environmental principles arise. There are only a few civil cases in which the principles arise and even fewer environmental criminal cases. This could be due to the fact that in most cases where the principles are referred to, the principles are incorporated in policies (and rarely in legislation), which, at least for civil and criminal courts, seems to restrict these principles to a very marginal testing.

With the exception of the precautionary principle, the other three 'European' environmental principles are seldom referred to explicitly. Where the majority of these principles, including the precautionary principle, are applied, it is mostly implicitly, as part of policy, via Article 3:2 Awb and sometimes Article 3:46 Awb (the general duty of care the justification principle). In only a very few cases are the European environmental principles in the context of Article 174(2) EC directly mentioned, and in no cases have they been applied in this context. The same position applies with the principles on the basis of international law.

In most of the cases where a principle is referred to explicitly, the parties (especially the appellants) refer to the principles. The few exceptions to this are the cases of 23rd April 1996, regarding the rectification at source principle, and possibly of 27th March 2002[123], regarding several environmental principles, both in the context of Article 174(2) EC. There the Administrative Law Division seems to refer *ex officio* to the principles Article 174(2) EC. When the precautionary principle was not referred to explicitly, but seems to be applied implicitly via Article 3:2 or 3:46 Awb, it may be argued that the court applied it *ex officio*. In none of the cases, have the courts rejected an appeal to a principle because an environmental group raised them. Similarly, it is rare that an appeal was dismissed prior to the intrinsic evaluation of the case. In these rare cases the objections entailing the principles had not been made prior to the appeal before the administrative courts, as a result whereof the principles played no role at the intrinsic evaluation of the cases.[124]

It can be concluded that, independent of the principles being explicitly or implicitly referred to in the cases, they can, in principle, have effect on the actual outcomes of the decisions of the court. The rate to which this occurs differs per principle, for example seldom for the polluter pays principle compared to the precautionary principle. The courts have not accepted that Article 6 EC has any

---

[123] ABRvS 27 March 2002, no. 200000690/1 en 200101670/1, note 39.

[124] An example is ABRvS 30 June 2000, no. E03.96.0477, *Vereniging tegen windturbines op Texel and Werkgroep Landschapszorg Texel* v. *Burgomaster and Aldermen of Texel*, www.rechtspraak.nl LJN AA6979, regarding an appeal against an EMA permit for windmills. There the appellants had not made the objection to the draft decision that the precautionary principle had wrongly not been applied. It is not clear from this case whether the basis of the precautionary principle was, Article 174(2) EC or national law.

potential effect at all. Non-observance of the principles can, in principle, lead to annulment of the appealed decisions. However, in most instances this will not be the case because of a violation of the principle itself, but because of a violation of Article 3:2 Awb (the general duty of care) or sometimes Article 3:46 Awb (the justification principle).

CHAPTER 10

The Application and Interpretation of the Core Environmental Principles by the Portuguese Courts

Alexandra Aragão

1 Introduction

Several references to the precautionary principle, the prevention principle, the integration principle and the polluter pays-principle can be
found in the main environmental case law of the Portuguese courts.[1] These have
been raised since the 1990's, mainly in disputes concerning locally unwanted
land uses and in the criminal prosecution of illegal activities. This chapter will
consider eleven cases ranging from administrative decisions regarding the
citing of noxious facilities (a landfill, an incinerator, a petrol pump), infrastructure construction (a bridge), the depletion of natural resources and pollution
emissions to water and soil.

2 Legal context

Although the core environmental principles do not appear as
such, in national constitutional provisions, they do appear in the framework
environmental legislation. The Portuguese Constitution provides it is a basic
responsibility of the State 'to protect nature and the environment, to preserve
natural resources and to ensure the proper planning of the national territory'
(Article 9 of the Portuguese Constitution), but the only principle expressly
mentioned in the sole environmental norm in the constitution is the 'principle
of solidarity between generations' (Article 66 on 'environment and quality of
life'[2]).

---

[1] The search was limited to official databases, covering all the superior Courts jurisprudence. Two
    internet sites were used: 'www.diramb.gov.pt', contains legislation (national, European, international
    and foreign) as well as jurisprudence and doctrine in the field of the environment. It is an official site
    supported by three public entities: *Direcção-Geral do Ambiente, Direcção-Geral dos Serviços de Informáti-
    cado Ministérioda Justiça and Centro de Estudos Judiciários.* 'www.dgsi.pt', contains Court decisions
    from the Supreme Court of Justice (40199 documents), the Constitucional Court (6107 documents),
    the Supreme Administrative Court (57351 documents), Second Instance Court of Oporto (34161 docu-
    ments), Second Instance Court of Lisboa (28381 documents), Second Instance Court of Coimbra (2293
    documents), Second Instance Court of Guimarães (179 documents) and the Central Administrative
    Court (3799 documents). It is an official site supported by a public Institute dependent upon the Minis-
    try of Justice: *Instituto das Tecnologias de Informação na Justiça.*

[2] Article 66 reads as follows:
    '1. Everyone has the right to a healthy and ecologically balanced human environment and the duty to
    defend it.
    2. In order to guarantee the right to such an environment, within the context of sustainable develop-
    ment, it is the duty of the State, acting through appropriate bodies and with the involvement and
    participation of the citizens:
    a. To prevent and control pollution, and its effects, and harmful forms of erosion;

As regards framework environmental legislation, the *Basis Environmental Law*[3], establishes the basis of environmental policy in Portugal (Article 1) and contains a catalogue of environmental principles. The eight 'specific principles' applicable to the protection of the environment are: the prevention principle, the equilibrium principle, the participation principle, the unity of management and action principle, the international cooperation principle, the search for a more adequate level of action principle, the recovery principle and the liability principle (Article 3).

The wording of the legislation provides how these principles are to be interpreted:

· The prevention principle: 'the actions having immediate or long term effects should be considered in an anticipatory way, reducing or eliminating the causes rather than correcting the effects of those actions, or activities likely to disturb the environmental quality, the polluter being obliged to correct or recover the environmental damage and bearing the resultant costs, and not being allowed to proceed with the polluting action'.

· The equilibrium principle: 'the adequate means must be created to assure the integration of nature conservation policies and social and economic growth policies, with the aim of an integrated, harmonic and sustainable development'.

· The participation principle: 'the different social groups must intervene in the definition and execution of the environmental and territorial planning policy, through the competent administrative [...] bodies'.

· The unity of management and action principle: 'a national body must be created with the responsibility for environmental and planning policies.[4] This body should engage the activities of public and private agents as a way of warranting the integration of environment, territorial and

---

b. To organise and promote national planning with the objectives of establishing proper locations for activities and a balance between economic and social development, while enhancing the landscape;

c. To establish and develop nature reserves and parks and recreation areas, and classify and protect the countryside in order to guarantee nature conservation and the preservation of cultural assets of historic or artistic interest;

d. To promote the rational use of natural resources, while safeguarding their capacity for renewal and ecological stability, respecting the principle of solidarity between generations;

e. To promote, in conjunction with the local authorities, the environmental quality of populated areas and urban life, specifically with regard to architecture and the protection of historical zones;

f. To promote the inclusion of environmental objectives in the various sectors of policy;

g. To promote environmental education and respect for environmental values;

h. To ensure that tax policy achieves compatibility between development and protection of the environment and quality of life'.

[3] Law n. 11/87, of the 7th April 1987.

[4] The Ministry of the Environment and Natural Resources was first created in 1990.

economic planning at the global and sectoral levels [...]'.
- The international cooperation principle: 'the problems of the environment and management of natural resources determines the search for solutions harmonised with other countries or international organisations'.
- The search for a more adequate level of action principle: 'implies that in the execution of environmental policies, consideration must be given to the most adequate level of action, be it international, national, local or sector level'.
- The recovery principle: 'urgent measures must be taken in order to reduce environmentally degrading processes in areas where they occur and promote the recovery of those areas, bearing in mind the equilibrium to be established with the surrounding area'.
- The liability principle: 'suggests that the polluters should assume the direct or indirect consequences of their actions over the natural resources, incurred by third parties.'

This law, which is still in force, was the first framework environmental law in Portugal; however, the national doctrine considers it as vague, inaccurate and even contradictory in certain parts. Above all, it reflects an old-fashioned perspective of environmental protection (in many ways more remedial than preventive) and contains principles of doubtful content and utility. However, this isn't the only law to include environmental principles. I will next consider some examples of laws containing the *classic* principles as well some less consensual principles.

The first example of laws containing these 'classic' principles is the National Water Plan[5]. This law distinguishes quite a few principles, organised in four categories: environmental principles, social principles, economic and financial principles and other general principles. The environmental principles include the precaution and prevention principles, a best technology principle and an integrated approach principle. This last principle means that policy makers have to draw up policy measures fixing both emission values and quality objectives, fixing quality and quantity objectives to surface as well as to underground waters. In addition to the environmental principles, the National Water Plan also highlights some social principles: the sustainability principle, the intergenerational solidarity principle and the national cohesion principle. The recognition of water as an economic good, efficient water use, the user-pays and the polluter pays principle are considered to be principles of economic and financial nature. Finally, the participation and the liability principles are the last and general principles listed.

---

[5]   Decree-law n. 112/2002, of the 17th April 2002.

A further example are the ten principles of the National Strategy for Nature and Biodiversity Conservation[6]: These principles include; the principle of the high level of protection, principle of sustainable use of biological resources, the precaution principle, the prevention principle, the recovery principle, the liability principle, the integration principle, the subsidiarity principle, the participation principle and the international cooperation principle. The National Strategy for Sustainable Development comprises (yet without defining) the sustainable development principle, the precaution principle, the prevention principle, the polluter pays principle, the user-pays principle, the diversity principle and the producer responsibility principle.

Further principles can be found in more specific environmental legislation, several other examples could be mentioned.[7] Aside from this, there is no additional Government official guidance on the interpretation of any of these principles.

3   The Portuguese cases

In five national court cases, one single principle alone was referred to. In the other six cases two or more principles were referred together. After a brief description of each case and some final remarks on the application of the principles by the Portuguese courts, table 1 outlines and synthesizes each case's main features.

---

[6]   Approved by the Council of Ministers Resolution n. 152/2001 of the 11th October.

[7]   Such as the law on integrated prevention and pollution control (Decree-law n. 194/2000, of the 21st August 2002), for instance, which mentions the precaution and prevention principles in regard to the best available techniques.

		(alone)				Prevention	
Precaution	Case					**Landfill-II**	
	Court					2 A	
	Year					2001	
	Dispute					Lulu	
Prevention	Case	**Mining**	**Dairy**	**Incinerator**	**Petrol**		
	Court	1 J	1 J	3 A	3 J		
	Year	1999	1994	1995	1996		
	Dispute	Water	Water	Lulu	Lulu		
Polluter-pays	Case	**Dyers**		**Storks**		**Landfill-I**	**Scrap**
	Court	1 J		1 J		3 J	2 J
	Year	1996		1990		1998	2001
	Dispute	Water		Nature		Lulu	Soil
Integration	Case					**Swallows**	**Bridge**
	Court					3 J	3 A
	Year					2000	1999
	Dispute					Nature	Lulu

Cases: Mining, Dairy, Incineration, Dyers, Storks, Landfill-I, Landfill-II, Scrap, Swallow, Bridge, Petrol.

Court: Judicial (J) Administrative (A) ; 1st instance (1), 2nd instance (2), Supreme (3).

Disputes: *Lulus*, illegalities (water, nature, soil).

Pro environmental decision	Decision against the environment

3.1   Illegal activities and the prevention principle: *Comital Mining* case[8] and *Azeméis Dairy* case[9]

In the Comital mining case, the prevention principle was relied upon in order to impose a fine on an illegal effluent emission. The plaintiff was *Companhia Mineira de Talco – COMITAL*, a mining company whose main activity is talc extraction in the centre of Portugal. The defendant was *Direcção Regional do Ambiente*, a decentralised organ of the Ministry of the Environment namely responsible for environmental inspection activities. In 1996, the *Direcção Regional do Ambiente* imposed a fine on the mining company for the illegal emission of wastewaters. As a consequence, *COMITAL* appealed to the Judicial Court of First Instance in Soure arguing that the responsibility should be imposed on the Municipality of Soure; who had planned and promised to build a wastewater management system for the whole of the industrial area of Soure, but this hadn't been constructed. On the basis of the law regulating

---

[8]   *Comital mining case* – Judicial Court of First Instance in Soure, 14th June 1999, process 1/97 *Companhia Mineira de Talco-COMITAL* v. *Direcção Regional do Ambiente*. Nature of decision: pro environmental.

[9]   *Azeméis dairy case* – Judicial Court of First Instance in Oliveira de Azeméis, 11th March 1994, process 18/93, *Lactícinios de Azeméis* v. *Direcção Geral de Ambiente*. Nature of decision: pro environmental.

industrial activities the Court recognized the company's liability for discharging wastewaters without previous treatment and without a permit and so, the Court maintained the imposed fine.

In the reasoning of the judgment, only the prevention principle was repeatedly mentioned: 'the plaintiff had the legal obligation to confine the materials in order to avoid interaction with the environment, even if these were the result of adverse weather conditions. The effects of weather conditions were predictable and could not have been ignored by the plaintiff, since it was not the first time that this happened [...]. Under the Portuguese law on industrial activities Decree-law n. 109/91 of the 15th March, and Decree-law n. 282/93 de 17th August [...] there is a general duty to prevent risks – the industrial manager should develop his activities according to the regulations applicable and should adopt preventive measures in order to eliminate or reduce the risks likely to affect people or goods, the working conditions or the environment [...]. Whenever he detects any irregularity in the functioning of the establishment, the industrial manager should take the necessary measures to correct the situation and, if necessary, suspend labour. This norm has to be understood in light of Article 26 of the environmental framework law which prohibits, in national territory, the emission, deposit or introduction in the water, soil, subsoil or atmosphere of any effluents, radioactive wastes or any other waste containing substances or micro-organisms likely to alter the characteristics or to render unsuitable for its uses those environmental components, thus contributing to environmental degradation'.[10]

The second case concerned, *Lacticínios de Azeméis* a dairy company in Oliveira de Azeméis who used to discharge untreated wastewater into a nearby river. They had a provisional six- month license that had already expired. They

---

[10] All translations are the author's responsibility. In the original version: '*Sobre a arguida recaía então a obrigação de confinar os materiais de molde a evitar as interacções com o ambiente, ainda que estas resultem das condições meteorológicas, mas cujos efeitos são previsíveis e, no caso em apreço, não podiam deixar de ser conhecidos da arguida uma vez que não era a primeira vez que tal sucedia. A este propósito o Dec. Lei n.° 109/91 de 15/3, com as alterações introduzidas pelo Dec. Lei n.° 282/93 de 17/8, introduz normas disciplinadoras do exercício da actividade industrial, [...] estabelece ainda um dever geral de prevenção de riscos – O industrial deve exercer a sua actividade de acordo com a regulamentação aplicável e adoptar medidas de prevenção no sentido de eliminar ou reduzir os riscos susceptíveis de afectar as pessoas e bens, as condições de trabalho e o ambiente [...] Sempre que detecte alguma anomalia no funcionamento do estabelecimento, o industrial deve tomar as medidas adequadas para corrigir a situação e, se necessário, proceder à suspensão da laboração. O preceito em análise deve ser compreendido à luz do art.° 26.° da Lei de Bases, nos termos do qual, em território nacional ou área sob jurisdição portuguesa é proibido lançar, depositar ou, por qualquer outra forma, introduzir nas águas, no solo, no subsolo ou na atmosfera efluentes, resíduos radioactivos e outros que contenham substâncias ou microorganismos que possam alterar as suas características ou tornar impróprios para as suas aplicações aqueles componentes ambientais e contribuam para a degradação do ambiente.*'

were obliged to install a wastewater treatment system, but the time limit for the construction had also expired.

In 1992, following an environmental inspection, *Direcção Geral do Ambiente* imposed a fine on *Lacticínios de Azeméis*. Reaffirming the point that preventative measures are needed in environmental matters, the Judicial Court of First Instance in Oliveira de Azeméis considered them guilty and issued the fine.

3.2 Locally unwanted land uses and the prevention principle: *Estarreja Incinerator* case[11] and *Maia Petrol Pump* case[12]

The prevention principle was also argued by a national environmental non- governmental organization, *Quercus*, to support its position on the Estarreja incinerator case. *Quercus* did not accept the Government's decision regarding the siting of an industrial waste incinerator in Estarreja, a small town in the north of Portugal. In 1995, *Quercus* brought an action against the Minister for Industry and Energy and the Minister for the Environment, who ratified the opinion of the environmental impact assessment Commission on the siting of the incinerator. Recognising the prevention principle as 'a fundamental and structural principle in this area', the Supreme Administrative Court relied on the conclusions of the environmental impact assessment (considered an indispensable tool to the application of the principle). In short, the Court concluded that damage to the environment was not likely to happen, after considering both the environmental impact assessment performed and the contents of the Council of Ministers Resolution, according to which the project would never proceed if the environmental requirements were not met.

In the *Maia Petrol Pump* case, Idetex, a firm that imports and distributes fuels, had obtained public authorisation to install a petrol pump in the vicinity of an elementary school at Maia. The parents association of children attending the public school decided to dispute this decision. The decision of the Court was as follows: 'Although the activity is licensed according to administrative law, the Common (civil) Court is competent to decide on the suspension of the activity based on the existence of an environmental danger. [...] Environmental law has constitutional force [...] [and] is preventive, by nature'. 'This field of law [environmental law] [...] has gained an ever increasing importance and its principles must influence juridical interpretation and, more than that, have to influence the application of the law, considering the unity of the legal order [...]. With due

---

[11] *Estarreja incinerator* – Supreme Administrative Court, 7th December 1995, process 38436/A/95 *Quercus e outros* v. *Ministro de Indústria e Energia e Ministra do Ambiente*. Nature of decision: against the environment.

[12] *Maia Petrol Pump* – Supreme Judicial Court, 2nd July 1996, process 483/96, *Associação de pais e encarregados de educação da Escola Primária da Maia* v. *Importação e Distribuição de combustíveis-Idetex*. Nature of decision: pro environmental.

respect it is obvious that a lack of harmony exists between the defendant and the environmental law [...] if we ignored the preventive character of environmental law (besides the identical character of the interim preventive measures) it would be allowing a situation where the public get ill first and protest later!'[13]

In summary, the Supreme Court considered they were competent to decide their claim by applying the Constitution (Article 66°), the European Community Treaty (Article 130R) the environmental framework law, the Civil Code and other pieces of legislation on facility siting. In terms of principles it relied on the prevention principle and on some other unnamed environmental principles.

3.3 The polluter pays principle: *Minderica Dyers*[14] and *Coruche Stork Nests* case[15]

The illegal emission of wastewaters was also the activity that leads the Ministry of the Environment to impose a penalty on the dyers factory *Tinturaria Minderica*, in 1995. In deciding the case, the Judicial Court of First Instance in Alcanena, recognised that *Minderica Dyers* were working illegally without an emission permit. The polluter pays principle was cited as the legal justification for the tax payment related to the emission of wastewaters.

A different approach was taken in the *Coruche Stork Nests* case.[16] In this case the plaintiff was the *Ministério Público*, the public prosecutor representing the State and the defendants were the landowners of a farm located in Coruche. The owners of a farm, called *Quinta Grande*, possessed three umbrella-pine trees, in which there were twenty-seven stork nests, containing in total 23 eggs. They were informed by the national environmental non-governmental organization,

---

[13] In the original language: *'Ainda que se trate de situação licenciada administrativamente, o Tribunal comum (cível) é materialmente competente para considerar e decidir pedido cautelar de suspensão de actividade base-ado em perigo ambiental; (...)a problemática do Direito de ambiente tem, hoje, foros de Direito constitucional [e] por natureza, preventivo;*

Este é um ramo do Direito [o Direito do Ambiente] (...) que tem vindo, nos últimos tempos, a adquirir uma importância cada vez maior e cujos princípios não podem deixar de influenciar a hermenêutica jurídica e, mais do que isso, a aplicação do Direito, na unidade da ordem jurídica (...).

E, salvo o devido respeito, é patente a dessintonização entre a problemática do Direito de ambiente e o pensamento da requerida, (...) fazendo tábua rasa do carácter preventivo do direito de ambiente, (para além de idêntico sentido genérico dos processos cautelares) como parecendo admitir que, neste âmbito, deveria acontecer algo do género adoeça primeiro e proteste depois!'

[14] *Minderica Dyers* – Judicial Court of First Instance in Alcanena, 15th November 1996, process 133/96 *Tinturaria Minderica* v. *Ministry of the Environment*. Nature of decision: pro environmental.

[15] *Coruche stork nests* – Judicial Court of First Instance in Coruche, 23rd February 1990, process 278/89 Ministério Público v. landowners. Nature of decision: pro environmental.

[16] *Ministério Público* v. *Landowners*, process: 278/89. Judgment 23/2/1990.

Quercus, that those storks were a legally protected species, according to national
and international law and further information was posted on placards on the
trunks of the trees. In spite of this, the pine-trees were sold and cut down by
timber-merchants, destroying both the nests and the eggs. The placards had
been ripped off the trees. The public prosecutor charged the landowners with
breach of a nature conservation law and asked for civil compensation. The landowners pleaded not guilty and blamed the timber-merchants for the offence.

The polluter pays principle was mentioned alongside applicable legislation, as the framework to judge the violation, to assess liability and the penalty
proportion. As grounds for repairing the damage, the Judicial Court of First
Instance in Coruche considered the polluter pays principle to mean 'charging
the costs of fighting and preventing pollution on the polluter' as well as 'the
effective responsibility of the polluter for the damages he causes [...]'[17]. Developing this last interpretation, the judge went even further and explained that
'damage compensation, according to the general liability principles and also
according with the principles in force in environmental law ("polluter-pays")
imposes, in the first place, the reconstitution of the situation that would have
existed if the fact that gave origin to the damage hadn't occurred [...].'[18]

In conclusion, the offenders were sentenced to 87 days imprisonment
(replaced by a 130.000$00 fine or 650 Euros, approximately) and ordered to pay
civil compensation of 30.000$00 plus VAT (more or less 150 Euros). This fine
was the corresponding price of the construction of alternative artificial pedestals
for the nests.

3.4 The polluter-pays and prevention principles: *first Póvoa de Lanhoso landfill* case[19]

In June 1997, the Court of First Instance in Póvoa de Lanhoso,
denied the request of the *Associação de Defesa do Ambiente – Terras de Lanhoso
(ADA-TL)*, a local environmental non governmental organization, to declare
the siting of a new sanitary landfill in Póvoa de Lanhoso as inappropriate. The
Court of Second Instance, in October 1997, agreed when deciding the appeal.
However, the Supreme Court of Justice seemed to be more sensitive to the

---

[17] In Portuguese: '(...) o "poluidor-pagador" *(traduzido, em sentido amplo, na imputação ao poluidor das
despesas inerentes ao combate e prevenção da poluição e ainda na efectiva responsabilidade do poluidor pelos
danos ecológicos a que der causa).'*

[18] *'A reparação dos danos, de acordo com os princípios gerais em matéria de responsabilidade civil e de acordo
também com os princípios que vigoram no Direito do Ambiente, (o "poluidor-pagador") impõe, em primeira
linha, a reconstituição da situação que existiria se não tivesse ocorrido o facto que originou o dano'.*

[19] *First Póvoa de Lanhoso landfill* – Supreme Court of Justice, 23rd September 1998, process 200/98 Associação de Defesa do Ambiente- Terras de Lanhoso (ADA-TL) v. BRAval. Nature of decision: pro environmental.

arguments of the plaintiff and declared the site as unsuitable for a municipal [solid] waste landfill. Based on Article 66 of the Portuguese Constitution, under several rues of framework law on the environment and in the environmental impact assessment law of 1990, the Supreme Court referred to, in its decision, five fundamental principles: prevention principle, polluter pays principle, participation principle, restoration principle and principle liability principle. Although the Court did not expressly establish the relationship, the identification and description of the principles was supposed to prove the existence of a 'grounded fear of damage'.[20] This 'grounded fear of damage' is recognised by the law and allows for the suspension of authorised activities, recognised as being in the public interest.

In the *Povoa* case, the burden of proving that there was a high probability of environmental degradation caused by the construction and functioning of the landfill was upon the non-governmental organization. The courts of first and second instance have declared the importance of key points, such as the avoidance of dangerous wastes, the urgent need to solve a serious environmental problem and the provision of security systems assuring risk acceptability. Contrary to the aforementioned decisions, the Supreme Court stated that the two-year gap between the commercial guarantee of the liners used to render the landfill impermeable (ten years) and the period foreseen for the functioning of the landfill (twelve years lifetime) was relevant. In conclusion, it decided there was a reasonably 'grounded fear of damage', declared the site inappropriate and suspended construction activity.

3.5 The principles of precaution and prevention: *Second Póvoa de Lanhoso Landfill* case[21]

The Póvoa de Lanhoso case also involved interim decisions. In 1998, following a request by the plaintiff non-governmental organization, a Court of first instance decided, in a provisional measure, to suspend any waste disposal activity developed by *BRAval.*, (the concessionary of the Portuguese State in the construction and exploitation of the municipal solid wastes management system in some northern municipalities). Furthermore, the Court decided to prohibit the resumption of the construction activities as well. The Supreme Courts confirmed these decisions.

BRAval requested the replacement of the provisional measure with the payment of a financial bond, a measure usually permitted under the Portuguese Civil Process Code. BRAval claimed that the construction and functioning of the

---

[20] *'Fundado receio de lesão,'* in portuguese.

[21] *Second Póvoa de Lanhoso Landfill* – Judicial Court of Second Instance in Oporto, 12th June 2001, process 422/00, *Associação de Defesa do Ambiente – Terras de Lanhoso (ADA-TL)* v. *BRAval*. Nature of decision: pro environmental.

sanitary landfill would not pose any danger to the environment and that consideration should be given to the fact that it was a holder of civil responsibility insurance of up to 100.000.000$00 (approximately 500.000 Euros). Confirming the views of the plaintiff, the reasoning of the judge can be considered almost revolutionary, in the global context of Portuguese jurisprudence:

'we have to learn from our mistakes and not get used to accepting the consequences. It's not time to cry over spilt milk, it's better to be safe than to be sorry.[22] It's urgent to correct the causes and not regret the effects because time is running and it's often too late for the environment [the judge goes on explaining the ozone layer hole problem as an effect of human activities in detail] [...] the principles of prevention as well as of precaution are fundamental principles in the domain of environmental law, meaning that confronted with the imminence of a human activity which will undoubtedly cause damage to the environment, in a serious and irreversible way, such intervention is necessary. [...]

The second principle [...] 'means that the benefit of the doubt must be used in favour of the environment, whenever there is uncertainty, lack of obvious scientific proof on the cause-effect relation between an activity and a certain form of pollution or of environmental degradation'. One promotes on one side: the anticipation of preventive action although there is no certainty on its need; and on the other side, the prohibition of potentially damaging activities, even if it is not scientifically certain.

On the other hand it has, from the procedural point of view, an important formulation, which is the inversion of the burden of proof. [...]

This principle has the effect of preferring an anticipatory protection, aiming at preventing the ecological damage before its occurrence.

The duty to prevent environmental degradation is at the basis of all international regulation, even if this principle is not very often explicitly mentioned.

The European Community has major influence on this matter: the main reason for the importance of prevention is that, most times, the damage caused to the environment cannot be repaired, but only compensated and, on the other side, though reconstituting a degraded environment is physically possible, its costs can be prohibitive and it is a very long term process.

The principle of precaution has to be understood as resulting from a qualified interpretation of the prevention principle (the most environmental friendly interpretation) [...] imposing a serious balancing of the environmental interest before other economic interests, considering Article 174(2) of the European Community Treaty, of which Portugal is a Member State. [...]

The response of the Court to the question raised, is that for precautionary reasons, the decision of the lower court was upheld, therefore upholding the values inherent in the protection of the environment, the inadequacies of the provisions for restoration of potential damage, considering the amounts at stake in the financial bond, consider-

---

[22] The expression used in portuguese is closer to the french *mieux veux prévenir que guérrir.*

ing that this is neither adequate nor sufficient to the prevention of the damage or to its full compensation [...]'.[23]

3.6 The principles of prevention and polluter-pays: *Cerveira Scrap-ground* case[24]

In the village of Cerveira, the owner of a scrap-yard allowed the disposal of scrap materials at his 2400 m² site, in return for payment. After losing his case in the Court of first instance, the owner of the Cerveira scrap-yard appealed to the second instance Court. The public prosecutor asked the

---

[23] *'É preciso que se aprenda com os erros e não habituarmo-nos à resignação das consequências. É tempo de, como se diz no adágio popular "não se chorar sobre o leite derramado" ou "mais vale prevenir que reme-diar". Urge corrigir as causas e não lamentar os efeitos porque o tempo está a escoar-se e pode ser tarde, [...] o princípio da prevenção é um dado adquirido no domínio do direito do ambiente bem como o princípio da precaução traduzindo-se o primeiro em, perante a iminência de uma actuação humana, a qual comprovada-mente lesará de forma grave e irreversível, bens ambientais, tal intervenção deve ser travada sendo o segundo, [...] "ele significa que o ambiente deve ter a seu favor o benefício da dúvida, quando haja incerteza, por falta de provas científicas evidentes, sobre o nexo causal entre uma actividade e um determinado fenómeno de poluição ou degradação ambiente". Incentiva-se, por um lado, a antecipação da acção preventiva, ainda que se não tenham certezas sobre a sua necessidade e por outro lado, a proibição de actuações potencialmente lesivas, mesmo que essa potencialidade não seja cientificamente indubitável. Tem por outro lado sob o ponto de vista processual uma importante concretização que é a inversão do ónus da prova.*

Resulta deste princípio a preferência por uma tutela antecipativa, visando prevenir o dano ecológico antes do seu aparecimento. O dever de prevenir a degradação do ambiente está na base de toda a regulamentação inter-nacional, sem que este princípio seja muitas vezes explicitado. Emana da CEE uma formulação que constitui autoridade na matéria: A principal razão da importância atribuída à prevenção é que, as mais das vezes, os danos causados ao ambiente não podem ser reparados, mas tão-somente indemnizados e, por outro lado, ainda que a reconstituição do ambiente degradado seja fisicamente possível, os seus custos podem ser proibitivos, além de constituir um processo a realizar a muito longo prazo.

O princípio da precaução deverá ser entendido como decorrente de uma interpretação qualificada do princípio da prevenção (a interpretação mais amiga do ambiente) [...], obrigando a uma ponderação agravada do interesse ambiental em face de outros interesses económicos nomeadamente e face ao disposto no artigo 174° n° 2 do Tratado da Comunidade Europeia de que Portugal é Estado membro.

Assim e perante a questão suscitada, a resposta deste Tribunal é indubitavelmente no sentido, por precaução, da confirmação da decisão proferida com sobreposição dos valores inerentes à defesa do ambiente direito essencialmente de natureza não patrimonial e de difícil reparação senão mesmo de todo impossível relativa-mente aos montantes patrimoniais em causa inerentes à prestação de caução uma vez que esta não se afigura adequada e muito menos suficiente para prevenir a lesão ou repará-la integralmente em substituição daqueles outros e que pudessem colmatá-los (...).'

[24] *Cerveira scrap-ground* – Judicial Court of Second Instance in Oporto, 8th February 2001, process 132-A/ 00, *Ministério Público* v. *Scrap industry in Vila Nova de Cerveira*. Nature of decision: pro environmental.

Judicial Court of Second Instance in Oporto, to prevent the owner scrap-yard
from proceeding with his polluting activities.

The judges considered that environmental degradation would be highly
likely and, on the basis of the prevention and the polluter pays principles, they
granted interim protection to the site, maintaining the previous judicial decisions. The decision was as follows: 'The above mentioned specific principle of
prevention establishes that actuations likely to have immediate or long term
effects in the environment should be considered in advance, reducing or eliminating the causes rather than correcting the effects of those actions or of those
activities likely to alter the quality of the environment; the polluter is obliged
to correct or restore the environment, bearing the consequent charges and not
being allowed to proceed with the polluting activity'.[25]

3.7   The principles of prevention and integration: *Nisa Swallow Nests case*[26] and *New Bridge* case[27]

Following the destruction of 400 swallow nests in a cleaning
operation at a Courthouse in Nisa, the national environmental non-governmental organization, *'Fundo para a Protecção dos Animais Selvagens' – (FAPAS)*,
brought an action against the State for breach of nature conservation law. They
sought interim measures, for the failure of the State to permit swallow nesting
and that devices intended to prevent the swallows (*Delichon Urbica*) from nesting in the walls of the Nisa Courthouse should be removed.

The Supreme Judicial Court recognised the plaintiff's arguments and
concluded that the requirements for authorising the removal of all devices were
present in this case; there was a 'grounded fear of damage' (for the swallows
still couldn't nest where they used to) and there was proportionality between the
prejudice caused by the interim measure and the damage that is to be avoided.
In the wording of its decision, the Court referred to a number of environmental
principles, as well as quoting a well-established national doctrine[28],

---

[25]   In Portuguese: *'Pelo referido princípio específico da* prevenção, *se estabelece que as actuações com efeitos
imediatos ou a prazo, no ambiente, devem ser consideradas de forma antecipativa, reduzindo ou eliminando
as suas causas prioritariamente à correcção dos efeitos dessas acções ou actividades susceptíveis de alterarem a
qualidade do ambiente, sendo o poluidor obrigado a corrigir ou recuperar o ambiente, suportando os encargos
daí resultantes, não lhe sendo permitido continuar a acção poluente'.*

[26]   *Nisa swallow nests* – Supreme Judicial Court, 27th June 2000, process 413/00, *Fundo para a Protecção
dos Animais Selvagens – FAPAS* v. *Portuguese State.* Nature of decision: pro environmental.

[27]   *New bridge* – Supreme Administrative Court, 14th October 1999, process 31535/99, *Liga para a Protecção
da Natureza-LPN* v. *Conselho de Ministros.* Nature of decision: against the environment.

[28]   Quoting Gomes Canotilho and Vital Moreira, in their anotation to the Portuguese Constitution, Coimbra Editora, 3rd edition, page 348.

'[...] a) the prevention principle, according to which the actions on the environment should, above all avoid the creation of pollution and nuisance at the source and
not fight the effects afterwards, since it's better to prevent environmental degradation
than to remedy it subsequently; b) the principle of collective participation, in other
words, the need of the different social groups interested in intervening in the formulation and execution of the environmental policy; c) the cooperation principle, point-
ing at the search for solutions in cooperation with other countries and international
organisations; d) the equilibrium principle which expresses the creation of adequate
means to assure the integration of the economic and social growth policies on the one
hand and environmental protection on the other [...]'[29]

The prevention principle is implicit in the judgment as far as the interim decision was intended to have the effect of safeguarding the utility and practical
effects of the final judgment on the substance of the dispute. The integration
principle, also named by the doctrine, as the 'equilibrium principle' is present
in the reasoning on the conflicts of rights and the balancing of interests. In the
wording of the Court:

'The Portuguese State can not approve the right to the environment in its Constitution, cannot defend an environmental policy, can not subscribe to international
treaties that are binding to it, can not make laws and decrees for the protection of
savage life and afterwards deny all this with its concrete behaviour. [...] The right to
the environment implies the State rendering certain services [to the community] [...]
[there are] means to harmonise the life of savage birds with the well being of man. [...]
The search of this technical means to avoid or minimise potential conflicts or colli-
sions of rights, is a task of the State, in view of the mentioned constitutional principles'.[30]

---

[29] In the original language: 'São princípios fundamentais de tal política: a) princípio da prevenção, segundo
o qual as acções incidentes sobre o meio ambiente devem evitar sobretudo a criação de poluições e pertur-
bações na origem e não apenas combater posteriormente os seus efeitos, sendo melhor prevenir a degradação
ambiental do que remediá-la à posteriori; b) o princípio da participação colectiva, ou seja, a necessidade de
os diferentes grupos sociais interessados intervirem na formulação e execução da política do ambiente: c) o
princípio da cooperação que aponta para a procura de soluções concertadas com outros países e organizações
internacionais; d) o princípio do equilíbrio que se traduz na criação de meios adequados a assegurar a inte-
gração das políticas de crescimento económico e social e de protecção da natureza – Profs. Gomes Canotilho e
Vital Moreira – "Constituição da República Portuguesa Anotada" 3ª edição, pág. 348'.

[30] In the exact wording of the Court: 'O Estado Português não pode consagrar constitucionalmente o direito ao
ambiente, defender uma política de ambiente, subscrever tratados internacionais que o vinculam, elaborar Leis
e Decretos-Lei de defesa da vida selvagem e depois com a sua actuação concreta negar tudo isso. [...] O direito
ao ambiente implica para o Estado a obrigação de determinadas prestações [...] [existem] meios adequados
para harmonizar a vida das aves selvagens com o bem estar dos homens. Essa procura de meios técnicos
capazes de minorar ou evitar eventuais conflitos ou colisões de direitos é, em primeiro lugar, tarefa do Estado,
face aos princípios constitucionais enunciados'.

In a further case, known as the New bridge case, the prevention and integration
principles supported the positions of the plaintiff, the national environmental
non-governmental organization *Liga para a Protecção da Natureza-LPN*. The *LPN*
disagreed, on environmental grounds, with the 1992 decision of the Council of
Ministers, which approved the siting of a new Bridge over theRiver Tagus, in
Lisbon and started proceedings against the Government. The Supreme Administrative Court, however, refused to suspend the Council of Ministers Resolution
considering that 'although one cannot forget the preventive concerns that prevail
in all environmental law, one cannot get to the point of rendering impracticable
each and every procedure and obstruct each and every undertaking whatever its
nature is.'[31] The Court believed that both the characteristics of the bridge and
the techniques to be used in its construction could still influence the environmental impacts of the bridge in such terms so as to determine its environmental
acceptability in spite of the lack of siting alternatives.

4   Final remarks on the national application of the principles

The prevention principle is, without question, the principle that
is used more often in the national courts. However, the other principles pose
more specific questions in the Portuguese legal context.

4.1   The precaution principle

A huge obstacle to the application of the precautionary principle is the concept of 'grounded fear of damage'. The existence of a 'grounded
fear of damage' is a legal requirement that has to be fulfilled in order to allow
the suspension of any potentially damaging activity, namely those activities that
are likely to damage the environment. In fact, the courts can order, as interim
preventive measures, immediate suspension of either public or private activities, although, in the later case this must be supported by an administrative
authorization. However, they can only do that if there is a 'grounded fear of
damage' to a legally protected interest or to a right, whose value is superior to
the public interest that is behind the public initiative or behind the authorised
activity. Furthermore, the burden of proof always rests on the person requesting
the suspension of the act, in other words, on the person who seeks to protect the
environment.

---

[31]   In Portuguese: '*Não se esquece a preocupação preventiva que domina todo o direito do ambiente, mas o que se
não pode é ir ao ponto de inviabilizar todo e qualquer procedimento e impedir toda e qualquer obra, seja qual
for a sua natureza.*'

4.2   The polluter pays principle

In Portuguese courts, the polluter pays principle is given a very wide interpretation. First, the underlying concept of pollution covers any damage to the environment. Second, the damaging activity is not only a pollution *strictu sensu*, but may also include any damage caused to particular species. Noticeable is the fact that, in the courts, the polluter pays principle is applied not only to justify the application of taxes, fines, or even to suspend polluting activities, but also to quantify the amount of damages to be paid in compensation. In the Coruche storks case, the polluter pays principle was at the core of the judges' reasoning when deciding the amount of indemnity. In this case, the amount the 'polluter' was fined, was not equivalent to the value of the measures necessary to remedy the damage, but the cost of the measures that had been necessary (if they had been taken in the right time) to prevent the damage. In practice, the consequence was a rather low payment although to this payment a criminal charge (fine) was added. Even if the Supreme Court of Justice didn't provide extensive justification for its decision, a similar reasoning underlies the first *Póvoa de Lanhoso Landfill* case.

4.3   The integration principle

There are three main interpretations of the integration principle in Portuguese case law; (i)the integration principle is the main basis for the State's special responsibility for the protection of the environment (*Nisa Swallow Nests* case); (ii) the integration principle is the justification for placing economic agents under an obligation to find the technical means to make environment and economic development compatible (*New Bridge* case); (iii) the integration principle is a solution for the balancing of conflicting interests (both cases).

5   Conclusion

Analysis of the main environmental jurisprudence in Portuguese courts reveals that, full application of environmental principles in the Portuguese courts is still in its infancy.

Environmental principles are seldom mentioned in the Court decisions, even when they are referred to in a case, the principles are not the main justification in reaching that decision. On the whole, we can say that the case solutions are exclusively grounded on legal norms. The principles are merely used to strengthen the reasoning.

This is the reason why the courts state the principles, but they don't really submit them to a detailed judicial interpretation.

Of all the environmental principles laid down in Portuguese legislation,
not many references are found in Court decisions, which tend to be based on
legal norms rather than on principles. Generally speaking, the principles are
used more as secondary sources for the decisions. And in most of the cases,
the courts handle them as freestanding principles. As a result of their status in
national legislation, they are not invoked by relying on the Treaty. In only one
case (*Póvoa de Lanhoso Landfill*, in the Court of Second Instance of Oporto) a
reference to the EC Treaty was made with regard to the prevention principle.

CHAPTER II

The Application of the Core EC Environmental
Principles by Spanish Courts

Angel-Manuel Moreno

1   Methodological remarks

EC Environmental principles are likely to play a little role in
the daily operation and reasoning of Spanish Courts. Several structural features
of the Spanish legal system must be summarily introduced here in order to
explain this belief.

On the one hand, the Spanish legal tradition is one of continental, 'roman'
law. Judge-made law and judicial precedents (*Jurisprudencia*, in Spanish) are
recognised by the Spanish Civil Code to also be a legal source, the law of the
land. However, the process by which they become binding is much more
complex and cumbersome than in a Common Law country. Judicial doctrines
are considered to be a 'complementary' or ancillary legal source and they are
subordinate to any form of written law. Far from being regarded as law-creators,
judges and courts are seeing as specialized, independent civil servants, who
limit themselves to applying the written law and to solving interpretative problems in a specific statute or administrative regulation. Normally, that institutional profile of judges, determines dramatically the decision-making process of
judges and courts. In general, a Spanish judge or court will be reluctant to use
a 'principle' as the exclusive or main ground for its reasoning, in isolation from
the relevant statute or regulation.

These general principles of law (*principios generales del Derecho*) are also
considered to be the law of the land in Spain, but several features have to be
taken into account: (a) they must be enshrined in a written norm, or formulated
by the case-law of the courts; (b) those principles usually respond to either classical legal aphorisms, going back to roman, private law (for instance: *ubi emolu-
mentum, ibi onus*) or are recognised in the Constitution; (c) legal principles lack
an essential or decisive importance, for they are regularly used by courts *obiter
dicta*, or as an additional support for judicial reasoning or statutory construction,
in order to affirm or uphold a given interpretation of the controlling statute, or to
accept or reject a legal claim. These general assumptions are perfectly applicable
to environmental law.

It may be suggested that, the 'principles' recognised by Articles 6 and 174
of the EC Treaty, may be considered authentic *principios generales del Derecho*,
under Spanish legal terminology. In our understanding, this is not the case, for
they are 'policy guidelines' addressed to policy-makers and law-creators.

Finally, EC Treaty principles are generally little known or little used as
grounds for legal arguments. The overall performance of Spanish courts, in
knowledge and application of EC Law, has been largely unsatisfactory for several
years.[1] In the field of EC-national law, Articles 6 and 174 of the EC Treaty are

---

[1]   For instance, the Spanish Constitutional Court has consistently refused to apply EC Law as a valid
ground for for ajudicating internal 'constitutional' disputes. What is more, the Spanish Supreme Court,
had, until the nineties, applied incorrectly a basic EC principle, such as the principle of 'direct effect'.
On this issue, see in general, A.M.Moreno, 'La Ejecución Administrativa del Derecho Comunitario'.
Régimen Europeo y Español (Madrid 1998).

primarily designed to bind the normative activity of the European Union. EC Treaty principles (Articles 6 and 174 EC) risk not being considered *'the law of the land'*, in the sense that they are mainly addressed to the Union's institutions (which, in strictly legal terms, is not a totally erroneous perception).

Consequently, the question of how Spanish courts apply the core EC environmental principles is not usually a subject for research, nor does it raise too much doctrinal attention.

Apart from that structural situation, ascertaining the actual role of EC environmental principles in Spanish courts' adjudication, raises other operational obstacles. First, it is almost impossible to 'research' accurately all the court' decisions, taking into consideration the high number of cases and judicial bodies. Contrary to Common-Law jurisdictions, the Spanish system of courts is very complex, for it comprises five different jurisdictional tracks, which are competent to adjudicate given litigation on the grounds of its subject-matter; civil and commercial courts, criminal, administrative, labour and military. All these jurisdictional tracks have at least three different territorial layers or instances. The jurisdictional track, which is more likely to apply environmental principles, is the administrative court. Civil and (to a minor extent) Criminal courts may also play some role in this field. The constitutional court may eventually be confronted with such principles.

Besides these 'ordinary' courts, there is also the 'constitutional' jurisdiction (constitutional court), which is separate from the regular track and is concentrated in one 'central' constitutional court. The number of judicial decisions is enormous; the Supreme Court alone handles more than 12.000 cases every year. On top of that, judicial decisions (except some presided over by the criminal courts) do not receive great publicity, nor are they a prominent subject for study in law schools. The cases decided by the lower courts are not always reported in full.

In the light of the aforementioned aspects, this paper represents the result of personal research, which has been conducted via the usual paper reports and electronic databases. This method, however, may prove to be insufficient sometimes, since search engines and report indexes are based on the main statutory provisions and concepts. There is also a risk that some decisions may be missed entirely.

2 EC environmental principles applied in jurisdictional 'environmental' adjudication

In spite of my previous remarks, it is possible to find a certain amount of judicial references to EC environmental principles.

2.1   The polluter pays principle (*el que contamina, paga*)

References to this principle are relatively frequent in court decisions. In general, rather that referring to it as an 'EC' principle, the courts make vague and imprecise references to it. The use of the *polluter pays* principle may likely be fostered by the fact that it is now considered enshrined in the Spanish Constitution. Article 45 establishes that environmental statutes may impose on law-breakers the duty to restore the impairment of the environment, as well as the obligation of paying for the actual damages caused: *'Para quienes violen lo dispuesto en el apartado anterior...se establecerán sanciones penales o, en su caso, administrativas, así como la obligación de reparar el daño causado'*. Although the wording of this constitutional provision is clearly reminiscent of the polluter pays principle, we should dispose of any direct link or influence of EC Law on the Constitution, since it was promulgated in 1978 and Spain only became a member of the Communities in 1986. It is, however, a happy coincidence, which reinforces the binding legal effect of the principle. Consequently, the courts may be citing the principle, without referring to the EC Treaty, but grounding it either on the controlling statute, or on the Constitution itself.

Another example of implicit reference to this principle may be found in the context of civil litigation for property damages. Here the courts may be more inclined to cite this principle as incorporated into the Spanish law of civil damages (civil code, section 1902 *et seq*.) or deriving from classical Roman law aphorisms, than in EC Law itself. As a rule, this principle is never used alone as a conclusive argument to settle a dispute, but as an additional force supporting the court's understanding of the case, or for assisting the final choice between two possible ways of interpreting a statute or a regulation.

I shall now consider examples of this principle in practice, derived both from the constitutional and the ordinary jurisdiction:

1) Constitutional case law

A good example of the role of the *polluter pays* principle in constitutional adjudication is the judgment of 30th November 2000.[2] In this case, the central government challenged a regional statute from the Parliament of Baleares, which established an environmental tax, on the grounds that the Region lacked constitutional powers to enact such legislation (under the Spanish Constitution, tax matters are reserved for the central parliament). It is noteworthy to say that the case does not concern a genuine 'environmental' adjudication, but a 'constitutional' issue, involving the allocation of powers between the state (central authorities) and the regions. However, the constitutional court made an explicit reference to the 'polluter pays' principle (in the fifth section of the judgment) as additional support for its final conclusion that the statute was unconstitutional.

---

[2]   Spanish Constitutional Court number 289/2000, of 30th November 2000. The text of the judgment (in Spanish) can be accessed at the Court's website: <http://www.tribunalconstitucional.es>.

According to the court, for a tax to be a genuine 'environmental' one, it should encourage 'environmentally friendly' behaviour, or discourage activities that are harmful to the environment; the 'polluter' should pay. However, when a tax is mainly designed as a 'flat' tax, when it is only used as a means to collect money for the general public budget and the person who is subject to it cannot avoid it, even if she follows an environmentally friendly behaviour, then the tax loses its 'environmental' spirit.

This was precisely the case in respect to the Balearic tax, since it was levied solely on companies that were running polluting activities, regardless of their actual 'environmental' impact or amount of pollution. In this case, the polluter was not confronted with the choice to pollute more or less, or to change its behaviour in an environmental way, but rather with the dilemma of running its installations or closing them. In that situation, the polluter pays principle would disappear and would be replaced by 'the owner pays' principle. In the text of the precedent, it has to be noted that the Constitutional Court does not refer to the polluter pays principle as an 'EC environmental principle', but just as a broad, vague 'principle'.

Of course, the case can not be fully understood outside of the technicalities of Spanish tax law, but at least it shows how the polluter pays principle may prove to be an important factor when it comes to the creation of 'genuine' environmental taxes. In order to be compatible with the principle, an environmental tax or charge has to fulfil at least two conditions. Firstly, the money collected out of this tax cannot be transferred or placed into the general public budget. Instead, it has to be dedicated to the specific purpose of restoring the environmental impact or damage that was a result of the taxed activity. It is supposed to be a sum of money "put aside" and dedicated to an exclusive and specific, environmental purpose. That is, the tax must be *'finalista'* (a Spanish word that can be translated by 'finalistic'). Secondly, the tax cannot be designed as a flat, universal one. Instead, it must leave some room for the polluter to modify its behaviour for the benefit of the environment. For instance, the polluter should be entitled to rate reductions or benefits if they reduce their pollution and should be penalized with a higher tax if pollution levels increase.

2) Administrative courts

Regular administrative courts may see the polluter pays principle raised in the context of litigation involving environmental taxes and charges.

One of the most important environmental charges in Spain is the one levied on water discharges (*canon de vertido*). The current Waters Act of 2001 regulates the charge. Taxes and charges on water discharges are collected by the River District Authorities (*Confederaciones hidrográficas*) and the money collected is supposed to be used by those Agencies to restore and improve the quality or rivers and lakes. When a corporation challenges the validity or extent of a given charge, it can sue the agency before the administrative courts. In that context, several administrative courts have applied the polluter pays principle in order to shed additional light on the legal dilemma, for the purpose of upholding or reversing the agency decision. Lawsuits must be first filed before the Administrative Chamber of the Regional High Courts (*Sala de lo contencioso-administrativo del Tribunal Superior de Justicia*). If the court upholds the agency decision, there is then the possibility to go to appeal before the Administrative Chamber of the Supreme Court (*Sala de lo contencioso-administrativo del Tribunal Supremo*). The case discussed below details an example of that litigation scheme.

2.a.) *Regional High Courts administrative litigation*

In the judgment of April 3rd 2002,[3] a corporation challenged the legality of a discharge tax, issued by the *Confederación hidrográfica del Guadalquivir* (The River Basin Management Authority of the Guadalquivir River). The plaintiff claimed that the tax resolution was invalid, because the agency had not determined the actual amount of pollution, or the actual volume of polluted waters, that had been discharged by the corporation. The court accepted that contention.

In a more than noticeable *obiter dictum*, the court included an extensive elaboration on the *polluter pays* principle, which was explicitly described as 'an EC principle' (*un principio comunitario*). What is more, the court referred to both (old) Articles 130R.2 and 130R.4 of the EC Treaty and to the Council Recommendation 75/436. On the other hand, the court saw a clear connection between this EC principle and the Spanish system of water discharges tax, for the national scheme was a way of implementing that principle. The court also found a connection between that 'community principle' and Article 45 of the Spanish constitution of 1978.

Another example is the judgment of October 11th 2001.[4] In this case, the facts were similar and the claim was disposed of in the same way. In this decision, however, there is mention of the polluter pays principle, although it is not presented explicitly as an 'EC principle'. It is presented as a rule or guideline (*regla*) with a connection to International Law ('*....técnicas, marcadas en el derecho internacional, recogidas en una pluralidad de principios, ... y en la regla de que quien contamina paga*').

In its decision of November 13th 1998[5], the court characterizes the polluter pays principle as stemming from the European policy on the protection of water, an essential and scarce resource (*el principio de que 'quien contamina paga', según se desprende de la política comunitaria de protección de un bien escaso e imprescindible como el agua*), while in the judgment issued on April 3rd 2002, the court states that the taxes levied on water discharges are based upon the 'community'

---

[3]   Regional High Court of Andalucia, administrative chamber, April 3rd 2002.

[4]   Regional High Court of Andalucia, administrative chamber, October 11th 2001.

[5]   Regional High Court of Andalucia, administrative chamber, November 13th 1998.

principle of polluter pays *(basándose tal canon en el principio comunitario de 'quien contamina paga')*. However, in other decisions from the same court, there is limited mention of the *polluter pays* principle, with no further elaboration: see, in this sense, the decisions of November 29th 2000, September 20th 2000 and March 5th 1999.[6]

Other territorial jurisdictions do apply the principle too. The judgment of July 15th 2002,[7] concerns a case, which is similar to the one, handled by the Constitutional Court on the Balearic Islands Tax, mentioned earlier. The present case involved another tax, established by a Regional statute of Galicia. The taxed corporation challenged the validity of the tax, claiming that the statute was unconstitutional, in the light of the abovementioned Constitutional Court decision. However, the High Court of Galicia rejected that claim and confirmed that the statute was constitutional. The court distinguished this case from the 'Balearic' one, for the Galician tax had a different set of features, which were in line with the Constitutional court requirements for those taxes (see, *supra*).

This case is relevant here because, the decision declares openly that the polluter pays principle is to be found in Article 45 of the Spanish Constitution. In addition, the Galician tax scheme is supported or legitimated by EC law and specifically by (former) Article 130R.2, as well as by the Council Recommendation 75/436 *(hay soporte constitucional, y aún conviene recordar el soporte de Derecho Comunitario, en concreto el art. 130R.2 del Tratado, así como la recomendación del Consejo 75/436 ...)*. The judge also mentions the 'rectification at source' principle.

The polluter pays principle is sometimes invoked with respect to taxes and fees charged by local or regional governments for the discharge of public services. The judgment of January 13th 2003[8] constitutes a good example of this. In Spain, the depuration of residual wastewater is a public service, which is the exclusive responsibility of local governments. Typically, the city council provides the service, but in turn it is entitled to charge its citizens a fee or tax *(tasa por prestación de servicio público)*. Spanish Tax and Local Government Law strictly regulates this city council entitlement. An essential requirement for the validity of any such a fee or charge, is that the total amount of money collected that scheme can not be higher than the actual cost of providing the service, there must be a balance. In other words, the actual fee or charge has to be calculated so that the city council does not make 'extra money' under the pretext that it is providing a municipal service.

In this case, a group challenged the validity of a local ordinance to commence charging in the town of Tarancón (province of Cuenca, in central

---

[6]   Regional High Court of Andalucia, adminstrative chamber, decisions of November 29th 2000, September 20th 2000 and March 5th 1999.

[7]   Regional High Court of Galicia, administrative chamber, July 15th 2002.

[8]   Regional High Court of Castilla-La Mancha, administrative chamber, January 13th 2003.

Spain). The fee had to be paid by the citizens, in return for the service of the depuration of residual wastewater. The plaintiffs claimed that the actual amount was too high and the total amount of money collected was greater than the real cost of the service. The court accepted that contention and struck down the local ordinance. The judge held in his decision, among other grounds, that this situation was tantamount to a breach of the 'Community polluter pays principle' (*se vulneraría el principio de justicia material [...] así como el principio comunitario de 'quien contamina, paga'*).

In this litigation context, we find another consequence of the principle; when it comes to financing public services, the polluter pays principle grounds the duty of the citizen to pay fees or charges to the body or agency providing the service, but not a single cent more than what is strictly necessary.

2.b) Supreme Court administrative litigation

In the past, many of the Supreme Court decisions have made reference to the polluter pays principle. As mentioned before, that mention usually takes place when the court has to adjudicate an appeal (*recurso de casación*) introduced against the judgment of a Regional High Court.

The Supreme Court decisions of February 2nd 2001, as well as the one of November 29th 2001[9], both have a similar background; an industrial corporation had allegedly discharged residual, polluted waters into a river. Furthermore, the discharge had produced some damages to the aquatic environment. Under the Spanish statute on Water management, the competent River Basin Management Authority (*Confederación hidrográfica*) has the power to unilaterally declare, that such damage exists. Once the facts are determined according to the appropriate administrative procedure, the Authority has the statutory power to both impose (in an executive way) a monetary penalty on the corporation and to order it to pay for the environmental damages actually produced.

In the case of February 2nd 2001, the River Basin Authority had ordered the plaintiff corporation to pay for the environmental damages caused by the discharge. The corporation challenged the Agency's decision because, in its view, the administrative body had failed to undertake sufficient fact-finding activities and had failed to produce evidence to demonstrate the actual volume of the discharge and damage resulting from it. The Supreme Court struck down the agency decision for that reason. It justified its reasoning by saying that it was not amounting to a denial of the polluter pays principle; it may deploy its effects only when the administrative agency has appropriately shown the facts, the causal link with the damages and the actual monetary value of those damages (*'no se niega la aplicación al caso de autos del principio "quien contamina paga", que inspira el régimen de protección medioambiental en materia de aguas [...] en el caso de autos no se llegaron a demostrar [...] la entidad de los vertidos [...] ni su traduc-*

---

[9] Judgments of the Supreme Court, administrative chamber.

ción económica'). Again in this case, there is a brief mention of the polluter pays principle, but without a specific reference to EC law or to any other legal basis whatsoever.

The Supreme Court decision of November 29th 2001, considered an appeal based on similar facts. In this case, a beer factory released several discharges of polluted water into the Júcar River (Autonomous Region of Valencia). The River Basin Authority opened an administrative inquiry in order to determine the legal responsibilities of the firm. As a result, the Agency ordered the firm to pay an amount of money, equivalent to the environmental damage produced by the discharges However, the agency failed to provide enough technical evidence to prove the exact quantities, characteristics and risks of the discharge. Accordingly, the Supreme Court reversed the Agency decision. In the words of the court, the lack of factual and documentary support, which had arisen in this case, rendered inoperative the polluter pays principle (*la falta de suficientes elementos de juicio aboca a la inoperatividad real del principio 'quien contamina, paga' como en este caso ocurrió*).

In conclusion, the case law may be summarised as follows; the polluter pays principle is an important support for accepting and exercising the power of sanctioning, on the side of Administrative Agencies. However, the principle cannot work as the sole support for those sanctions, since they must be supported by a conclusive evidentiary basis.

2.c) Criminal law litigation

Since 1995, the Spanish criminal code has included 'environmental crime' (*delito ecológico*). A criminal court may sentence a person guilty of causing serious environmental damage to a term of imprisonment. When the offence is committed by a corporation, the general manager, or the person in charge, is imprisoned. However, the firm may still be held liable for the damages actually caused, whenever the sentenced person cannot pay for them (*responsabilidad civil subsidiaria*). This secondary, monetary obligation of the firm is usually seen as a result of or practical implementation of the polluter pays principle. See, for example, the judgment of the criminal court of first instance of Zaragoza, of January 14th 2003.

2.2 The principle of prevention/precaution (*principio de cautela y acción preventiva*)

In recent years, the principle of precaution/prevention has been repeatedly invoked before the Spanish administrative courts (in a relatively open manner) in litigation involving the construction, installation and operation of telephone aerials and antennas. This issue has triggered considerable public debate and there has been a strong reaction on behalf of citizens groups and some local bodies, when confronted with the interests of telecommunications operators.

Usually, the litigation involves the following steps; (a) the telephone company applies for a municipal permit to build or install an infrastructure for telephone waves (aerials, antennas, etc). This structure is to be built on the roof of a private building (apartments building, industries), on the company's own premises, or on public spaces; (b) the city council refuses to grant such a permit, on the grounds that there is no scientific certainty of the risks posed by those types of structures for the locale, or because insufficient studies have been carried out; (c) in other cases, the process is controlled by a municipal ordinance, which prevents construction, or imposes strong restrictions on those infrastructures, there may be a two-year time limit on the permit, or a minimum distance required between the equipment and residential areas; (d) the company appeals the administrative decision before the competent court, either claiming that the administrative decision is ultra vires or that the municipal ordinance is illegal, on the ground that it is too stringent or disproportionate.

In most of these cases, the risks posed by the aerials are usually in question, both during the administrative process and litigation. The claims and counter-claims usually trigger a more or less implicit reference to the precautionary/preventive action principle. In order to provide some examples, the following court decisions may be cited:

1) Supreme court decision of June 18th 2001;[10]
2) Regional High Courts decisions:
   i) Decision of February 8th 2001;[11].
   ii) Decision of April 9th 2002 and decision of February 28th 2002;[12]
   iii) Decision of March 17th 2003.[13]

The most important features of this litigation can be summed up as follows:
   a) There is always a relatively clear claim, that aerials and antennas might be dangerous and this fact should have weight in the administrative agency's decision;
   b) Courts usually understand that local councils cannot impose an absolute ban on those infrastructures;

---

[10] Judgment of the Supreme Court, administrative chamber, June 18th 2001, *Telefónica* v. *City Council of Barcelona*.

[11] Regional High Court of Castilla y León, adminisatrative chamber, February 8th 2001, *Telefónica* v. *City Council of Santa Marta de Tormes*. This judicial decision has already been analysed by commentators, from the perspective of the precautionary principle. See. A. Fortes. 'Licencia de instalación de una torre para soporte de antenas de telefonía móvil: la aplicación del principio de precaución ante los riesgos para el medio ambiente y la salud y seguridad de las personas', in the environmental review: *Gestión Ambiental*, December 2001, pp. 74-78.

[12] Regional High Court of Madrid, administrative chamber, April 9th 2002, *Retevisión* v. *City Council of Manzanares el Real* and February 28th 2002, *Telefónica* v. *City Council of Chinchón*.

[13] Regional High Court of Valencia, administrative chamber, March 17th 2003, *Telefónica* v. *City Council of Albaterra*.

c) In some cases, the court upholds the refusal of the permit by the local council, because the company has not produced conclusive evidence that the planned infrastructure is completely safe for any surrounding neighbours. A perfect example of this doctrine is the decision of February 8th 2001,[14] which was decided prior to the promulgation of the national regulation on telecommunications mentioned below. At that time, there was no national legislation regulating the general precautions in the matter. In that context, the court found that there were serious suspicions that this activity could be dangerous for the public at large and that the city council had the discretion to impose on the company the duty to produce detailed evidence that the infrastructure was not dangerous. The decision is also important because the Courts refused to control agency discretion in the assessment of the evidence produced by the applicant;

d) However, the courts do sometimes find that the restrictions and limitations imposed on companies by city councils are too stringent. Unfortunately, that conclusion is rarely backed by any further conceptual or dogmatic elaboration;

e) The whole legal framework of this litigation was, however, dramatically altered in 2001, when the central government approved a new regulatory scheme on this issue; Royal Decree of September 28th, 2001. Currently, most courts find that the legal questions raised by these health hazards, have since been reduced by this piece of national legislation. Consequently, any further restriction or limitation imposed unilaterally on telecommunications companies by city councils (for instance, minimum distances) will be found unlawful by the courts, if they are not in accordance with that national legislation. In exceptional cases, a local council can impose such conditions, provided that the body produced conclusive arguments, based on the specific circumstances of a given town. With the new regulation, telecommunication operators must be granted the permits, as long as they comply with that piece of legislation. It seems that the burden of evidence has been shifted to administrative agencies, if they decide to impose more stringent standards (a side effect of the BATNEEC principle?).

It is noteworthy to mention that litigants and courts do not usually refer openly to the precautionary principle as an 'EC Law' principle. However, they refer frequently in the same litigation to EC telecommunications directives (such as Directive 96/19) and other technical and environmental, materials and studies. For instance, the decision of March 17th 2003[15], refers to the Recommendations

---

[14] *Op cit.*, note 11.

[15] *Op cit.*, note 13.

of the Council (Health matters) of July 12th 1999 and the decision of October 22nd 2002,[16] refers to a report made by the Health Council of the Nederlands in 2001 as additional evidence to support the conclusion that the risks of standard telephone stations is low.

2.3 Rectification at source, producer or extended responsibility, regional variations, scientific base, and the 'integration' principle

It has not been possible to find reported cases making a detailed reference to these principles.

3 Environmental principles enshrined in Spanish legislation

As mentioned at the beginning of this chapter, it is possible to find a role for EC environmental principles in an *indirect way*, that is to say, when any such principle has been included or enshrined in an EC Directive or regulation. In the case of EC Directives, the Spanish statutes and administrative regulations that transpose those norms into the Spanish legal system, also mention in the explanatory memorandum (*exposición de motivos*) that they are based or informed by a given EC principle. Consequently, some Spanish environmental statutes also mention explicitly those environmental principles, either in specific articles, or, more frequently, in their explanatory memorandum (*exposición de motivos*). The Spanish statutes on waste, or the national IPPC statute of 2002 constitutes an example of such an approach.

Once the Spanish statute or administrative regulation has been promulgated and becomes the *'law of the land'*, the principle on which it is supposed to be based may be invoked under a Spanish court. Of course, the Spanish judge will interpret and, eventually, apply the *Spanish* principle (embodied in the Spanish regulation), however, in reality they will be applying the original EC one.

4 Conclusions

In the light of my previous discussion, it is possible to draw some conclusions. Firstly, in general, EC Environmental principles play a little role in the daily operations of Spanish courts, at least at first glance. In other words, a Spanish court will be usually reluctant to apply 'directly' any of the

---

[16] Regional High Court of Andalucia, administrative chamber, October 22nd 2002.

indents of Article 174 of the EC Treaty, or Article 6 itself. This situation is not exclusive to the environmental domain, for it is grounded in general, structural features of the Spanish legal system.

Secondly, when an EC environmental principle is invoked or applied by the courts, judges do not usually refer to it as an "EC principle", or an "Article174, EC Treaty principle", but just as a 'principle', or as a principle enshrined in the Constitution, a national statute, administrative regulation, or in international law. The best example is the polluter pays principle, which most courts view as enshrined in Article 45 of the Spanish constitution. In some cases, however, it is still possible to find judicial decisions where an 'EC Environmental principle' is explicitly referred to as such, or with a direct reference to the Treaty.

Thirdly, there are particular subject matters where EC Environmental principles have been predominantly raised. In the case of the polluter pays rule, it is mainly used in tax matters, either as a ground for challenging a tax statute or a specific tax, charge or fee (especially in the field of water management, inspection and [depuration]). The principle of prevention is clearly raised in the process of licensing and planning telephone infrastructures. Unfortunately, no significant mentions were found of the remaining principles.

Finally, it is expected that the role of EC environmental principles will be greater in the future; judicial references to them have increased significantly in recent years and EC environmental law becomes more and more important in the daily operations of lawyers and judges.

CHAPTER 12

Environmental Principles in the United Kingdom

Richard Macrory and Ian Havercroft

1 Principles in UK legislation

The United Kingdom represents a legal jurisdiction steeped in common law tradition where traditionally the judiciary have considerable freedom to develop and apply legal principles quite independently from their expression in legislation. Yet the number of cases where the core environmental principles such as the 'polluter pays principle' and the 'precautionary principle' have proved decisive in shaping outcomes have to date been surprisingly low. One reason for this may be that the vast majority of modern environmental litigation concerns the interpretation of complex provisions contained in legislation (and now often implementing European Community legislation), and the courts are likely to feel more comfortable in seeking solutions within the body of the legislation rather that striking out, as it were, with their own principles. We should start, then, by considering the extent to which the principles themselves are reflected in national legislation.

Before the introduction of the nineteenth century fore-runners of modern regulatory machinery, environmental law was largely based on the existence of private legal remedies designed largely to protect property and various powers available to public authority to deal with specific nuisance problems that already existed, and impose the clean up causes on the person responsible. Both types of legal remedies could be said to be implicitly based in notions of the polluter pays principle. Prevention and even less precaution, however, played little role, and proof of damage was a sina qua non for invoking such remedies. Even today, it is near impossible to secure a court injunction in a private nuisance action before at least some damage has occurred. The first UK legislation introducing specialized consent requirements in respect of industrial emissions into the air was the Alkali Act 1863. It was based on a Parliamentary investigation into air pollution, which found that preventative technology existed and was economic but that reliance on private legal remedies was insufficient to force industry to take effective preventative measures. Since then there have developed many examples of environmental law based on consent/licence type and where prevention can be said to underlie their rationale. The original Alkali Act contained statutory emission limits, but as the legislation was extended to other classes of industry, the duties became broader, and unusually contained an explicit duty of prevention. The Alkali etc Works Regulation Act 1881 contained a general duty on operators of industries falling within the ambit of the legislation to employ the 'best practicable means' for preventing all offensive gases being emitted, or rendering them harmless when released. Gradually this evolved into a triple duty of prevention of emissions, or if that was not practicable, reduction of emissions to a minimum or rendering them harmless, a formulation which found itself reflected in contemporary environmental legislation such as that relating to integrated pollution control under Part I Environmental Protection Act 1990. Other contemporary environmental law initiatives, such as liability regimes and special taxation regimes such as landfill tax, are, at least implicitly, influenced and justified by the notion of polluters pay.[1]

Whatever the underlying motivation of developments in environmental legislation, it remains the case that principles rarely find their expression in the body of the legislation itself. This is in part a characteristic in the British style of legislative drafting, which has tended to avoid the use of wide-sweeping principles or policy goals. As recently as 1990 a leading UK expert of the drafting of legislation noted, 'The truth is that the pragmatic British are chary of statements of principle. They distrust them because they almost invariably have to be qualified by exceptions and conditions to fit them for real life. What is the use of a principle than cannot stand on its win?'[2] In the environmental field, the difference in US and UK style of legal drafting in environmental laws in this respect has been explained in part by the fact that in the United Kingdom, Government dominates the legislative process. The Executive, as do most administrative bodies, largely wishes retain as much discretion as possible in how new legislation will be applied and implemented, and the avoidance of broad statements of principle, which could give rise to litigation and judicial intervention reinforces this goal. This characteristic was reinforced in the field of pollution control, by a long-standing policy and scientific belief that pollutants could be effectively dispersed and assimilated in the physical environment by natural processes. Going back to the original Alkali legislation, two features are striking. The interpretation and application of the controls was largely left to the discretion of the regulatory agency, dominated by engineers rather than lawyers, the court played little or no part in the interpretation of the legislation. More significantly, perhaps, although 'prevention' is expressed in the legislation as the first and prime duty of industrial operators subject to the controls, this duty in practice received little real emphasis by the regulatory bodies who favoured rendering emissions 'harmless' by dispersion. It was only in the late 1980s and early 1990s that regulators gave more emphasis to the duty of prevention – environmental cause celebres such as acid rain and low level radioactive disposal in the Irish sea had dented policy confidence in the dispersion theories and the expression in the European Treaty of the principle of prevention assisted those UK administrators who wish to give the concept greater emphasis.

Drafting style in the United Kingdom is changing a little. The use of 'purpose' clauses explaining the general objective of the legislation on question is now more prevalent and encouraged.[3] There is example where one sees explicit expression of underlying principles contained in legislation. A notable example was the introduction of new rules governing court procedures in civil

---

[1] See, for example, Morrow (2000) Nuisance and Environmental Protection, in Lowry and Edmunds (eds.) *Environmental Protection and the Common Law*, Hart Publishers, Oxford at p. 140.

[2] Bennion, F (1990) *Statute Law*, 3rd ed., Longmans, London, p. 25.

[3] See, *e.g.* Thornton (1996) *Legislative Drafting*, Butterworths, London.

cases, which open by stating boldly that the rules have 'the overriding objective of enabling the court to deal with cases justly'[4], a principle reinforced by the an express obligation of courts to seek to give effect to this overriding requirement when interpreting the rules and exercising any powers connected with them.[5] The Human Rights Act 1998, implementing within the United Kingdom the European Convention on Human Rights, has introduced a set of general principles of a scope unseen before in UK legislation. Furthermore, the need for UK judges to interpret European Community legislation has required them to become much more familiar and comfortable with a different approach towards the interpretation of legislation, often drafted in a distinct style, and containing principles and preambles of a type not traditionally found in national legislation.

2 Environmental principles in UK legislation and policy

Despite the tentative changes in the style of legislative drafting, it remains the case that there are few expressions of general environmental principles in national legislation. Where this does take place, it generally reflects the requirements of transposing European Community legislation. For example, regulations governing the licensing of waste disposal installations specify a number of objectives, which the relevant authorities must seek to achieve when carrying out their functions. These include the establishment of a network of waste disposal installations which enables 'waste to be disposed of in one of the nearest appropriate installations..'[6] The plan making functions include objectives of 'encouraging the prevention or reduction of waste production.'[7] The 'polluter pays' principle does not appear to have been transposed into any legislation, and only two references to the 'precautionary principle' can be found. The first concerns the detailed transposition of chemical substances regulations.[8] The second is more noteworthy and reflects the underlying political significance of the principle. Following devolution, certain aspects of the regulation of genetically manipulated organisms have been delegated to the Welsh (and other) regional assemblies. In transposing the EC Directive on deliberate releases, the Welsh Assembly makes expressly clear in the legislation that, in exercising any review powers to revoke or modify consents, 'the National Assembly for Wales is to take into account the precautionary principle.'[9] In the accompanying notes,

---

[4] Civil Procedure Rules 1998, r 1.1.

[5] *Ibid* r. 1.2.

[6] Waste management Licencing Regulations 1994 SI 1994/1056, Sched. 4 para 4(2).

[7] *Ibid*, para 4(3).

[8] The Notification of New Substances (Amendment) Regulations, 2002, SI 2002/ 2176, definition of 'exposure'.

[9] The Genetically Modified Organisms (Deliberate Release) (Wales) Regulations, 2002, Welsh Statutory Instrument 2002 / 3188 (W.304), reg. 38.

it is stated that this derives from Article 174 EC and the fact that the preamble to the Directive states that the principle is to be taken into account in its implementation.

However, there appears to be no legal requirement that this provision of the pre-amble is to transposed into national implementing legislation and the equivalent legislation covering England contains no such reference. Clearly, its inclusion in the Welsh provisions reflects a political antagonism within Welsh towards the development of GMO crops.

3   Environmental principles in policy documents

The precautionary principle was first endorsed and firmly stated, albeit in rather qualified terms, in an official Government policy document in 1990 in the Government's White Paper on the Environment, the first comprehensive Government state of environmental policy. This stated that, 'Where there are significant risks of damage to the environment, the Government will be prepared to take precautionary action to limit the use of potentially dangerous materials or the spread of potentially dangerous pollutants, even where scientific knowledge is not conclusive, if the balance of likely costs and benefits justifies it.'[10] The first UK Strategy of Sustainable Development[11] contained a chapter devoted to principles of sustainable development. In the context of precaution, it stated that the Government was committed to basing action 'on fact not fantasy', but that 'when potential damage to the environment is both uncertain and significant, it is necessary to act on the basis of the precautionary principle.'[12] The statement in the 1990 White Paper was then repeated. The Sustainable Development Strategy also endorsed in general terms the polluter pays principle.

In 1999 the new Labour Government produced a new Strategy for Sustainable Development for the United Kingdom.[13] This contained a chapter, which was more explicit on guiding principles and stated, 'the Government's policies will also take account of ten principles and approaches'. These included the precautionary principle, with the definition in the Rio declaration quoted and 'Making the polluter pay.' The polluter pays principle is further elaborated in an accompanying box which states that 'There are no hard and fast rules on when to take action: each case has to be considered carefully.' Since the Strategy was published, the status of the Strategy has become more complex because many areas of policy now fall within the devolved governments of Scotland, Wales and

---

[10]   This Common Inheritance – Britain's Environmental Strategy, Cm 1200 HMSO, London 1990.

[11]   Sustainable Development – The UK Strategy C m 2426, HMSO, London, 1994.

[12]   Para 3.12 *ibid*.

[13]   A Better Quality of Life – a Strategy for Sustainable Development, Cm 4345 HMSO, London 1999.

Northern Ireland. The Scottish Executive and the National Assembly of Wales have produced their own sustainable development strategies.[14] These also reflect the core environmental principles. The most recent plan of the Welsh Assembly, for example, states that the Assembly is committed to, *inter alia*, 'applying the precautionary principle that cost-effective measures to prevent possibly serious environmental damage should not be postponed just because of scientific uncertainty about how serious the risk is.' and 'preventing pollution as far as possible, and making the polluter pay for the damage done by pollution, and more generally trying to ensure that costs are met by those whose actions incur them.' In contrast, the Scottish Executive's Strategy does not expressly refer to the precautionary principle or the polluter pays principle, but states only three guiding principles: to have regard for others who do not have access to the same level of resources, and the wealth generated; to minimise the impact of actions on future generations by radically reducing the use of resources and by minimising environmental impacts; and to live within the capacity of the planet to sustain human activities and to replenish resources which are used. In the light of these developments at devolved levels of government and the changing policy agenda, the Government has recently issued a consultation paper, with the aim of developing a new strategic framework for sustainable development to be agreed by the UK government and the devolved administrations by 2005.[15] The consultation document repeats the ten guiding principles and approaches in the 1999 Strategy, but asks what should be the guiding principles for decision-makers and how can they be made more widely practical and relevant, both within and beyond government.

It is clear then, that a number of the core environmental principles are entering the language of official national policy documents, if not the actual body of legislation.

The question, then, arises as to their legal significance. A White Paper or a Command Paper[16] is not legally binding in the sense of a law or regulation, but has been deemed by government of sufficient importance to present before Parliament. As distinct from the UK Sustainable Strategies and those of other regional administrations, the Welsh Sustainable Development scheme (which currently contains endorsements of core environmental principles) is legally required to be made by the Welsh Assembly.[17] The legislation requires an annual report on implementation of the strategy to be made and while the provisions

---

[14] Meeting the Needs. Priorities, Actions and Targets for Sustainable Development. Scottish Executive, April 2002; Learning to Live Differently National Assembly for Wales, November 2000, now replaced by Starting to Live Differently, March 2004.

[15] Taking it On – Developing UK sustainable development strategy Together: A Consultation Paper Dept of Environment, Food, and Rural Affairs, 2004.

[16] A 'White Paper' is one form of various categories of Command Papers.

[17] S 121 Government of Wales Act 1998.

do not state that the contents are legally binding as such, it is arguable that the legislative requirement gives it heightened status.[18] Nor can a statement in a White Paper dictate how a court should interpret legislation, whether at national and even more so at European level. See, for example, the decision in *Friends of the Earth* v. *Secretary of State for Environment, Food and Rural Affairs*, [2001] EWCA Civ 1847 where the court was required to interpret the provision of a Euratom Directive, and considered the content of a Government White Paper. The Court noted that, 'The White Paper cannot in any event dictate the correct approach to Article 6'.

Many White Papers containing the Government policy thinking behind proposed new legislation, and have been used by the Courts to assist them in the interpretation of the laws subsequently passed. Papers such as the UK Sustainable Development Strategy are, however, rather distinct and in essence represent an official statement of Government policy thinking rather than proposals for new laws. As a high level statement, indicated by the decision to present it in the form of a Command Paper, it is certainly likely to be highly relevant in administrative law proceedings where, say, a Government decision is being challenged before the courts on the grounds that the Government misdirected itself as to its policy. However, the language in which endorsements of principle, such as that of precaution, is chosen with care and hedged with qualifications and exceptions, in order to avoid it being treated as a binding commitment with legal force.

4 Significant case law involving environmental principles

4. 1 Polluter pays principle

There have been few cases to date before the UK courts where the polluter pays principle has been considered at any length or in any great detail. The case law that exists within this select group is both diverse and broad in its scope and encompasses areas of the law that might not be thought of as typically environmental.

Designation of nitrate vulnerable zones
The most noteworthy case to date remains the cases of ex parte *H.A. Standley and Others and D.G.D. Metson and Others*[19], which, following the judicial review hearing discussed here, was referred to the ECJ for a preliminary ruling under Article 177.[20] Two farmers and others, who sought to challenge the Secre-

---

[18] Though see the decision in Goldfinch v. National Assembly for Wales, noted below.

[19] *R.* v. *Secretary of State for the Environment and Another* ex parte *H.A. Standley and Others and D.G.D. Metson and Others*, Queens Bench Division (Crown Office List), CO/2057/96. .

[20] Case C-293/97, 29 April 1999.

tary of State's implementation of the Nitrates Directive[21], brought the application for judicial review. The farmers argued that the Government had failed to apply the polluter pays principle when they had identified waters under Article 3(1) of the Directive because they could not prove that all the nitrate pollution in the areas derived from agricultural operations (other sources included traffic emissions), with the result that farmers would bear the cost of removing nitrates which were not all due to them. In the alternative, they argued that if the Government were permitted to do so under Article 3, the directive itself was in breach of the polluters pay principle. The farmers raised the principle as an aid to the interpretation of the Directive's provisions, and, in addition the court was asked to consider the principle as 'an obligation under the Treaty with effect from July 1987'.[22]

The case was referred to the ECJ. Essentially the ECJ held that the Directive did not infringe the polluters pay principle in that while the process of designation of waters depended on nitrate concentrates and did not require sources of nitrates to be identified, the Directive did not require that farmers bear all the costs of removing the nitrates. The principle of proportionality was invoked and was held to be reflected in the polluter pays principle, and Member States were therefore required 'not to impose on farmers costs of eliminated pollution that are unnecessary.' Formally, the farmers lost the case they brought, but in practice they won the tactical victory they were seeking in that the Government's approach towards the imposition of burdens following designation was constrained.

Insolvency law and waste sites

The polluter pays principle has twice been raised in cases discussing apparent conflicts between insolvency and environmental law, where companies operating waste sites have become insolvent. Modern waste management law under the Environmental Protection Act 1990 (EPA 1990) tries to prevent waste management companies running away from their obligations to complete or restore a site after operations have ceased. It requires, for example, that a licence cannot be given up until the environmental regulator, the Environment Agency, is satisfied that all obligations have been fulfilled. Financial bonds and the equivalent are also used. Once a company has become formally insolvent, however, insolvency law gives extensive discretion and obligations to liquidators to 'disclaim' existing responsibilities in order to maximize assets for creditors. The general principle is that unless the legislation is absolutely clear on obligations than cannot be disclaimed in this manner (which it is on certain matters such as tax debts) then future obligations can all be disclaimed. Unfortunately,

---

[21] Directive 91/676.

[22] Judgment of Potts J, Official Transcript, 7th May 1997.

the waste management legislation never made explicit the position on liquidation of a waste management company – probably a legislative oversight.

In Re *Mineral Resources Ltd*[23] the High Court examined the ability of a liquidator of a company to disclaim a waste management licence and 'the consequences of such a licence being capable or incapable, as the case may be, of disclaimer'.[24] Mr Justice Neuberger acknowledged in his judgment, that there was a conflict between the EPA 1990 the Insolvency Act 1986. In discussing why the EPA 1990 should prevail over the IA 1986, the judge raised the polluter pays principle saying; 'it appears to me that there is considerable public interest in the maintenance of a healthy environment, and in the principle pithily expressed as the polluter must pay. It is the view which prevails both in the popular perception and in the legislative system in this country and indeed, in most of the developed world.'[25]

The judgment went further, however, stating that the importance of the principle was not only reflected in the EPA 1990, but also in the terms of the Council's Directive on Waste.[26] The emphasis placed upon the principle of EC law is reflected in Neuberger J's final statement on the point; 'at least in the absence of strong factors the other way, that the interest in the protection of the environment should prevail over the fair and orderly winding up of companies.'[27] It seems clear from the judgment that the principle is to hold an elevated status in these circumstances, thus prevailing over the provisions of the Insolvency Act 1986. In addition, it appears that the High Court was suggesting that this principle is well established in domestic law as well as EC law. Further reasoning behind the application of the principle in this case is to be found later in his judgment where he states; 'by virtue of the conditions imposed in the licence for the benefit of the environment, the loser as a result of the disclaimer of the licence would not so much be the [Environment] Agency as the general public.'[28]

Re *Celtic Extraction (in liquidation) and Re Bluestone Chemicals Ltd (in liquidation)*[29] was a similar case on the facts and initially heard by Mr Justice Neuberger, who came to a similar conclusion. In this case the liquidator appealed to the Court of Appeal which overruled his decision, thus allowing a liquidator to disclaim a waste management licence.

---

[23] *Re: Mineral Resources Ltd, Environment Agency* v. *Stout* [1999] 1 All ER 746, [1999] 2 BCLC 516.

[24] Judgment of Neuberger J, 30th April 1998.

[25] *Ibid.*

[26] Council Directive 75/442, as amended by Council Directive 91/156.

[27] Judgment of Neuberger J, 30th April 1998.

[28] *Ibid.*

[29] *Official Receiver (as liquidator of Celtic Extraction Ltd and Bluestone Chemicals Ltd)* v. *Environment Agency* [1999] 2 BCLC 555.

The appeal court judges analysed the judgment of Neuberger J and held that there was no inconsistency between the 1990 Act and the 1986 Act. In his judgment Morrit LJ too considered the principle and held that the European Directive on Waste; 'enunciated a principle of 'polluter pays' and required member states to take the necessary measures.'[30] This stated, however, he noted that the Directive did not go into any detail as to the consequences if the polluter was insolvent; 'there is nothing in the directive to suggest that the polluter pays principle is to be applied to cases where the polluter cannot pay so as to require that the unsecured creditors of the polluter should pay.'[31]

Essentially the Court reverted back to earlier general principles, that legislation must be absolutely explicit if it is prevent a liquidator from disclaiming obligations and held that it was a matter for the legislature if provisions were to be made. The result of the case caused considerable concern to the Environment Agency who is now pressing Government to make the necessary legislative changes.

Interpretation of landfill tax legislation

In 1996 the British Government introduced special taxes on the landfill of wastes in order to bias the costs of waste disposal in favour of recycling and incineration. The 2002 *Parkwood Landfill*[32] case was the first decision of the High Court concerning the interpretation of the tax provisions. The argument concerned whether landfill operators should be taxed on waste, sent to sites but used there for recycling operations such as foundations for roads. There was little discussion within the case as to the principle itself, but the Court of Appeal acknowledged the existence of the principle within UK environmental policy regarding landfill. Reference was made to a policy White Paper of 1995 that preceded the imposition of landfill tax in the UK, where an indirect reference was made to the principle.

The case primarily concerned the definition of waste and who would in fact be liable for the relevant duties, but the eventual decision made by the Court of Appeal may be said to adopt the principle. Lord Justice Aldous stated; 'The tax bites upon the person who discards not who recycles.'[33] Significantly, the Court seems to have accepted that the principle was now part of national policy and law, and it should be noted that the landfill tax was a purely national initiative and not one derived from EC law.

---

[30] Judgment of Morritt LJ, para. 10, 14th July 1999.

[31] Judgment of Morritt LJ, para. 39, 14th July 1999.

[32] *Customs and Excise Commissioners* v. *Parkwood Landfill Ltd* [2002] EWCA Civ 1707.

[33] Judgment of Aldous LJ, para. 30, 28th November 2002.

[34] [1994] AC 264.

Civil liability for damage

Under UK law, the courts through individual cases have largely developed the core principles for civil liability between private parties for personal or physical damage. In 1993 in *Cambridge Water Company* v. *Eastern Leather Counties plc*[34] the House of Lords considered these principles in the context of major water contamination caused by the defendants over a number of years, through seepages of minor chemical spillages on their sites. It was accepted that at the time the spillages took place the type of damage that occurred was not reasonably foreseeable. The Court of Appeal revived earlier Victorian cases on water pollution and held the company strictly liable, but the House of Lords reversed this decision, holding that in deciding the extent of damage for which the company was liable, the principle of reasonably foreseeability should be applied in all cases in the absence of any particular legislation. Lord Goff acknowledged that much of the thrust of modern environmental policy was to establish, 'legislation which will promote the protection of the environment, and make the polluter pay for damage to the environment for which he is responsible.' But the very existence of such activity by policy makers and legislatures meant it was undesirable for the courts themselves to duplicate these efforts: 'Given that so much well-informed and carefully structured legislation is now being put in place for this purpose, there is less need for the courts to develop a common law principle to achieve the same end, and indeed it may well be undesirable that they should do so.'

4.2   The precautionary principle

The precautionary principle has been raised in a greater number of cases before the UK courts though it has the reputation of being, 'the fuzziest of environmental principles'[35] and it has been suggested that, 'while courts in the UK and other common law jurisdictions have been willing to recognise the principle and uphold precautionary decisions they have not, in most cases, been willing to accept it as a justification for substantive and intensive review.'[36] Much of the case law is to be found within the traditional areas encompassed by environmental law, typically planning law, conservation and issues involving public health.

Government duties to protect public from low level magnetic fields

The leading case in domestic law, where the principle was considered in great detail is the 1995 decision of ex parte *Duddridge and Others*.[37] The case was an application for judicial review, which claimed that the Secretary of State

---

[35]   D. Hughes, *Journal of Environmental Law*, Vol 7(2), 1995, at p. 238.

[36]   E. Fisher, *Journal of Environmental Law*, Vol 13(3), 2001, at p. 315.

[37]   *R.* v. *Secretary of State for Trade and Industry* ex parte *Duddridge and Others*, *Journal of Environmental Law*, Vol 7(2), 1995, at p. 224. [Court of Appeal decision, The Times, 26th October 1995] .

for Trade and Industry was obliged to protect residents, living in the vicinity of high-voltage power lines, from possible effects of low level magnetic fields. The Secretary of State had the power to lay down regulations specifying thresholds of exposure from power lines, but had not done since the scientific evidence for exposure and effects was still highly contested.

The applicants' argument centred upon the contention that the Secretary of State was obliged to make regulations, because he was legally bound by the precautionary principle under both EC law and the government's policy reflected in the White Paper of 1990[38]. The evidence from the expert scientific panel suggested that there was a 'possibility' of an increased risk to human health from the exposure to the large electrical forces and thus the precautionary principle was relevant here.

The presiding judge, Mr Justice Smith, stated; 'I am prepared to accept that, if the Secretary of State is shown to be under a legal obligation to apply the precautionary principle to legislation concerned with health and the environment, the possibility of harm raised by the existing state of scientific knowledge is such as would oblige him to apply it in considering whether to issue regulations to restrict exposure to EMFs.'[39]

He then considered the basis upon which the applicants' submissions were made and concluded that the application would only succeed if the court was satisfied there was a duty imposed upon the Secretary of State by EC law. Counsel for both sides discussed the obligations raised under EC law by Article 130, in particular Article 130r. Mr Justice Smith accepted the submissions for the Secretary of State that, when considered in conjunction with Articles 130s and 130t, Article 130r merely 'lays down the principles upon which Community policy on the environment shall be based.'[40] Here, there was no Community policy or law governing threshold emissions for power cables, and the regulations were purely a matter of national law. He held that Article 130r did not create an obligation upon a member State to take specific action and that; 'in accepting the provisions of Article 130r, a Member State has done no more than to indicate in advance its consent in principle to the formulation of a policy governed by the objectives there stated.'[41] Although the Government had endorsed the precautionary principle in a Government policy paper, this was not considered sufficient to impose any legal obligations on him.

The views of Mr Justice Smith were upheld in the Court of Appeal, where leave to appeal against the decision was dismissed. As noted above, the principle had been endorsed in the 1990 Government White Paper on the Environment and Mr Justice Smith acknowledged the existence of the principle in Interna-

---

[38] 'This Common Inheritance', Cm 1200.

[39] Judgment of Smith J, *Journal of Environmental Law*, Vol. 7(2), 1995, at p. 230.

[40] *Ibid*, at p. 233.

[41] *Ibid*, at p. 234.

tional, Community and domestic policy, but was unable to find it possessing more status than as a guide to policy objectives.

Transfrontier waste legislation

The case of ex parte *Dockgrange Limited*[42] considered the precautionary principle, two years after the decision in *Duddridge*. The case was an expedited application for judicial review with respect to the interpretation of a European regulation concerning the shipment of waste.[43] Essentially wastes on the 'green' list were considered non-hazardous, while those on 'amber' and 'red' lists were treated as hazardous and required much more extensive controls. The regulations provided that if a waste category did not appear on any list, it was to be treated as a 'red' list waste, a provision which itself reflects the precautionary principle.

The applicant was a recycling firm who imported mixed consignments of green waste categories (mainly crushed cars and white goods). All the constituent parts of the waste were green listed wastes, but because a mixture of these categories was not listed in the Regulation lists, the Environment Agency treated it as a Red List, the 'red list' procedures causing considerable potential harm to the applicants' business.

The Environment Agency raised the precautionary principle as grounds for the adjustment to the procedure stating that; 'the Regulation must be interpreted in accordance with the governing 'precautionary principle' laid down by the treaty.'[44] Mr Justice (now Lord Justice) Carnwath, however, dismissed the issue of the principle here and clearly felt that the result of the Agency's approach was a bureaucratic nonsense; 'where there is legitimate room for uncertainty, then the precautionary principle argues in favour of a more restrictive approach until the facts are known. However, that is no justification for applying a restrictive approach, where, as here, the facts are known.'[45]It is clear from judgment that; the court accepted the existence of the principle as an aid to the interpretation of the disputed regulation, and the judgment rejects the principle only on the basis that it cannot be applied in the circumstances surrounding that particular case.

Land use planning decisions

The principle has also been raised in planning cases; the case of *R* v. *Derbyshire County Council*[46] provides an example of how it has been handled by the

---

[42] *R. v. Environment Agency*, ex parte *Dockgrange Limited and Another,* The Times, 21st June 1997.

[43] Regulation No. 259/93.

[44] Judgment of Carnwath J, 22nd May 1997.

[45] *Ibid.*

[46] *R. (on the application of Murray)* v. *Derbyshire County Council,* CO/1493/2000, 6th October 2000, The Times 8th November 2000.

courts. This case was an application for judicial review in the High Court by a local resident of the decision by the local authority, to grant planning permission for the extension of a known landfill site. The third ground sited by the applicant in his application was the failure of the council to 'give effect to the precautionary principle'. Counsel for the applicant suggested it was 'incumbent' upon the Council to give effect to the Community principles under Article 174 of the EC Treaty and sited the precautionary principle as being of particular relevance here.

Mr Justice Kay held that the precautionary principle was reflected in both the Waste Framework Directive and the regulations that transposed the directive into domestic law. He stated; 'although it is said to illuminate the waste Framework directive and the implementing provisions of the 1994 Regulations, it does not in my view take any further the arguments already considered in relation to those matters.' [47] He refused to consider the principle as one that was justiciable in isolation, but saw it as an integral part of national and EC legislation. Thus, it was held that by following the procedure in both the Waste Framework Directive and the implementing legislation, the inspector in the case had complied with the requirements of Article 174 EC.

The principle was raised in argument in *Goldfinch (Projects) Ltd* v. *National Assembly for Wales and Flintshire County Council*[48], a decision, which emphasises the extent to which the courts will be influenced by the location of the principle within a hierarchy of norms. The planning application for housing development in Wales had originally been granted in 1996, but because development was never commenced, a fresh application was submitted but refused in 2001. The key question of law was whether sufficient changes had occurred in the intervening years to justify such a change in decision. The government argued that the policy context had changed significantly. The Land Use Plan for the area, approved in 1991, was argued to be to out of date, although it made reference to sustainable development. The government pointed in particular to the increasing emphasis on sustainability and the new legal duty of the National Assembly to produced a sustainability development plan. It also noted that the new draft land use planning policy guidance for Wales (adopted by the Assembly in 2002) noted that the Assembly 'will be prepared to take precautionary action and on the basis of the precautionary principle to limit environmental damage even where scientific knowledge is not conclusive.'

The judge was not convinced that enough had changed to warrant the new decision in law. The planning legislation requires individual decisions to be in accordance with the existing development plan, unless material considerations indicate otherwise and that the decision-maker has regard to the development plan and any other considerations. The Court was prepared to accept that a draft

---

[47] Judgment of Kay J, para. 17, 6th October 2000.

[48] High Court, Co/4855/01, 21 June 2002.

planning policy (such as that concerning the precautionary principle) might be a material consideration in law, but felt that the second decision had paid insufficiently attention to the reasons for granting permission in 1996. In relation to sustainability, he noted, 'There was in my judgment no fundamental difference in the principle to be applied to this planning application between 1996 and 2001. Sustainability was already a familiar concept in 1996, it did not provide a basis for departing in 1991 from an earlier decision.'[49]

Pesticide regulation

In a more recent case, *Amvac Chemical UK Ltd*[50], the High Court considered the significance of the principle in relation to a regulatory procedure concerning pesticides. The action, brought by a pesticide manufacturer, sought to challenge the Government decision to suspend regulatory approvals for a chemical used in pesticides known as 'dichlorvos'. One of the grounds of challenge concerned the precautionary principle, though, given that those challenging were the manufacturers, it was raised in a peculiar way. The claimants did not argue that the Government was under any legal duty to apply the precautionary principle, but that they had in fact purported to do so in reaching their decision and had failed to apply an appropriate risk assessment in doing so. As the judge noted, in order to succeed, the claimants had to show that (a) there were mechanisms in place to apply appropriate risk assessments in applying the precautionary principle in the context of pesticide approval (b) the Government had purported to apply the principle and the mechanisms in place and (c) there had been a failure to do so.

Mr Justice Crane considered the legislative and political background to the precautionary principle and its relevance to the UK legal system. He noted, inter alia, the references to the precautionary principle in the 1999 Sustainable Development Strategy, referred to in para 3 above, the EU Communication on the subject, the December 2000 Resolution of the EU Council of Ministers, together with various other official references. He also noted that the relevant Government scientific committee making the key recommendations in this case had in 2001 considered a paper on the precautionary principle, which clearly indicated that how it should be applied in practice in this context was still unfinished business. The court rejected the claimant's case on the basis that, 'there is – at least so far – no settled, specific or identifiable mechanism of risk assessment in the field of pesticide approval that the Claimant is entitled to rely on as part of the precautionary principle, viewed as a separate basis for challenging a decision.'[51]

---

[49] Scott Baker J at para 23.

[50] *R (on the application of Amvac Chemical UK Ltd) v. Secretary of State for Environment, Food and Rural Affairs and Others* [2001] EWHC Admin 1011, CO/3087/2001.

[51] *Ibid.*

[52] Judgment of Crane J, para 84, 3rd December 2001.

However, the judge considered the decision in *R v. Derbyshire County Council* discussed above and states; 'I am prepared to accept that on a substantive challenge to a regulatory decision, it may in some cases be relevant to take into account the precautionary principle and, more important its limitations.'[52] This decision suggested that the judiciary might now be encouraged to consider, to a greater extent, the principle in relation to particular regulatory challenges. The reference to the precautionary principle in official Government policy statements such as the Sustainable Development Strategy seems to have been of influence and indicates that the clear distinction in the *Duddridge* case, between the precautionary principle having legal force in the context of EC legislation and none at purely national level is now no longer so sound. Nevertheless, in the absence of more detailed methodologies for its application, which are practiced by Government, the courts may still find it difficult to give the principle genuine legal bite.

4. 3   Prevention at source

There appears to be no reported case to date where this principle, or words equivalent to it, is referred to expressly in judgments.

4.4   Producer or extended responsibility

The concept of producer or extended responsibility is not strictly part of the provisions of the EC Treaty, though; it may be seen as an elaboration of both the polluter pays principle and rectification at source. There is at present very little case law to be found upon this notion, but it has been considered to some extent within the UK courts.

Packaging regulations
There have to date been two leading cases concerning the interpretation of the 1997 Producer Responsibility Obligations (Packaging Waste) Regulations[53] which implemented 1994 EC Directive on the subject. Both turn on the interpretation of specific provisions in the Regulation and Directive, but against the underling policy background.

Davies and Hillier Nurseries[54] was a dispute between the Environment Agency and the operator of a number of garden centres selling plants in plastic pots. The Agency argued that the pots were packaging within the meaning of the legislation and therefore the operators were subject to producer obliga-

---

[53]   Producer Responsibility Obligations (Packaging Waste) Regulations 1997.

[54]   *Davies v. Hillier Nurseries* [2001] EWHC Admin 28, CO/3149/00.

[55]   *R. (on the application of Valpak) v. Environment Agency* [2002] Env L.R 36.

tions. The Court held that it was quite possible for such containers to have dual purposes – both as a growing medium and a form of sales unit – and therefore such pots could be considered as packaging within the meaning of the law. A similar case was *R on the application of Valpak v. Environment Agency*[55] which was concerned with whether drink sold in bottles to be consumed on the premises of pubs or restaurants, fell within the concept of packaging and whether the operators of the pubs could be considered as producers, rather than the wholesalers who supplied them. The case was brought by one of the packaging recovery facilitators who wished to test the Agency's contention that suppliers to pubs and restaurants were still responsible producers. The Agency argued that the bottles were opened and drinks poured before supply, thus making the operators of the pubs no longer producers within the meaning of the legislation. The High Court disagreed, arguing that a more generous interpretation was more consistent with the basic aims of the Directive to improve collection and recovery, with the result that responsibility was pushed onto the owners and operators of pubs and restaurants.

Extending the notion of producer responsibility

The concept of *'producer responsibility'* in its wider application places legal responsibility on parties 'further up the chain', than might be traditionally thought liable. In the field of pollution control we have identified two fields where this concept has been developed though the terminology, 'producer responsibility' was not used as such.

Supermarket prosecuted for abandoned shopping trolleys dumped in local river

The background to this 2001 case was a joint clean up operation by the Environment Agency and a local council of a river running through the town of Chelmsford in Essex. During this operation, the authorities recovered 237 shopping trolleys of which 197 were found to belong to a local supermarket branch of Tesco's. No one knows who actually dumped the abandoned trolleys there, but presumably it was local vandals who could not be identified.

Tesco's had no deposit, local-up system for their trolleys, and the Environment Agency decided to prosecute them under the water pollution law which makes it an offence to *'knowingly permit'* the deposit of pollutants or substances in a river without a licence. Previous court decisions on the meaning of this phrase have tended to be concerned with industrial pollution where the company failed to prevent pollution with actual knowledge. What was unusual here was that Tesco's clearly had no actual control or knowledge over the vandals who dumped trolleys inn the river which was not on their land. The Environment Agency, however, decided that that failure to implement any sort of preventative system to discourage dumping was sufficient to impose liability.

In the event, Tesco's decided to plead guilty before local magistrates, who sent the case for sentencing to a higher court where the company was fined

£30,000 plus legal costs. Shortly before the case was heard, the local store management fitted 'coin in the slot' locks on trolleys. The case received considerable coverage and can be expected to have encourage other stores to fit similar preventative systems.

Responsibility for noise nuisance on owners of buildings with poor sound insulation
Legislation gives power to local authorities to serve 'statutory nuisance' orders to stop or prevent particular sources of pollution, especially noise levels. The legislation requires the notice to be served on the person *'responsible'* for the nuisance, a term not defined in the legislation. In relation to domestic noise nuisances, notices are generally served on the individual directly causing the noise (hosting a party, etc.), but some local authorities have argued in cases where those disturbed are immediate neighbours in blocks of flats, that the person really responsible was not the immediate individuals but the landlord or the owner of the building who failed to provide adequate sound insulation. There have been isolated successful cases in local magistrates, but the point has never been tested in the higher courts to date.

Only since 1985 have building regulations required standards of sound insulation and the issue is focussed on older, multi-occupied flats. In a leading case[56], the House of Lords considered the issue in relation to the legal obligations of landlords generally. The case concerned a poorly insulated block of flats let by a local authority, where even the ordinary sounds of people walking about and talking caused disturbance to others living there, so poor was the sound insulation. The tenancy agreement included an obligation on the landlord to take steps to prevent other tenants committing a nuisance, but the House of Lords could not see that it could be invoked here. The landlord had not expressly authorized any nuisance, and could not see that the normal use of a flat could be a nuisance in law. According to Lord Hoffman, 'if the neighbours are not committing a nuisance, the councils cannot be liable for authorizing them to commit one.' The local authority was under no contractual or statutory obligation to insulate the building.

The decision was not directly concerned with the meaning of 'responsible' under the statutory nuisance legislation, but may well inhibit further use of those provisions. The decision in some respects is a conservative interpretation, but one that reflects the courts unease with the social and financial consequences of a court ruling which should really be the responsibility of Parliament and Government. Apparently, within the one London Borough concerned, the costs of bringing up its existing stock of building to modern sound insulation standards would be £1.27 billion, against an annual budget (mainly from Central Government funding) of less than £55 million for major housing schemes.

---

[56] *London Borough of Southwark* v. *Mills and others*, [2001] 1 A.C. 1, 21 October 1999.

5 Conclusions

The core environmental principles as expressed in the EU
Treaty clearly have legal significance at European level, and would be equally relevant to a UK national court dealing with European Community environmental
legislation. Yet the case law to date, suggests that principles such as polluters pay
or the precautionary principle do not have significant independent legal weight
in the determination of purely national decisions. Some commentators would
put this down to a lack of environmental sympathy or understanding by the judiciary and have called for a more specialist environmental court.[57] There may be
some truth in this, but the more compelling reasons lie in the relationship of the
judiciary with the executive and the legislature.

Core environmental principles are not expressed in the body of national
legislation, nor have the European Treaty provisions been transposed into
national law. Unlike the European Court of Justice, the national courts cannot
rely upon a nationally legally binding instrument containing these principles. If
we were dealing with areas of law where the development of underlying principles were largely the responsibility of the judiciary, then one might expect more
express reliance on environmental principles by the courts. Most contemporary
areas of environmental law are now dominated by legislation (not least because
of the need to transpose European Community obligations) and it is hardly
surprising if courts expect the legislation to contain such principles if that is
the aim of government or parliament; if they do not, it is not the function of the
courts to fill such policy gaps.

Even in the field of civil liability, traditionally dominated by principles developed independently by the courts, the courts have indicated that the density of
modern environmental legislation means that new principles of environmental
liability should be the preserve of the executive and legislature rather than the
courts.[58] The role of the courts is to interpret and apply, rather than to create.
Ironically then, the greater the success in developing contemporary environmental legislation, the less will be the role of courts in developing environmental
principles. It does not follow, though, that in the absence of express transposition into legislation, these principles are devoid of effect. The more that they are
referred to in Government policy documents or plans – and there is an increasing tendency in this respect – the more that the courts will feel entitled to regard
them as policy considerations which cannot be disregarded by decision-makers.
The weight that is given to the principles in any particular case is likely to
remain within the discretion of decision-maker, but the courts can ensure that
at least they cannot be ignored.

---

[57] Environmental Justice Report 2004.

[58] *Cambridge Water Co v. Eastern County Leathers, supra.*

CHAPTER 13

Environmental Principles – Experiences of Transition Countries

Gyula Bándi

The principles of environmental law are relevant to those countries where environmental legislation is at a relatively early stage, the level of detail is not always present and where the implementation of such principles in practice may not always be a future prospect. I have had the pleasure, during the past 10 years, of participating in different studies and projects, related to the experiences of developing environmental legislation in the transition countries – first in Central and East European (CEE) countries and in the past 2-3 years in South-East European (SEE) countries. My views of the role and place of environmental principles, in countries in economic and environmental transition, are based on knowledge generated during these ventures. As a preliminary statement, or introduction to the following chapter, it may be suggested that there has been an escalation of environmental principles within the past 10 years in the CEE and SEE countries. Of course, this rise is not unique to transition economies, but may also be seen as the experience within Europe as a whole. 'The 90s have shown an enormous proliferation of and dedication to laying down objectives and principles of environmental law and policy in legal and non-legal instruments.'[1]

In transition countries, such principles mostly appear in general or framework environmental acts, adopted by a country's Parliament. Often there is pretence that environmental protection is well developed and has a high priority. The question is, whether this is the actual case, or whether the increasing numbers of principles remain the only sign of environmental concern. In this chapter seeks to address this question and explain why principles play a role in the evolution of legislation in this part of Europe.

Environmental law is still a relatively new field of legislation and jurisprudence should develop its own theoretical foundations. The principles may be perceived in the scientific works of environmental policy and legal scholars, but they may also form a part of an official environmental policy document or a legal regulation – as was the case with the environmental action programmes of the Community. This last option is even more important in those cases where the regulation itself is of a framework nature, lacking details in terms of environmental institutions, means and measures. Legal principles are therefore explicitly or indirectly part of the legal regulation in all European countries, as well as the environmental policy of international organisations.

We may distinguish between at least three basic roles, to which all principles aspire:

     a)   to provide guidance for further regulation and a framework for further policy or legislative action;

---

[1]   N. Dhondt, *Integration of Environmental Protection into other EC Policies*, Europa Law Publishing, Groningen, (2003), p. 123.

b) to provide guidance for implementation and enforcement, sometimes filling the gap between real-life problems and loopholes within legislation; and

c) to also assist in research and education.

The emergence of principles is not a unique attribute of transition countries. Principles have determined the development of international law and for the purposes of this chapter international environmental law. 'Nonetheless, even now certain principles may be considered an established part of the common law of environmental protection'.[2] These principles may also occur in domestic environmental law. 'Certain principles, techniques and practices are or could be extended from one level to others providing dynamic and creative solutions to environmental problems.'[3]

The environmental principles may be divided into three categories, in connection with the manifestation of environmental characteristics and their practical implementation:

· the principles of environmental policy in a broader sense, which are sometimes identical but not always similar with the legal principles, which instead define the general framework of environmental protection;

· the principles of environmental law, determining the development of the structure of the legal system and also the main lines of implementation;

· finally, the principles of specific environmental areas, covering conceptual grounds for the improvement of regulation of different environmental media or means of environmental uses.

It may also be added, that the above three categories do not exhibit strict differences; there are a great number of principles which form a part of all the three groups. Prevention or precaution is relevant in all the fields of environmental policy and law, while proximity is only appropriate in waste management and cooperation with the developing countries is a component of EC environmental policy.

The Model Act drafted by the Council of Europe (presented in its final format in 1994[4]) after referring to the right to a stable environment, mentions the following principles in Article 4:

---

[2] A. Kiss and D. Shelton, *International Environmental Law*, Transnational, Ardsley, New York, (2000) p. 43.

[3] A. Kiss and D. Shelton, *op. cit.* note 2, p. 45.

[4] In 1991, at the first meeting of eastern and western experts on environmental law under the auspices of the Council of Europe Directorate for Environmental and Local Authorities, the idea to establish a Model Act on the protection of the environment was born. At that time the Model Act was designed for the Central and Eastern European countries. At the end of the drafting process in 1994, it turned out

a) precautionary principle,
b) substitution,
c) maintenance of biodiversity,
d) non-degradation of natural resources,
e) polluter pays,
f) right of the public to information and participation,
g) cooperation.

The Model Act was created for CEE countries at the beginning of the 1990s, thus it is worthwhile to examine these transition countries first. Some of these transition countries became members of the EU in 2004. A comparative study, published at the beginning of 1996 lists 10 countries in transition[5]. If we take the example of Estonia from among them, then we find the following principles listed in the Act on Sustainable Development, adopted in 1992:

a) preservation, protection and improvement of the quality of the environment;
b) protection of human health (presented indirectly);
c) prudent and rational use of natural resources;
d) control of pollution at source;
e) integration of environmental issues into other sectoral policies.[6]

In Slovenia, where the Council of Europe model played an important role in drafting the Environmental Protection Act (the EPA), a new framework environmental protection law based on the new Slovenian Constitution, was adopted in 1993. This act lists the following principles:

a) principle of sustainable development;
b) principle of comprehensiveness;
c) principle of cooperation;
d) principle of prevention;
e) principle of precaution;
f) principle of liability of the party responsible for 'environmental strain/impact';
g) principle of restitution for 'environmental strain/impact';
h) principle of mandatory insurance;

---

that the Model Act might be taken as a model for drafting environmental laws in general, without any reference to the target group. Although this Model Act has not been adopted by any body of the Council of Europe, this organization takes it as being their own.

5 Approximation of European Environmental Law, Case studies of Bulgaria, Czech Republic, Estonia, Hungary, Latvia, Lithuania, Poland, Romania, Slovak Republic and Slovenia, The Regional Environmental Centre, Budapest, January, (1996).

6 Ibid, pp. 57-59.

i) principle of mandatory subsidiarity measures;
j) principle of freedom of environmental information;
k) principle of protection of rights (legal remedies for environmental rights).[7]

I was a member of the editorial board, who authored the 1996 study. During the preparatory works of the report, we were looking for the reasons and consequences of the increase of such sophisticated and progressive ideas and we came to the subsequent conclusions:

'Because most countries in the region adopted new environmental laws and other principal regulations in the last few years, the field of general environmental policy is one of the more advanced in terms of its stage of approximation [...].

The easiest way was to adopt the principles of environmental law, but some of these principles, such as rectifying pollution at its source or implementing the precautionary principle, required further elaboration. When looking at the details of one of these principles, the polluter-pays-principle, the overall level of similarity is much less favourable. Taking the polluter-pays-principle as an important element of the market-oriented approach to environmental protection, certain elements are often missing in domestic legal systems.'[8]

Several years have passed since the 1996 study and at the beginning of this decade, the first round of transition countries, the CEE countries, are close to EU membership and may nominate ECJ judges. Other SEE and NIS countries are eagerly anticipating membership, as they aspire to become part of the European family.

A good example, is the 1996 Framework Environmental Protection Act of the Republic of Montenegro, the 1992 Constitution which in its Article 1 refers to Montenegro as 'a democratic, social and ecological state', describes the objectives and basic principles of environmental protection as follows:

a) conservation of natural resources;
b) preservation of biological diversity;
c) reduction of environmental risks;
d) environmental impact assessment;
e) alternative solutions;
f) substitution of chemicals;
g) reuse and recycling;

---

[7] M. Mirkovic, Slovenian Framework Environmental Law – Structure, Elements and Policy Choices at Seminar of Framework Environmental Law Drafting, in *Countries in Transition, Jahorinia, Bosnia and Herzegovina*, The Regional Environmental Centre, (1998) pp 51-52.

[8] Approximation of European Environmental Law, *op. cit.* note 6, p. 13.

h)   the polluter pays;
i)   the user/consumer pays;
j)   mandatory pollution insurance;
k)   public access and involvement; and
l)   public information on the state of the environment.[9]

The list above, is a mixture of general and media specific objectives, regulatory methodological considerations and principles, but is also a characteristic example of legal development and environmental law drafting of the South-East European region. Here the comments of Nele Dhondt are relevant to the situation: '... there is also an extremely confusing terminology use in relation to the provisions. Terms such as rules, principles, legal principles, objectives and guidelines are used incoherently, to mean both similar and different things.'[10] Here we may also add, that even general and sectoral problems, alternative solutions and substitution of chemicals, are shown together and there is also the conceptual combination of principles, see for example, polluter pays together with user/consumer pays, but without mentioning producers' responsibility.

The REC (Regional Environmental Centre) report summarizes the most important lessons learned: 'There are some environmental laws adopted on the parliamentary of governmental level, sometimes with good ideas, principles, phrases and general provisions, which have never been implemented because the necessary detailed regulations – how to set the standards, how to issue a permit, what are the reporting obligations, etc. – have not been enacted.'[11]

The latest development in environmental law in Bosnia and Herzegovina is governed by several legislative aid projects, mostly based on EU resources, which take approximation to Community environmental law as the guiding principle. For example, 'on July 25th 2002, the National Assembly of Republika Srpska (one of the two entities of Bosnia and Herzegovina) adopted a series of new environmental laws. Along with the Framework Law, which included permitting (Official Gazette No. 53/02), there was water quality legislation (53/02), air quality protection (53/02), law governing waste (53/02), nature protection (50/02) and an Eco-fund (51/02).'[12] All these newly adopted laws were products of international assistance and are all based upon the EU requirements of:

· sustainable development;
· precaution and prevention;
· substitution;

---

[9]   *Assessing Environmental Law Drafting Needs in South Eastern Europe* REReP 1.3, Phase One Report, Drafted by G. Bándi and C. Kiss, (ed) T. Tsvetelina Borissova, The Regional Environmental Centre (2003) p. 60.

[10]   N. Dhondt, *op. cit.* note 1, p. 125.

[11]   REReP 1.3 Report, *op. cit.* note 9, p. 24.

[12]   REReP 1.3 Report, *op. cit.* note 9, p. 45.

· integration;
· public participation and access to information;
· polluter pays principle.

The question here, is why all these CEE and later SEE countries find principles so important as to they list them extensively throughout their major environmental laws? One possible reason is their wish to join the EU; consequently all these countries take approximation of environmental law as one major task. As these, or similar, principles also emerge in Community policy and law, their use in domestic law is a direct outcome of that desire. However, what is the legal significance of Community environmental principles?

'The question is, whether also the environmental principles of Article 174(2) EC are such principles, which Community legislation may not infringe. In my opinion, this is not the case. Rather, they constitute guiding principles for political or legislative decisions and may be used – as a sort of leitmotif – to explain or justify a decision, which was taken. [...]

Even where the principles of Article 174 are seen as general guidelines for Community policy, they have some indirect legal significance. They place an obligation on the Community to base its policy on these principles and to plan policy and measure accordingly.'[13]

The CEE and SEE countries have referred to principles in such a broad way, that they only have a minor legal significance and justify decisions in an indirect way. Thus, one may question, whether it is necessary to use such a broad approach. 'To a large extent such a statement of broad principle, even though expressed in legal language, is bound to be more a expression of policy aspiration than a specific legally binding requirement capable of enforcement by conventional legal routes.'[14] At that stage of environmental maturity where the CEE countries could stand in the 90s and where SEE countries are 10 years later, even this political aspiration could have great importance. [For some decades environmental protection was only taken as an all-purpose reference, if any, without direct, implementable meaning. The manifestation of new political interests, new alliances require a gradual transposition of innovative legal order.]

The REC Report summarizes the situation in a straightforward way: 'Most SEE countries/entities have a framework act as the main source of environmental legislation, dated in most the cases to the beginning of the 1990s. These original framework laws are usually too general and do not reflect the need of

---

[13] L. Krämer, *EC Environmental Law*, 5th Ed, Thomson, Sweet and Maxwell, London, (2003) pp. 14-15.

[14] R. Macrory, *The Scope of Environmental Law in European Environmental Law – A Comparative Perspective*, ed. G. Winter, Dartmouth, Aldershot, (1995) p. 8.

and effective environmental policy. [...] The principles and general provisions in force in the original environmental acts of the 1990s reflect the present state of environmental legislation in Europe, but the details, the set of instruments, the methods of legislation, the right of the public, the liability measures, and other issues, need further elaboration.'[15]

Jans' summary on the real meaning and importance of environmental principles at Community level may also be interpreted as an explanation for the boom in environmental principles in the rest of Europe: 'Establishing the legal basis of a proposed Community measure on the environment is important for at least three reasons. In the first place because, under Community law, the Community's institutions do not have the unlimited competences of the national legislators to take whatever measures they please. ...In the second place, deciding the legal basis is relevant for the decision-making procedure to be followed when adopting a particular environmental measure. ... in the third place, the choice of legal basis affects the extent to which Member States are entitled to adopt more stringent environmental measures than those on which agreement has been reached within the Community.'[16]

Of course, the first reason in Jans' list in not relevant to domestic law, but the remaining two are essential in our scope of interest. Summing up the different, but mostly comparable, views of the authors and also adding our own experiences of the region, it is easy to catalogue some of the main motives, supporting the actual values of environmental principles in countries in transition:

1. First of all, these principles are reflections of political will. Macrory pointed to issues of 'political aspiration', which are not necessarily strong enough to be demonstrated by further detailed rules or effective implementation. In the early stage of environmental legal evolution, the political aspiration may be taken as a value. If it is coupled with the interest of approximation to the EU, then the future improvement is even more likely.

2. A greater number of countries are willing to make use of the experiences and guidance of different international organisations; these include the Council of Europe, OECD and the European Union. In addition to the first point, this may even go beyond a vague political interest and be taken as a strong commitment.

3. Having once established the political interest or the commitment, it is much easier to begin with broad guidelines than with detailed rules. Principles illustrate the future of legislation, but still leave some time for elaboration. Usually they indicate that legislation has been started, but still requires more to be done. Later, when detailed rules of imple-

---

[15] REReP 1.3. Report, *op. cit.* note 9, (2003) p. 23.

[16] Jan H. Jans, *European Environmental Law*, Europa Law Publishing, Groningen, 2000, pp. 10-11.

mentation are in place, this meaning can be changed to a more practical, interpretative position. In the CEE and SEE regions, principles are usually exhibited as parts of framework laws and thus may be used as a point of reference.

4. Principles are extremely important when we are in the design phase of environmental legislation. As Jans pointed out above: 'deciding the legal basis is relevant for the decision-making procedure'. Taking prevention as a basis, the different forms of authorisation can then be developed. The polluter pays principle refers to the need of using wide a variety of instruments, among others financial measures. Public participation requires access to information or to justice, for example.

5. Following the reasoning above, principles may also be used for developing the details of legal regulations, cooperation or shared responsibility may give rise to regulating the legal grounds of administrative contract or voluntary agreements. The polluter pays principle is better implemented if there is some assistance for the victim of pollution, a scheme of strict liability instead of a fault-based one, compulsory insurance or other means of financial guarantees, presumptions of liability, are just a few examples.

6. Finally, principles offer a handy tool for effective implementation, or in case of legal disputes, illuminating the reasons behind written requirements, linking different elements of legislation. This may also be the case in the first period of legislative development, when there are less direct environmental rules in place. For this reason, constitutional courts may benefit from principles. A good example is the Hungarian Constitutional Court decision, issued even before the adoption of the 1995 framework environmental act. One paragraph of the 1994 decision[17], interpreting the environmental rights articles of the Hungarian Constitution, explains that prevention has priority over sanctions in the field of environmental protection. Prevention as a requirement can only be effective if the legal framework for effective protection is made. The lack of preventive measures was one reason for the decision. The outcome was that some paragraphs of the privatisation act were repealed.

Notwithstanding the fact that the practical implementation of principles of environmental law is mostly limited to constitutional court decisions or to some individual cases, these principles have a very important role to play in the development phase of environmental legislation in the transition period. This is an important aspect of turning environmental principles into practice.

---

[17] Decision No. 28/1994.(V.20.) of the Hungarian Constitutional Court.

CHAPTER 14

Environmental Principles, Modern and Post-modern Law

Nicolas de Sadeleer

1   Introduction

Environmental principles are increasingly treated as the common denominators around which environmental law and policy are organized. The focus of this chapter will be to compare the modern and post-modern law paradigms with a view to emphasize the role of several environmental principles on the evolution of those models.

The following analysis is based on a theoretical research that I carried out between 1994 and 2002, whilst I was director of the Environmental Law Center in Brussels. In a book recently published by Oxford University Press,[1] I explained the purpose of the principles of the polluter-pays, prevention and precaution, how each of those principles link with one another and what legal issues entail. In so doing, I drew attention to the specificity and legitimacy of this group of new environmental principles that, while far from similar to traditional General Principles of International Law, are necessary to ensure the regulation and management of environmental risks. Hence, I made a distinction between General Principles of Law, which are characteristic of modernity and the cluster of new environmental principles, which are better suited to adapting the shifting and convoluted forms that characterize contemporary or post-modern environmental law. Nevertheless, I showed that the principles of the polluter-pays, prevention and precaution did not represent a complete break with modernity, since they eventually re-establish rationality.

I will not embark on a discussion regarding the definition of the terms modernity and post modernity. A complete discussion on those terms is not possible in the space available here, furthermore, another lawyer has recently summarized the various meanings of those terms.[2] After a brief look at the substance of the modern and post-modern law and the principles related to each of those two models, I will turn to the functions of a new set of environmental principles that signal a shift in emphasis away from the completeness and the coherence of the legal system towards a more convoluted regulatory process.

2   Modern law

Modern law, which rests on the fixed standards of traditional rulemaking, reflects the character of modern societies. Modern law is represented as an autonomous system made up of general and abstract rules; in other words a system which is deemed to be rational, complete and coherent.

---

[1]   N. de Sadeleer, *Environmental Principles: from Political Slogans to Legal Rules*, Oxford University Press, Oxford, (2002).

[2]   B. Edgeworth, Law, *Modernity, Postmodernity: Legal Change in the Contracting State*, Ashgate Publishing, Aldershot, (2003).

In a liberal vision, the function of modern law is to provide for the coexistence of individual freedoms: each person has the right to enjoy maximum freedom to pursue his own interests, as long as he does not impinge upon the freedom of others. In order to provide every person with the maximum degree of freedom, modern law concentrates political power in the hands of the State. In that context, the need for legal certainty and foreseeability has led relations between individuals to be bound by general rules that refer to abstract concepts grouped together in general categories. Both generality and abstraction guarantee impartiality by drawing a veil of indifference between a rule and specific situations.

In addition, modern law presents itself from a Kelsenian perspective, as a pyramidal construction, with the most general rules at the apex. It thus appears to constitute a coherent whole that is a system of hierarchical rules linked to each other by logical and necessary relationships. This systematization confers upon the law the attributes of clarity, simplicity and certainty. Furthermore, its axiological neutrality characterizes modern law. Indeed, modern law seeks clearly to distinguish itself from non-legal spheres. The rule of law in the modern perspective has to be seen as completely autonomous in relation to extra-legal disciplines such as economics or political sciences.

Whether they are called *principes généraux du droit, principios general del derecho, Rechtsbeginselen* or *Rechtsprinzipien*, the General Principles of Law have been central to modern law. General principles of law have been called upon to fill possible lacunae.[3] At the level of international, EC and national legal orders, courts regularly find themselves confronting gaps in written sources. To the extent that courts must rectify such deficiencies to rule on a case, they will do so by deducing a relevant principle from a mass of rules. Once it has been enunciated, the principle will be applied as an autonomous norm to resolve the dispute. Subsequently, that same principle can be applied in other cases. In so doing, courts make the law a consistent system in the sense that they make it possible to ensure systematic unity of the law amid the disorder of positive rules. The demand is more conspicuous in the international community, where there is no central lawmaking body. According to Cassesse, 'in this community, general principles constitute both the backbone of the body of law governing international dealings and the potent cement that binds together the various and often disparate cogs and wheels of the normative framework of the community'.[4]

In addition, principles of customary law play a significant role as an autonomous source of international law, albeit the fact international courts can invoke them only if specific conditions are fulfilled. Indeed, only substantive and

---

[3]   T. Tridimas, *The General Principles of EC Law*, Oxford University Press, Oxford, (2000), p. 9; P. Birnie and A. Boyle, *International Law and the Environment*, Oxford University Press, Oxford, (2002), p. 19.

[4]   A. Cassesse, *Principles of International Environmental Law*, 2nd Edition, Cambridge University Press, Cambridge, (2002), p. 151.

repeated uses of State practice as well as *opinio iuris* are likely to transform an emerging norm into a customary principle. Some customary principles, such as international cooperation, simply reflect the application of general international law principles to environmental issues.[5] Others, like the obligation not to cause environmental harm, are specific to international environmental law. On the other hand, principles that are not yet supported by significant practice, through repetitive use in an international legal context, cannot give rise to a legal remedy (*e.g.*, the right to a healthy environment, the principles of common but differentiated responsibility and of subsidiarity). As a result, there are hitherto few general principles or customary principles of international law. For instance, Birnie and Boyle conclude that, in practice, the most frequent use of general principles by international courts 'derives from the drawing of analogies with domestic law concerning rules of procedure, evidence, and jurisdiction and these are only marginally useful in an environmental context'.[6]

3 Post modern law

Jean-François Lyotard has defined post-modernity in his book *The Post-Modern Condition* as 'incredulity toward meta-narratives'.[7] It follows that all metadiscourses, whether in the social or in the natural sciences, are suspected. Nevertheless, after more than twenty years of discussions among social scientists, post-modernism still remains an incomplete intellectual construct within which a large number of concepts – divergent as well as convergent – jostle each other.

Applied to law, post-modernity emphasizes the pragmatic, gradual, unstable change nature of contemporary law. We support the thesis that post-modernity applied to law should not be understood in a deconstructionist perspective as social scientists are keen to do. Rather it must be seen as a means of analysing the emergence of a new legal culture.

By contrast to other legal disciplines, environmental law has taken a distinct post-modern identity. Indeed, this new legal discipline has undergone, during the past two decades, more transformations than any other field of law. These transformations have brought environmental law far from the premises of modern law described above. It is with the issue of the different factors that have contributed to modern law losing the attributes of generality, systematicity and autonomy, thus hastening the passage of contemporary environmental law to the

---

[5] P. Sands, *Principles of International Environmental Law*, 2nd Edition, Cambridge University Press, Cambridge, (2003), p. 232.

[6] P. Birnie and A. Boyle, *op. cit.* note 3, p. 24.

[7] J.F. Lyotard, *The Postmodern Condition, A Report on Knowledge (Theory and History of Literature)*, University of Minnesota Press, Minneapolis, (1984), xxiv.

post-modern sphere, that this section is concerned. The issue of the functions of the environmental principles will be addressed in the next section.

3.1 Dispersion of the law makers

The sovereign State has given way to a plurality of institutions, which are as much infra national as supranational, as the number of regulators has increased dramatically in the past thirty years. 'Upstream', inter-governmental institutions such as the WTO, the EC and NAFTA, directly influence the elaboration of environmental rules at national level. In addition, as environmental problems have worsened, it has become necessary to develop at the international level a body of law more specifically aimed at reducing environmental impairment. 'Downstream', public policies concerning environmental education, health, land-planning natural resources, nature protection, generally fall within the competence of the numerous national actors (regions, provinces, Lander, communities, ...) most closely involved with the areas being regulated, thus increasing the number of relevant regulators even further. Furthermore, standard-setting bodies (ISO, CEN, Codex alimentarius) have established their own functional norms and procedures, thereby giving rise to a non-state law that vies with State law. Those standards can even be incorporated to some extent in hard law.[8] Hence, as Sands points out 'lawmaking is decentralized with legislative initiatives being developed in literally dozens of different intergovernmental organizations at the global, regional and sub-regional level. Coordination between the various initiatives is inadequate, leading to measures which are often duplicative and sometimes inconsistent'.[9]

3.2 Fragmentation of law

Lack of time and means, the complexity and changeability of the questions to be addressed, pressure from lobbies, lack of interest in legal questions – these difficulties are giving rise to a proliferation of specific laws edited in haste and littered with gaps and contradictions, whose duration dwindles in direct proportion to their mediocrity. The need to adopt new legislation often rests on a permanent state of reluctance to apply existing legislation. Thus,

---

[8] According to the new approach for technical normalisation, the institutions of normalisation (CEN, CENELEC) can find themselves entrusted with the task of developing technical specifications *'needed for the production and placing on the market of products conforming to the essential requirements established by the Directives'* adopted on the basis of Article 95 of the EC Treaty.

[9] P. Sands, Environmental Protection in the XXIst Century: Sustainable Development, International Law, in R.L. Revesez et al, *Environmental Law, the Economy and Sustainable Development*: The United States, the European Union and the International Community, Cambridge University Press, Cambridge, (2000), p. 372.

environmental regimes in most countries are teeming with hundreds of laws whose effectiveness leaves a great deal to be desired, owing to their precarious and confused nature.

In addition, environmental law challenges well-established boundaries between private and public law[10] and international and national law.[11] It does not have an overall focus or objective. Instead, it has tended to develop in a haphazard fashion, responding to particular needs, in the light of new ecological crises. By the same token, the line between soft law and hard law is becoming indistinct, as treaty mechanisms increasingly turn towards 'soft' obligations[12] and non-binding instruments, in turn, incorporate mechanisms traditionally found in hard-law texts. Furthermore, environmental law encompasses both more and less than the law of sustainable development. Even though the objectives are by no means identical, 'there is a major overlap in rules, principles and techniques'.[13] It follows that environmental law does not form a coherent whole.

3.3   Acceleration of time

Environmental law is experiencing a true flight forward. The speed at which norms are produced has accelerated drastically. The ineffectiveness of existing regulatory regimes is compelling legislators to constantly adopt new rules. Time is no longer a measure of duration; radically accelerated, it reduces the long term to a short term and continuance to immediacy. As a result, lawmakers favour flexibility over long-term action. Reflecting this, the legal universe has become one of short-term programmes and constant change. The legitimacy of the State is no longer acquired as of right, but is rather a function of the relevance of State-generated programmes. Furthermore, those post-modern policies based on programmes are designed to achieve concrete ends in a way that general, impersonal rules are intended not to be.

---

[10] See, for instance, the proposed Environmental Liability directive, which entails mainly administrative obligations rather than civil liability schemes.

[11] EC law and the ECHR tend to merge into the legal orders of the States members of the European Community and the Council of Europe. Thanks to direct effect, several obligations laid down in those international agreements can be invoked before national courts. As a result, it has become difficult in Europe to deal with environmental law through a purely national approach, without taking into account the obligations laid down in those two international agreements.

[12] See, for instance, the 1992 Convention on Biological Diversity allows for its own further development through a wealth of recommendations and decisions.

[13] P. Birnie and A. Boyle, *op. cit.* note 3, p. 2.

3.4   Decline of State authority

As hinted as above, at the international level, 'soft law', is replacing the 'hard law', advocated by those who support control and command systems. At national level and even at EC level, more flexible, incentive-driven and consensual instruments are gradually replacing classical command and control mechanisms. A new form of co-regulation replaces the "thou shalt not" approach. For instance, voluntary participation by those whom the State intends to regulate has in this way come to replace classical forms of State intervention, in the name of 'shared responsibility'.[14] Self-regulatory mechanisms (*e.g.*, voluntary labels, eco-audits, tradable pollution rights), under which those being administered are considered fully involved actors ('stakeholders'), play a major role in most of these new environmental policies. This trend is already entrenched both at municipal and at EC level.

The result of this approach is that it affords greater autonomy to the private undertakings. In addition, it tends to downplay the role of legislation and to dilute the responsibility of public authorities in formulating and implementing public policies. Inversely, the decline of State authority is often associated with an increased political role for civil society. New rights to information, participation and access to justice have been accorded to citizens, in order both to integrate them into the process of defining and implementing public policies and to facilitate the subsequent acceptance of negotiated norms. In parallel to this trend, lawmakers at both the international and national levels have become increasingly open to the influence of human rights advocates, environmental NGOs and other activist groups.

3.5   Increasing dependence of the law on extra-legal spheres

While modern law seeks to distinguish itself from non-legal disciplines, rules of law in the post-modern perspective are no longer seen as being completely autonomous in relation to the extra-legal sphere. Rather, a much greater openness towards the economic, ethical and policy spheres characterise post-modern law. In this respect, Sands is of the view that "over the past decades the rules of international law have become increasingly complex and technical as environmental considerations are increasingly addressed in economic and social fields".[15]

---

[14]   Edgeworth asserts that environmental law is a typical example of this novel regulatory practice. B. Edgeworth, *op. cit.* note 5, p. 153.

[15]   P. Sands, *op. cit.* note 5, p. 69.

3.6 The undermining of the premises of modern law

As a result of these upheavals, post-modern law is going
through a process that is radically different from any of those that characterize modern law. Rigidity (hard law) has given way to flexibility (*e.g.*, contracts);
abstraction (law of general ambit) to individual decisions (environmental agreement, concluded with a particular undertaking, on a case by case approach);
the continuity (based on abstract and general rules) to timeliness (obligation to
update the regulation, ephemeral programmes); and authority (command and
control instruments) to co-regulation (negotiation with stakeholders).

Needless to say that these significant changes are seriously undermining
the foundations of modern law (*e.g.*, hierarchy between legislative and executive
norms, autonomy of the legal system, identity of the legal subject).

4 Environmental principles represent the interface between modern law and post modern law

Whilst modern law is devoid of precise objectives, contemporary laws are goal-oriented. Hence, most environmental international agreements and national environmental codes are characterised not only by the
proclamation of legal objectives, but also by the embodiment of principles
(precaution, prevention, the polluter-pays, sustainability, substitution, self-sufficiency, proximity, integration, participation, reduction of pollution at source,
cooperation, stand-still) meant to set various social and political actors in
motion.

Compared to other legal disciplines, environmental law is a prime example
of a goal-oriented discipline, marked by the presence of an array of principles.
For instance, from their origins as vague political slogans, the principles of
the polluter-pays, prevention and precaution have been recently incorporated
into different legal instruments, ranging from the 1998 Swedish and the 2000
French environmental codes to more sophisticated protocols. By contrast to
other chapters of the EC Treaty, the environmental chapter (Title XIX) lists at
least five principles (prevention, precaution, polluter-pays, rectification at source,
high level of protection), some having decisive influence on some hard case
rulings by the CFI and the ECJ.[16] In the process of codifying their national laws,
national lawmakers set forth principles that are already embedded in international agreements.

Those principles are strikingly different from the General Principles of Law
that we described above. While the latter are applied by the courts through an

---

[16] N. de Sadeleer, *op. cit.* note 1, pp. 119-124.

induction process, the former have been set forth in statute provisions, with a view to be applied by public authorities.

The presence of those principles in both soft and hard law is due precisely to the fact that environmental law is more strongly characterised by post-modern elements than any other legal disciplines. In particular, the polluter-pays, preventive and precautionary principles are emblematic of the functions that principles must assume in the context of post-modern law that stresses flexibility, adaptability and pluralism. First and foremost, by openly proclaiming new orientations, these directing principles enrich the formulation and implementation of environment law by State authorities within a post-modern perspective. In other words, they can stimulate new public policies (section 4.1). By more clearly defining the limits, within which public administrations exercise their discretionary powers, these principles provide authorities with a more coherent orientation and consequently legitimise their actions (section 4.2). By freeing courts from the constraint of an overly literal interpretation of texts, they have also an interpretative function (section 4.3). Finally, we will see that these principles may play a determining role in balancing interests – an activity which plays an important part in post-modern law – by helping courts to understand the specific value of environmental protection measures (section 4.4). As a result, those principles are highly characteristic of post-modern law.

4.1 Enabling function

Principles are never sufficient on their own. The lawmaker cannot merely set forth principles in the form of a wish list without engaging in concrete legislative revisions. Rather, he must legislate area by area, procedure by procedure – in order to give full expression to those principles.[17]

Therefore, principles are in the first instance meant to enable the legislator, who must breathe life into them by adopting specific implementing laws. At the national level, the lawmaker then implements the principles through specific legislation. The same is true for international environment law, with protocols being guided by the basic principles set out in framework conventions. In EC law, several directives and regulations are deemed to implement the various principles set out in Article 174(2) of the EC Treaty. For instance, when there is uncertainty as to the existence or extent of risks to human health, the precautionary principle enables EC institutions to take protective measures 'without having to wait until the reality and seriousness of those risks become fully apparent'.[18] In addition, the principle of integration plays an important role in

---

[17] N. de Sadeleer, *Les principes du polluer-payeur, de prévention et de précaution*, Bruylant, Brussels, (1999).

[18] Case C-157/96, *The Queen v. Ministry of Agriculture, Fisheries and Food*, ex parte *National Farmers' Union a.o. United Kingdom v. Commision of the European Communities* [1998] ECR I-2265.

the choice of the proper legal basis of environmental measures.[19] Last but not least, this enabling function can justify encroachments on fundamental rights such as the right of property.[20] For instance, the polluter-pays principle, which requires the abatement of nitrates produced by intensive farming activities, can justify encroachment on property rights, in so far as the interference is not disproportionate or intolerable.[21] By the same token, the precautionary principle has been recognised as a justification under Article 30 of the EC Treaty with a view to restricting fundamental rights to trade freely, chemicals hazardous to human health.[22]

In addition, the flexibility of the environmental principles enables rule makers to make less detailed rules.[23] Put another way, principles allow the legislator to achieve economies of scale, thus replacing a *pointilliste* regulatory technique that finds expression through a multitude of detailed rules. Such flexibility has the added advantage of making it easier to adapt rules to changing circumstances, ensuring for the principles, the type of sustained use that more precise and complete rules no longer enjoy. Being malleable, principles do not need to be formally modified when circumstances change. Principles could similarly serve to temper the increase in legal precariousness that typified post-modernity. Malleable and adaptable by nature, those principles function within a long-term perspective absent from more precise rules, which must be formally modified every time circumstances change. Yet while specific rules are continually being modified to conform to changing situations, directing principles remain imperturbable.

4.2   Directing function

When the law-maker proclaims the polluter-pays, preventive and precautionary principles, he is also addressing subordinate administrations: regulatory as well as individual decisions will henceforth be required to conform to the principles set out in the law. These principles will thus serve as guides and signals for the use of discretionary powers by administrative authorities. For instance, Winter points out that principles set forth in Article 174 of the EC

---

[19]   N. Dhondt, *Integration of Environmental Protection into Other EC Policies: Legal Theory and Practice*, Avosetta Series, Europa Law Publishing, Groningen, (2002), p. 170.

[20]   G. Winter, Environmental Principles in Community Law, in J. Jans, *The European Convention and the Future of EC Environmental Law*, Europa Law Publishing, Groningen, (2003), p. 5.

[21]   Case C-293/97, *The Queen v. Secretary of State for the Environment, Minister of Agriculture, Fisheries and Food, ex parte: H.A. Standley and Others, D.G.D. Metson and Others*, [1999] ECR I-2603.

[22]   Case C-473/98, *Kemikalieinspektionen and Toolex Alpha AB*, [2000] ECR I-5702.

[23]   N. de Sadeleer, *op. cit.* note 20, p. 302; J. Verschuuren, *Principles of Environmental Law, The Ideal of Sustainable Development and the Role of Principles of International, European and National Environmental Law*, Nomos Verlagsgeschellschaft, Baden-Baden, (2003), pp. 40 and 134.

Treaty can be attributed a 'directive function'.[24] This function entails among others the obligation to handle complex environmental cases comprehensively and not incrementally.[25] In my book on Environmental Principles, I have deliberately chosen the term 'directing principles' instead of the usual term 'policy principles' which, in my view, does not convey this particular legal function.

This function is fully justified in the light of postmodern developments explained above. Public authorities increasingly require guidance as they find themselves having to balance interests that demand the use of wide discretionary powers on a daily basis. I will give a few examples. When authorising a project with significant effects on a protected natural area, national authorities must, according to Directive 92/43/EC, balance the 'imperative reasons of overriding public interest' that justify the project against the obligation to prevent irreversible damage to biodiversity. The obligation to use best available technologies under the 96/61/EC IPPC Directive also leads to some weighing of environmental and economic interests. When the European Commission must decide individual requests for exemption from the prohibition on anti-competitive practices under Article 81(3) of the EC Treaty, it should not exempt practices with harmful consequences for the environment; at the same time, it should adopt greater flexibility regarding projects that would be favorable to the environment.

4.3 Interpretrative function

Principles can be seen as a link between ideals and rules[26] Indeed, principles differ from rules in the sense that the latter can be more easily applied in an individual case. However, administrations and courts alike, can use principles in the process of interpreting statutory rules in concrete cases, especially when those rules are vague and open.[27] An interesting example is the differentiation between waste and product, which has been the subject of much heated academic debate as well as litigation in EC law. According to the ECJ, the concept of waste must be interpreted in light of the aim of Directive 75/442/EEC, which is to protect human health and the environment against harmful effects caused by waste. Furthermore, the ECJ has pointed out that, pursuant to Article 174(2) of the EC Treaty, EC policy on the environment is to aim at a high level of protection and must be based, in particular, on the precautionary principle and the principle that preventive action should be taken.[28] It follows that the concept of waste cannot be interpreted restrictively.

---

[24] G. Winter, *op. cit.* note 20, p. 11.

[25] G. Winter, *ibid*, pp. 7-8.

[26] J. Verschuuren, *op. cit.* note 23, p. 25.

[27] J. Verschuuren, *Ibid*, pages 38 and 131.

[28] Cases C-418/97 and C-419/97, *ARCO Chemie Nederland*, [2000] ECR I-4512, para. 39.

If it is true that some environmental principles such as the precautionary principle increase the freedom of interpretation enjoyed by the courts, the latter nonetheless remain bound to find solutions in harmony with the spirit of the legal system. Moreover, courts only have recourse to principles such as prevention or precaution when they see the need to make one interpretation prevail over another. In addition, principles are always used in tandem with more precise rules, which serves to reduce the threat of legal uncertainty even further.

4.4   Weighing the conflicting interests

As we have seen above, from the perspective of modern law, both national and international courts fulfill an important role by elaborating general principles of law in order to fill gaps in the legal system. From the perspective of post-modern law, courts certainly have to apply principles set out in legal texts such as framework conventions or framework laws (directing principles) rather than principles derived from case-law (general principles of law). The role of the court is thus shifting from judge-made principles to the implementation of principles recognized by the legislator.

Recourse to these principles is therefore encouraged to the extent that, unlike precise rules, they make it possible for divergent interests to coexist, by providing the flexibility needed for adaptations; they are able to balance all the interests that must be taken into consideration in a given case. Overly precise rules are far too decisive to support multiple public policies liable to contradict each other at every turn. Considering their vagueness, the principles of the polluter-pays, prevention and precaution thus allow courts to weigh and reconcile highly divergent interests with maximum flexibility. Furthermore, by shedding new light on an environmental measure when it comes into conflict with intersecting interests, the environmental principles may serve to tilt the scales more strongly in the direction of environmental protection. In sum, those environmental principles constitute key means by which to mitigate contradictions and antagonisms.

5   Conclusions

Several principles of environmental law mark a shift between modern law, which rests on fixed standards of rule-making and post-modern law, which emphasizes the pragmatic, gradual, unstable, and reversible nature of rules. If in a modern perspective, there has been a long clear distinction between law and the other spheres, this is no longer the case today. From a post-modern perspective, environmental law is more likely to be organized around an array of principles that will provide the basis for conciliating conflicting interests. Of course, post-modern law is less of a phenomenon, whose beginnings can be pinpointed at a precise moment of modern history; rather than a complex process built up incrementally as the result of the upheavals that at regular intervals have shaken the order of modern law. In addition, the shift from modernity to post-modernity is not a radical one. Indeed, the two models continue to coexist. Finally, although set out in law, the principles characterising contemporary environmental law, suggest a certain fragility. Even when they are recognized in framework conventions or environmental codes, they are never secure from the forces of circumstance, since nothing prevents the lawmaker from renouncing their use. Similarly, they may at any time be contradicted by the protocols or the regulations intended to put them into effect, because they occupy the same level in the hierarchy of norms. If they were to play a significant role in guiding lawmakers, it would be preferable to set them out at the highest level of the legal order – in the case of Continental legal regimes, the Constitution.

Table of Cases

European Court of Human Rights (ECHR)

Belgium

Court of Arbitration

Council of State

Courts of Appeal

Tribunals

Denmark

Supreme Court

Nature Appeal Board

Index

Contributors

Maria Alexandra de Sousa Aragão

Maria Alexandra de Sousa Aragão is Assistant Lecturer at the Faculty of Law of the University of Coimbra where she teaches European Environmental Law (European Module Jean Monnet) and Waste Law. She obtained the masters degree in European Integration in 1995, with a thesis on the Polluter-Pays Principle and is currently preparing her PhD thesis on the High Level of Environmental Protection Principle.

Gyula Bándi

Gyula Bándi (C.S.c, Dr. habil.) is Professor of law and head of the Environmental Law Chair of the Pázmány Peter Catholic University, Budapest, Hungary. Professor Bandi is a member of the editorial board of the Environmental Encyclopaedia, the European Law Review and chairman of the editorial board of the Hungarian Environmental Protection Review. He is founder and president of the Environmental Management and Law Association.

Stefano Grassi

Stefano Grassi is Professor of constitutional and administrative law at the Faculty of Law of the University of Florence. He is director of the Environmental Law Observatory of Ceradi-Luiss Guuido Carli in Rome. He is also a practising barrister and a legal advisor to several institutions.

Ian Havercroft

Ian Havercroft is currently a Research Fellow at the Centre for Law and the Environment, University College London. He has an LL.M in environmental law (University College London) and was called to the Bar of England and Wales in 2002.

Ludwig Krämer

Ludwig Krämer is a lawyer who works in the Environmental Department of the European Commission, where he is head of the unit on governance. He is a judge at the Landgericht Kiel, Lecturer at the College of Europe in Bruges (Belgium), Visiting Professor at University College London and Honorary Professor at Bremen University. He has extensively published on EC environmental law, most recently EC Environmental Law, 5th ed. 2003 and Casebook on EU Environmental Law, 2002.

Luc Lavrysen

Prof. Dr. L. Lavrysen is a part-time Professor at Ghent University, Belgium, where he is Director of the Environmental Law Centre. He is editor-in-chief of the Tijdschrift voor Milieurecht, a Flemish Environmental Law Review and member of the Belgian Federal Council for Sustainable Development, a multi-stakeholder advisory body. Professor Lavrysen is a Judge in the

Court of Arbitration, the Belgian Constitutional Court, and in that capacity he is involved in UNEP's Global Judges Project on Sustainable Development and the Role of Law.

Richard Macrory

Richard Macrory is Professor of environmental law at the Faculty of Laws, University College London, where he is director of the Centre for Law and the Environment. He is currently a board member of the Environment Agency, which is responsible for key areas of environmental regulation in England and Wales and was elected President of the National Society for Clean Air and Environmental Protection from 2004. Between 1992 and 2003 he was a member of the UK Royal Commission on Environmental Pollution, and was chair of the steering committee of the European Environmental Advisory Councils between 2001 and 2002. Professor Macrory is editor in chief of the Journal of Environmental Law.

Liselotte Smorenburg-van Middelkoop

Liselotte Smorenburg-van Middelkoop is a PhD student supervised by Professor H.G. Sevenster, at the Centre for Environmental Law, University of Amsterdam. Her main area of research concerns the interaction between Dutch environmental conflicts before the courts and European law. Prior to commencing her research work, she graduated from the University of Leiden and worked as a lawyer at Baker & McKenzie, specialising in environmental, administrative and real estate law.

Massimiliano Montini

Massimiliano Montini holds a law degree (J.D.) from the University of Siena (1994) and an LL.M. in European Law from University College London (1996). He is currently a Lecturer at the University of Siena in the fields of International Law and European Union Law. He is the co-ordinator of a postgraduate course in environmental law, organised annually by the University of Siena. He is also a fully qualified, practising lawyer and a member of the Italian Bar

Angel-Manuel Moreno

Angel-Manuel Moreno, LLM (Harvard Law School), Dr.iur, is a Professor of law at Carlos III University of Madrid, where he teaches administrative and environmental law, both at national and at EU level. Apart from these subjects, he has also published several works in the domain of local government law and the U.S. federal agencies.

Peter Pagh

Peter Pagh is an Associate Professor at the Law Faculty of the University of Copenhagen, where he currently teaches liability and contract law and EU environmental law. Professor Pagh has written books on EU environmental law, EU law and public procurement and has published a comprehensive study comparing US environmental law with EU and Danish environmental law.

Ray Purdy

Ray Purdy is Senior Research Fellow in environmental law at the Centre for Law and the Environment, University College London. He has previously held academic positions at Imperial College London and the University of Oxford, His main research interest, is the legal and social implications of the use of satellite remote sensing to monitor and enforce environmental laws.

Nicolas de Sadeleer

Nicolas de Sadeleer was awarded the first Marie Curie Chair by the European Commission in February 2004 and located at the University of Oslo. Professor de Sadeleer is also a Professor of environmental law at the Facultés universitaires Saint-Louis and at the Institut d'études européennes de l'Université catholique de Louvain and post-doctoral Research Fellow at the Faculty of Law of the Vrijie Universiteit. He was Director, from 1990 to 2003, of the Environmental Law Center at the Facultés Universitaires Saint-Louis and acted as a legal adviser for different environmental departments in Belgium, France and Luxemburg.

Joanne Scott

Joanne Scott is Reader in European law and Deputy Chair of the Cambridge Law Faculty. She is a Fellow of Clare College Cambridge. She writes in the areas of EU law and WTO law, with specific interests in environmental law and new approaches to governance in the EU.

Bernhard W. Wegener

Bernhard Wegener was appointed Professor in public law at the University of Erlangen-Nürnberg in 2004. Prior to this appointment, he was at the University of Bielefeld (Der geheime Staat – Arkantradition und Informationsfreiheit in Deutschland) and between 1997 and 2002; he was an assistant to Prof. Dr. Gertrude Lübbe-Wolf (now a judge at the Federal Constitutional Court). During the period between 1993 and 1994 he was assistant Professor at the Academy for Public Administration of Nordrheinwestfahlen.